Practical Magic in the Northern Tradition

Fig. 1 Irminsul, the Cosmic Pillar of the Saxons, at Stonehenge, symbolizing the unity in diversity of the Northern Tradition.

Practical Magic in the Northern Tradition

Nigel Pennick

THE AQUARIAN PRESS

First published 1989

British Library Cataloguing in Publication Data

Pennick, Nigel, *1946*
Practical magic in the northern tradition.
1. Northern Europe. Occultism
I. Title 133'.094

ISBN 0-85030-757-0

The Aquarian Press is part of the Thorsons
Publishing Group, Wellingborough,
Northamptonshire, NN8 2RQ, England

Typeset by Burns & Smith, Derby
Printed in Great Britain by Biddles Limited, Guildford, Surrey

1 3 5 7 9 10 8 6 4 2

No, my children; by chance you are all mista'en,
For here I find myself, I am not slain:
But I will rise, your sport for to advance,
And with you all, brave boys, I'll have a dance.

Lincolnshire Revesby Play

Contents

Introduction   9
I   Basic Perceptions: Space, Time, and Directions   15
II   Natural Lore   60
III   The Magic of the North   110
IV   Tools and Equipment   160
V   Protective Techniques and Objects   194
VI   Ceremonies and Rituals   228
Conclusion   256
Appendix 1   259
Appendix 2   264
Appendix 3   273
Appendix 4   276
Select Bibliography   278
Index   283

NOTE ON ILLUSTRATIONS

All illustrations were drawn by the author, except where
noted, when they come from the author's collection. Figure 5
is by courtesy of Robert J. M. Rickard.

Introduction

This book is about the beliefs and spiritual techniques indigenous to northern Europe, known as the *Northern Tradition*. It explores the basic aspects of the spiritual experience rooted in the lands of the North. This is the area of human consciousness sought out and entered by meditators and holy men, martial artists, magicians and shamans, wise women, cunning men, and, in times of personal crisis, by 'ordinary' people. Through the ages and in many different countries and cultures, this human experience has been described and understood in many different ways, conditioned by local beliefs and language. The Northern Tradition, then, is appropriate to the climate, culture and peoples of northern Europe. There can be no real appreciation of our culture or history without a proper understanding of this tradition.

The tradition dealt with in this work is a sacred and magical world-view which is a part of the ancient Indo-European way of life. Indian Hinduism is the eastern end of this observance, and the Northern Tradition is the north-western end. It is distinct from what is called the *Western Tradition*, as that has the specific meaning of a magical tradition influenced by and containing much Egyptian and Judaeo-Christian mythology and magical praxis. The Northern Tradition comprises mainly Germanic, Baltic, Norse and Celtic strands, along with some Etruscan and Graeco-Roman Pagan elements. It covers the area from Austria and Bohemia (Czechoslovakia) in the east, through Switzerland, Germany and northern France, including Brittany, in the west. In the north it covers Ireland, Britain, Iceland, Scandinavia and the Baltic countries (northern Poland and the western USSR). Although there are local variations between separate observances, for example Druidism and Asatrú, these are the kind of variations we can

see in the Hindu religion between devotion to Krishna or Kali
or worship of trees, rocks and natural features. A parallel in
the classical world was the Graeco-Roman religion, where
worship of various gods and goddesses, spirits and principles
went on in separate temples in the same cities. In the Northern Tradition, the devotion to various gods and goddesses,
local and universal, contained elements of the same ideal.
One can be a follower of a certain faith, or a devotee of a goddess, whilst allowing others to follow their own paths, and
this is the only way that peace and harmony, or at least
tolerance, can exist.

My own place in this spiritual tradition originates in my
own person and nationality: I am English, descended from
ancestors from most parts of Britain, and some from France,
Holland and the Baltic lands. Britain is a land with two basic
ancient traditions, the Celtic and the Germanic, of which I am
an inheritor of both, especially its East Anglian form. The
Celtic is a mixture of the Pagan traditions of Central Europe
and Gaul, Wales and Ireland, and the Germanic is of both
strands—Saxon and Norse, mainly Danish. Thus the tradition of magic and worship in England is basically Saxon but
with the overlay of the years, which includes a Judaeo-
Christian interpretation of indigenous material and, in this
century, Egyptian, Indian, Chinese and native American
input.

In the Northern Tradition, we can trace the same themes,
the same traditions, the same practices and the same deities,
under different names. The design of sacred sites, the games,
the festivals, the means of measurement, all differ slightly,
but are of the same roots. The variation of names for the same
principles, deities and sprites is just the same as the different
names for the same thing in different languages. The thing
described is the same, but the means of description varies according to cultural factors. For example, the god called Odin
in the Norse is Wotan in the German, Woden in English and
Gwydion in the Welsh Tradition. Thor in Norse is Thunor in
English, Taranis in the Gallic, and Perkunas in the Prussian
tradition, etc. Here, we are dealing with personalized
manifestations of forces, feelings and the way things happen.
The Celtic and the Norse blend in Ireland, as in Normandy
and parts of England and Scotland, to produce a special
culture using elements from both systems.

The underlying principles which we are dealing with are

indentical, for they come out of the same environmental conditions. They have links with northern shamanism, a system of magical evocation and heightened consciousness which was once practised all across the northern hemisphere, from Frisia to Lappland, in Siberia, central Asia and by the Northern American natives. The runes, especially, are the northern European key to these mysteries, having been obtained by shamanistic methods. They are one means to this, specially adapted to the circumstances of Germanic-Saxon world-views, just as oghams are their Celtic counterpart; however, in the Celtic world, runes were also used. The Coelbren Y Beirdd (Alphabet of the Bards) of ancient Wales is derived from runic and ogham, and Irish manuscripts of the thirteenth century describe various runic rows.

Like all human cultures, the Northern Tradition is expressed in the interaction betwen the inner experiences of human spirituality, which are universal for all humans, and the exterior experiences of climate and landscape, which are specific to this part of the world. The Northern Tradition, then, includes the observances, customs and practices of several distinct national or linguistic groupings of northern Europe. It is the essential spiritual observance of the Celtic, Anglo-Saxon, Frisian, Germanic, Norse and Baltic regions, originating in prehistoric times and continuing in a modified and updated form until the present day as folk-custom, the veneration of saints, household magic and rural practices. Although within this area there are local differences, expressed as different names for deities, festivals and sacred observances, they are nevertheless linked with one another through common transcendent themes. Most importantly, as in all systems originating in pre-industrial times, the Northern Tradition is one in which there is no distinction betwen the sacred and the secular; the world and our part in it are seen equally as elements of the sacred. Every living and inanimate thing is part of the universal whole, and each has, in varying degree, part of the essence of the divine creative power from which it originated and to which it will, one day, return.

Of course, at the core of things, the matter is universal, transcending local belief and custom, for at its roots is the human condition and the nature of things. Regardless of their origins and outward observances, all religions and philosophies are fundamentally concerned with the nature of the universe, and our place in it. Their interpretations are the logical result of our common condition. We are present on the Earth, and clearly our bodies are made of the material which also composes the Earth. Our sustenance comes from eating other living beings, whether plant or animal, and they, too, are of the Earth, subject as we are to its complex cycles of the seasons, birth, life and death. The Earth, in turn, is part of a greater whole, the material-space-time continuum of the universe, itself part of a more complex and bewildering existence, the multiverse: an eternal, cyclic existence without beginning or end, within which the gods, as with all things, are part of the natural order. It is clear that the inner essence of all religions is the adoration of the same transcendental reality, perceived in different ways and associated with different explanatory mythologies. The great spiritual teachers of the world like Confucius, Lao-Tse, Gautama, Orpheus, Pythagoras and Apollonius have recognized and taught this reality.

Unfortunately, despite their teachings, countless wars have been fought, and many atrocities committed in the name of a god or gods. Their devotees could not understand that their deity was just their own tribal, national, linguistic or cultural interpretation of the same power or quality followed under another name by their supposed opponents. They have not recognized that what is important is essence, not form, and that while the corresponding deity of another culture may have a considerably different form, its essence is the same. They have failed to see that that which they believe in and support is no *better* than someone else's, merely an appropriate *form* for them, personally or collectivity. Because of this, militant religions have always used armed force to compel people to believe. The forcible advance of militant religions at different times in history has never meant that conquered people have adopted the new faith unchanged. In no country have the traditions of the older faith been obliterated completely. On the contrary, it has always been customary for newer beliefs to absorb most of the shrines, festivals and observances of the older ones, creating a version appropriate to the country or locality. Old gods and goddesses of pre-Buddhist, pre-Christian and pre-Islamic faiths became the saints or demons of the newer faith, expressing the same essences and often very similar forms. The shrines of the Elder Faith were converted into temples, churches, chapels or mosques, often retaining some special character of the former shrine. The new festivals, celebrated on the same date as the old ones, retained the underlying essential character of the former observances. Our own celebration of Christmas is a perfect example of this continuity, where Pagan and Christian elements are merged to create a spiritually rich celebration of midwinter and rebirth. This merging-together of the older with newer elements to create a locally-appropriate version is the only way that the newer can work. Local belief and custom are the forms appropriate for the locality in which they have arisen, expressing the essence of the place. As they are the outcome of human interaction with the immediate local environment, both seen and unseen, they enable those who use them to live there more easily. All over the world, local belief is intimately connected with local deities and places of power, which are often, but not always, linked with tribal or national gods. At different times in history, these deities, entities, powers, forces or qualities will have been given different names and interpretations, yet they have been ever-present, and are essentially the same.

This quality of local belief is complicated by the historical process of expansion and development. This is where, over the years, tribal or local gods have developed from being exclusively associated with a specific locality or ethnic grouping to become identified as the transcendent creator, of which they were, in any case, a part, but not the whole. This process of expansion is visible all around us today, where place-names that had arisen from single objects or small areas, have become applied to whole districts, even nation-states. In London, King's Cross is a good example, beginning as a single stone cross at a road junction, and ending up as a district known by millions for its rail terminus, and even exported across the globe to Australia, where it is a part of the city of Sydney. Even whole countries may take the name of a relatively small place, such as Zimbabwe, named after the ruins of an ancient settlement covering a few dozen acres. This process has occured time and again in the past when local sanctuaries become tribal, then national and eventually international shrines. Jerusalem, the Vatican and Mecca are well-documented examples of this process.

In its fullest expression, a deity, whether localized at a holy well or generalized as the power immanent in the universe, embodies a complex of traditional standpoints, practices and observances, part of the everyday life of those aware of it. The thread which links the various elements in the Northern Tradition is one of harmony with the natural environment, which, in the North, is one of a contrast between long, light, productive summers and cold, dark, harsh winters. Within this framework of the seasons, a system of natural lore arose which enabled the people of a pre-industrial era to come to terms with the good and bad things of life, and to find meaning within their lives. The forces of nature, personified first as spirits and gods, and later as saints of the Church, become approachable when visualized in this way, giving us the means for a dynamic interaction between ourselves and their workings, so long as we work for the good of all, and do not subvert the free will of others. The Northern Tradition is a vital corpus of appropriate natural lore, tried and tested over thousands of years, which anyone today can make use of.

In this book, I write of the ceremonies and customs in the present tense, for even where some of them have lapsed, it is not appropriate to consider that they have ceased for all time. Every year, ceremonies and customs exist only on the days that they are conducted. At other times, they exist only in the collective memory. Even if a ceremony is conducted once more after a break of a century, as with the Rochester sweeps' festivities on May Day, then the gap in observance has been a little longer than usual. That is all. They are still valid parts of tradition which can be reinstated at any time; in fact, they are rising, revitalized, once again from a low point. This ran from the 1940s until the late 1960s, when I received my teaching from an old East Anglian master, when another generation recognized its fundamental importance. By following the festivals and customs of the Northern Tradition today, we can attune ourselves to the natural cycles of the seasons and harmonize better with both nature and our fellow human beings.

Nigel Pennick
Bar Hill
Merrymoon, 1988

I

Basic Perceptions: Space, Time and Direction

Creation works ceaselessly through man. But man does not create, he discovers. Those who seek out the Laws of Nature as support for their new work collaborate with the Creation. Those who copy are not collaborators. For this reason, originality consists in returning to the origin.

Antoni Gaudí (1856–1926)

The Eight Airts: the circle of time and space

Our most basic perception of what we see around us is a circle; out of doors, it is the circle of the horizon, and indoors the 360 degrees formed by the four walls of a room. Our human perception makes it necessary for us to make distinctions or divisions in order to make some sense of our surroundings. The natural division of a circle is in four parts which correspond with the arrangement of our bodies, with a front and back, left and right sides. This is the quartered circle or *sunwheel*, archetypal symbol of completion and wholeness. Although this is the basic division, it is not of much practical use as it stands, so the tradition of the North divides it once more, cutting it into eight sectors, eighths known as *aett* or *airts*.

The best known example of this eightfold division is in the compass rose, which has the cardinal directions (*airts*) of North, East, South and West, and the intercardinal directions of North-East, South-East, South-West and North-West. The *airt* lines formed by the intercardinal directions define the four quarters of the earth and heavens. The northern quarter runs from North-West to North-East; the eastern quarter from North-East to South-East; the southern quarter from South-East to South-West, and the western quarter from

South-West to North-West. The square formed by connecting the lines towards these intercardinal directions is the *foursquare* pattern for traditional house and sacred grid layout.

Because of the apparent daily motion of the sun, these directions correspond to times of day. When we tell the time by the sun, as our ancestors did, we do so by noting the direction of the sun, either directly by the sun's position or indirectly via a sundial. For example, the most basic observation is that when the sun stands due south, that is noon or midday. Regardless of the season, noon is exactly halfway between the positions of sunrise and sunset, always being due south. The positions of sunrise and sunset, however, vary with the seasons. At the equinoxes, when the length of day and night are the same, the sun rises in the due east and sunsets in the due west, making a daylight period lasting exactly half of the 24-hour cycle. At the winter solstice, day length is shortest, and both sunrise and sunset are at their most southerly points.

Conversely, at the midsummer solstice, day length is the longest, and both sunrise and sunset are at their most northerly points. Between these extremes, sunrises and sunsets occur progressively northwards after the winter solstice and southwards after the summer. Until the advent of sundials and then clocks, time was told by the position of the sun in relation to marks visible from a central viewing-place. Prominent mountain and hill-tops, cairns, standing stones, artificial notches in the horizon and other landmarks were used as day-markers. When the sun rose, set or stood over them, then it was the corresponding time of day. Thus, to those who knew, the whole landscape was a means of time-telling. Similarly, as sunrise and sunsets occur at certain places corresponding with the time of year, these markers, too, were indicators of the seasons and festivals. Although no longer in use, and scarcely recognized, many of these ancient markers still exist within the landscape, and can be found by those who go looking for them.

The apparent motion of the sun's course is in the direction we call *sunwise*, *clockwise* or *deiseil*. The hands of clocks go this way in imitation of the shadow cast by the *gnomon* of a sundial. The direction of *deiseil* is very significant in the Northern Tradition, representing things being done with right orderliness, in harmony with the natural order. The opposite direction, *widdershins*, is considered unlucky, and is associated with black magic. It is considered bad luck to wind wool or anything *widdershins*, and also after sunset, as rotation is to do with the day, not the night. Anything wound up during the day should be done *deiseil*. Stirring anything, from a cup of tea to a pudding, should be done sunwise. Rope, string and thread should also be wound in a sunwise direction, so that the spindle onto which it is wound will move sunwise when the thread is unwound again. This tradition is adhered to today in modern equipment like records. Dances and other secular or magical activities which involve circular motion should be done *deiseil*.

The country calendar

The rural tradition of northern Europe recognizes a number of festivals related to the various different but related natural cycles of the year. In the Northern Tradition, the calendar is seen as an annual spiritual and physical renewal of the cycles of life. In sacred terms, the festivals which are commemorated on special days in the year cycle in proper sequence re-enact the mysteries of birth, life, death and rebirth. The modern calendar, with which we are most familiar, is a solar astronomical calendar which has been modified over the centuries and drifted away from a strict correlation with solar phenomena. But it is clear that its intention is to begin at the winter solstice, with the summer solstice halfway through. The original form of the modern calendar, then, is one which begins at the shortest day, has increase of daylength until the middle, then declines to the end of the old year, when a new one begins. The alternative version of this is the year which begins at midsummer, and has midwinter as its mid-point, where the first half of the year is declining light, and the second half, increase. The other common solar year is the equinoctial one, which runs from either equinox, having the other equinox as the mid-point. The British financial year, which begins in April, is a relic of an old equinoctial year beginning at the vernal equinox. The short-lived *Revolutionary Calendar*, instituted in 1792 by the French revolutionaries in an attempt to create a new conception of the year, began at the autumnal equinox.

In addition to years which relate to the sun, whose progress are marked by the equinoxes and solstices, there are 'years' based on the vegetation cycle. While the solar years relate to daylight, the 'vegetation years' relate more directly to the seasonal temperatures, which lag behind the sun owing to the slow cooling and heating of the Earth. Vegetation years may be divided into two parts, the 'flower year' and the 'harvest year', their important points being marked by the so-called *cross-quarter days* or *Fire Festivals* of rural tradition. The flower year begins with or has its middle in May, traditional commencement of summer, when flowers attain their most luxuriant bloom and vegetation is growing at its maximum rate. The harvest year begins in August, when the grain harvest is taking place, and has February, the most wintry low point of vegetation, as its mid-point. The other version of this year starts at the low-point of February, and has harvest-time as its apex.

There are eight possibilities inherent in these cycles, which can be summarized as follows:

SOLAR YEARS

Solsticial solar years
1 December — June — December
2 June — December — June

Equinoctial solar years
3 September — March — September
4 March — September — March

VEGETATION YEARS

Flower years
5 November — May — November
6 May — November — May

Harvest years
7 August — February — August
8 February — August — February

The vegetation years are marked by the ancient festivals of the Northern Tradition which have had many names during their existence, going back to archaic times. In the Celtic tradition, the February festival is *Imbolc* or *Brigantia*; May is *Beltane*; August is *Lughnassadh*; and November is *Samhain*. In the Christian Church year, the February festival is Candlemas; there is no May festival, though in England, St George's Day (23 April) has many of its attributes; August is Lammas and

All Saints' Day is 1 November. The seasons are defined by these festivals: spring begins at Imbolc, summer at Beltane, autumn at Lughnassadh and winter at Samhain. In the full cycle, the solar year is observed along with the vegetation year, creating the eight festivals of the year cycle. In this way, each season is divided into two parts by an equinox or solstice—early spring, for instance, runs from Imbolc to the vernal equinox, whilst late spring runs from the equinox until Beltane.

An important part of the vegetation year is the harvest cycle, culminating in the season of autumn. The passage of the autumn season, 'the back-end of the year', is marked by the *Three Harvests*: the First Harvest is Lammas, when the grain crop is cut; the Second Harvest is the autumnal equinox, when the fruits are ready; and the Third is Samhain, when it was traditional to slaughter animals to prepare preserved meat for the harsh days of the coming winter.

The lunar cycles

In the passing of time, there are three time periods which have no common measure: the week, the lunar month and the solar year. Perfect harmony between the week and the lunar month is not possible, for the lunar month is 29 days, 12 hours, 44 minutes, 2.87 seconds in length, a day and a half longer than the 28 days of four weeks. In Anglo-Saxon and Norse tradition, there are two different kinds of month. One is the Common Law month of 28 days composed of four seven-day weeks, conveniently close to the sidereal month of the lunar cycle when compared with the fixed stars, which is 27.3 days in length. Various practical measurements of duration, for example the payment of a fine, or the submission of evidence in Common Law, was generally reckoned in 28-day periods. The second month is the moon month, the synodal month of approximately $29\frac{1}{2}$ days between similar lunar phases. This lunar division was used by the priests of the early Church, who held their monthly *synods* every 29 or 30 days in the style of the Elder Faith from which they had adopted it. The complex calendar of the Faeroe Islands, which survived until the early part of this century, used lunar months adapted and altered as necessary to fit in with the equinox-solstice solar year. Before 1926, in Britain the lunar month was the legal month, but in that year, the calendar month became the legal definition of a month.

To modern astronomy, *new moon* and *full moon* are the precise second of conjunction and opposition between the sun and the moon. But in ancient times, and to rural inhabitants without the benefit of astronomical instruments and tables, the new moon was measured from the first visible appearance of the crescent moon in the evening sky. This was the commencement of a new lunar month. But although it is more accurately observable than the solar year, the lunar calendar is not directly related to it. The 13 full moons of each cycle do not coincide with the solar cycle. The cycles only come together every 19 years, when the same phase of the moon as before coincides with any designated solar festival. However, the seasons are regulated by the motion of the Earth around the sun, and only a solar calendar can ensure that the essential functions of agriculture can be performed at the right time. So the 13 months of the lunar cycle had to be subordinate to the solar cycle, which was divided into eight periods for the purposes of agriculture and sacred festivals, and 12 periods for more precise accounting of dates. These 12 periods, roughly coinciding with lunar months, are the solar months, called *months* from *moons*! These 12 months divide the $365\frac{1}{4}$ days of the year as best they can, and, over the years, various means have been applied to the calendar to keep it in step with the real cycles, none of which occur in a 'round number' of days, causing a gradual drift away from accuracy over the years.

The day and its tides

As with the year, is is possible to begin 'days' at various notable times. Nowadays, most people think of the day itself as identical with the calendar day, beginning at midnight. However, traditionally, this has not always been the definition of a day. Even now, the word *day* has three distinct meanings: the 24-hour period, ascribed a weekday name; the period which runs from sunrise to sunrise, or from sunset to sunset; and the period of *daytime* when it is light. In ancient Greece, the day was held to commence at dawn—daybreak. In the Northern Tradition, on the contrary, the day begins at sunset and continues through the night and the next period of daylight until the following sunset. This is why even today the ancient festivals of the year are usually prefaced with the previous *eve*—New Year's Eve, May Eve, Allhallow's Eve (Hallowe'en) and Christmas Eve—to name but a few. The confusion caused by calendar dates has meant that conceptually the evening before the festival has become thought of as taking place on a separate 'day', whereas customarily, the evening is the first part of the festival, and a prelude to the morning's daylight festivities or observances. Symbolically, the gestation of the festive day is in the darkness before the daylight; the night is equivalent to the enclosure of the foetus in the womb, or the seed in the ground, before its birth with the light of dawn.

The eightfold division of the directions is independent of this eve-beginning definition of the day, being based upon

HOROLOGII ICONISMUS.

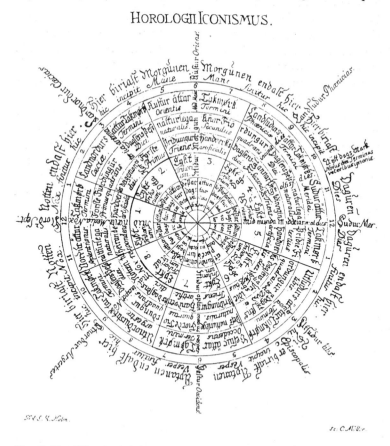

Fig. 2 The Wheel of the Day showing its 8-, 16-, and 24-fold division. (From Stephán Björnsson's *Rimbegla*, Copenhagen, 1780.)

the apparent motion of the sun. During the hours of light, the sun's position is visible with regard to the horizon, and likewise, at night, although invisible 'beneath the Earth', the sun has a direction from the place or person. Because of this, the day as defined by a complete solar cycle is divisible by eight and in the Northern Tradition it is customary to divide it into the eight *tides* of the day, *ættir* or *airts*. These are not related to the tides of the sea, which have a cycle influenced mainly by the moon and its phases. Each of these tides of the day is three hours in length, with an *ætting* at the middle of each tide. For example, Noon, due south, is the middle of Noontide or High Day; Midnight, 12 p.m., is the middle of the tide of Midnight. These *ættings* are special times. People born at these points, of 3, 6, 9, 12, 15, 18, 21 and 24 hours (known today as the *chime hours*), have always been considered to be in possession of powers of foretelling the future and seeing supernatural beings.

As time is continuous, there is no conventional starting point for the tides of the day. Here, I will begin at Midnight, which runs from 10.30 p.m. until 1.30 a.m.; *Uht*, from 1.30 to 4.30 p.m. (a time called *Rismal* or Rising Time). The next tide is Morningtide, from 4.30 until 7.30 (*Dagmal*). Next comes Undernoon or Forenoon, from 7.30 until 10.30, at which time Noontide commences. After Noontide, at 1.30 p.m., begins Undorne, which ends at a time called Eykt, 4.30 p.m. In the summer half of the year, this was the traditional time to stop work. At Eykt, Eventide begins, passing mid-evening at 6 p.m. and ending at 7.30. Finally, the tide of Night begins, lasting the final three hours until Midnight begins again at 10.30 p.m. Each tide of the day has its own correspondences to the directions, times of the year, certain runes and other magical qualities. A summary of the tides and alternative names is below.

Times	English	Anglo-Saxon
04.30–07.30	Morntide	Morgan
07.30–10.30	Daytide	Dæg Mæl (Undertid, Oander)
10.30–13.30	Mid Day	Mid Dæg
13.30–16.30	Undorne	Ofanverthr Dagr (Oern)
16.30–19.30	Eventide	Midaften
19.30–22.30	Nighttide	Ondverth Nott (Cwyl-tid)
22.30–01.30	Midnight	Mid Niht
01.30–04.30	Uht	Ofanverth Nott (Uhten-tid)

The important marks of the day's tides are:

00.00	Midnight (Bull's Noon or Low Noon)	
04.30	Rising	Rismæl
07.30	Daymark	Dæg Mæl
12.00	Noon (High Noon)	Mid Dæg
16.30	Eykt	Eykt
19.30	Suppertime	

The tides of the day have correspondences with activities ruled by the quality inherent in the time of day:

Morntide	Arousing, awakening, fertility, life
Daytide	Gentleness, earning, gain, increase, money
Mid Day	Sustaining, personal will, continuance, perseverance
Undorne	Receptiveness, transformation, replication, parenting
Eventide	Joyousness, spirituality, family, children
Nighttide	Creativity, teaching, gaining knowledge and insights
Midnight	Static, healing, regeneration, recovery
Uht	Stillness, sleep, death

The week

In modern English, the days of the week are named after the deities of the Elder Faith who rule them. All of the qualities of these deities, who are equivalent to the sun, moon and five major planets, are extra-powerful on these days, and corresponding activities are more likely to succeed then.

Sunday is dedicated to the sun, envisioned as the goddess Sól, who rides in the Chariot of the Sun drawn by the horse Aarvak. In East Anglian tradition, the sun goddess is called Phoebe. The Celtic version is the god Ogmios, though in Scottish tradition, the sun is said to '… rise up on the quiet wave, Like a young queen in flower'. The depiction of the deity is as holding a burning sun-wheel before his or her breast. Pointing at the sun brings bad fortune on the pointer, being an insult to the goddess. Sweepings should not be thrown in the direction of the sun—they are also an insult to her, and bad luck will follow. The military salute is derived from the traditional gesture for hailing the rising or setting sun, a shadowing of the eyes from her brilliance whilst looking towards her bounteous light.

Fig. 3 The lunar goddess. (From R. Verstigan's *A Restitution of Decayed Intelligence*, Antwerp, 1605.)

Monday is the sacred day of the moon goddess, Mani (or Eostre in her spring guise), depicted as a woman in a short coat, wearing a hood with two long hare's ears, crescent moon in hand. Figure 3, drawn from R. Verstigan's *A Restitution of Decayed Intelligence*, published at Antwerp in 1605, is a classic rendering of Mani. The hare is the sacred animal of the moon, being one of the favourite forms for Wiccan *hamfarir* (travelling in a shape-changed form), and the 'Easter bunny' or mad March hare of Eostre.

When a full moon falls on a Monday, then the lunar powers are at their most potent. A traditional rhyme recommends invoking the moon at her fullness:

Pray to the moon when she is round,
Luck with you will then abound,
What you seek for shall be found,
On the sea or solid ground.

Tuesday is the day of the god who has been known under the names of Tîwaz, Tiw, Tuisco or Tyr, the defender-god who is also a sage, equivalent to Mars in the southern European pantheon. As Tvisto or Tuisco, he is the ancestor-god of northern Europeans. Traditionally, he is depicted as an old sage, bearing a sceptre in his right hand, and dressed in an animal skin.

Wednesday is the day of Woden or Odin, an aspect of the Allfather, god of wisdom, energy, enlightenment and battle, equivalent to Hermes-Mercury. Woden is often shown as a bold, martial figure, wearing armour and wielding a broadsword, though his weapon is usually the ash-handled spear called Gungnir.

Thursday is the day dedicated to Thor, the god of thunder, equivalent to Thunor, Taranis and Perkunas, and Zeus-Jupiter of the southern European pantheon. Thor was sometimes shown as a red-bearded figure, seated on a throne, wearing a crown of gold with a circle in front and bearing two bright burnished gold stars, and a regal sceptre and a hammer (or axe) in his hands. Thursday is a sacred day in the Northern Tradition, just as the Muslims worship on Friday, the Jews on Saturday and the Christians on Sunday. Traditional rhymes always promise something good for Thursday, such as 'Thursday's child has far to go', 'Cut nails on Thursday for wealth', or 'Sneeze on Thursday, something better'. As Thor is a weather-deity, among other things, Thursday also has some elements of foretelling what weather is to come:

On Thursday at three
Look out and you'll see
What Friday will be.

Friday is the day dedicated to the goddesses Frigg or Freyja (Venus in the southern European pantheon). Frigg is shown as a goddess with a drawn sword in her right hand, and a bow in her left. In her agrarian aspect, her tool is the distaff, symbol of femininity and the transformation of natural materials into human artifacts. It has always been considered unwise to take the risk of making a journey or beginning new things on a Friday, especially if it bears the date 13th. According to Great Yarmouth folklore, a fisherman named Friday had the keel of his new lugger laid on a Friday, carried out the completion ceremonies on a Friday, launched it on a Friday, and named it *Friday* to defy superstition. The *Friday's* maiden voyage was on a Friday and, to everyone's surprise, the vessel returned with a fine catch of herrings. On the next Friday, it set sail again and returned once more with not only a magnificent haul of fish but valuable salvage. The *Friday* was lost with all hands on the third trip.

Rather than always being considered bad in itself, it is often thought of as dangerously unpredictable, as in this old East Anglian adage:

Friday's the day will have its trick,
The fairest or foulest day of the week.

Fisherman Friday found that out the hard way!

Saturday is dedicated to Sætere or Seater, equivalent to the god Saturn, and is a day also associated with the Norns, the Three Fates, and the trickster-god Loki. Seater's image shows him dressed in a long coat, girded with linen. He is leaning against a perch with a sharp back, his head uncovered, lean visage, in his left hand a wheel, and in his right, a container of water, with flowers and fruit.

The descriptions of the customary way of depicting the deities comes from 'A Short Account of the Saxon Idols', from an obscure work entitled *History, Topography and Directory of Bedfordshire, Huntingdonshire, Hertfordshire, etc.*, published anonymously in London in 1863. Like the work of Verstigan, it demonstrates that there has always been an unbroken knowledge of the attributes and qualities of the deities of the elder faith, ever-present in the days of the week. Further examples of this exist in week-lore, where a traditional rhyme tells of the qualities or omens of things done or happening on each day of the week. Some express the Christian prohibition of work on Sunday, having a dire consequence for doing so. But others just express the different qualities of the days. For example. hearing thunder on a specific day is said to portend certain things:

Monday's thunder tells the death of unmarried girls and women.
Tuesday's thunder promises there will be plenty of bread.
Wednesday's thunder brings death to harlots, whores and other bloodshed.
Thursday's thunder brings no misfortune.
Friday's thunder brings the slaughter of a great man, and other murders.
Saturday's thunder brings pestilence and plague, and great death.
Sunday's thunder tells the death of judges and learned men.

The day on which a baby is born, and thus the ruling

deity's attribute, is said to govern his or her fortune:

Monday's child is fair of face,
Tuesday's child is full of grace,
Wednesday's child is full of woe,
Thurday's child has far to go,
Friday's child is loving and giving,
Saturday's child works hard for a living.
But the child that is born on the Sabbath Day
Is blithe and bonny, good and gay.

   Weddings held on different days are said to have different
results:

Monday for wealth,
Tuesday for health,
Wednesday, the best day of all.
Thursday for losses,
Friday for crosses,
And Saturday, no luck at all.

Also, everyday things like doing the washing or cutting
finger and toe nails:

Cut nails on Monday, cut them for news,
Cut them on Tuesday, a new pair of shoes,
Cut them on Wednesday, cut them for health,
Cut them on Thursday, cut them for wealth.
Cut them on Friday, cut them for woe,
Cut them on Saturday, a journey to go,
Cut them on Sunday, cut them for evil.
The rest of the week you'll be ruled by the Devil.

Calendars old and new

Although we must use the present-day calendar in our everyday doings, we must remember that it is not perfectly fitted to
the natural cycles on which Northern Tradition practices are
based. Before the Roman conquest, there were a number of
calendars used in Britain, about which little is known. The
best preserved non-Roman calendar, which must be similar if
not identical to those used in Britain, is the Gallic *Coligny
Calendar*, found in France and dated at around 50 BC. This
was a lunar-solar system which had 12 months of alternating
29 and 30 days' duration, with an additional 13th month to
bring it into line with the solar year. There are fragmentary re-

mains of other systems, too. But it was the old Roman calendar that formed the basis of European calendars ever since it was set up by Julius Caesar in the year 45 BC. In the Pagan tradition, calendars were set up by rulers in their capacity as high priest, or by the high priests themselves. When the Roman Catholic religion became the state faith of the Roman Empire, then it was natural that the popes, high priests of the new religion, should take over this function. Known as the *Julian Calendar*, Caesar's system was slightly inaccurate in its record of the year. Every fourth or leap year was too long by 11 minutes 10.3 seconds, and, because of the way it was arranged, there was no provision for rectifying this error.

By 1582, the accumulated error had become 10 days, so Pope Gregory altered the calendar to the present one, known as the *Gregorian Calendar*. In fact, the change was long overdue. For example, at the beginning, the vernal equinox had fallen, correctly, on 21 March but, by 1582, it was falling on 11 March. In that year, in connection with the new calendar, Gregory decreed that 4 October was to be followed by 15 October, to bring the calendar into line with the solar year. Roman Catholic countries adopted the new calendar immediately but, because Gregory was head of the Catholic Church, countries ruled by Protestant or Orthodox monarchs would not accept the change, and so it stayed for many years.

Finally, in 1752, Britain changed over, adding 11 days on. The 2 September was followed by 14 September, which caused protest demonstrations throughout the country. There were several reasons for the protests. Some people had a sectarian objection, and saw it as 'changing the style to popery'. Others seem to have believed that the government had actually stolen 11 days out of their lives. But the main objection was from country people, whose livelihood depended upon an observance of the old country calendar. This calendar, derived from pre-Christian times, accommodated Christian festivals with the observances of the Elder Faith. When the Gregorian calendar was imposed, many people continued to observe the festivals according to the *Old Style* or Julian calendar.

Today, some people observe the festivals on the corresponding day of the Gregorian, and others, the Julian, calendar. Thus, Michaelmas Day in the present calendar is observed on 29 September, but in Old Style, it is on 11 October. The only official survival is in the financial year. The first day of the financial year is 5 April, Old Lady Day—before 1752, the first day of the calendar year. Even in 1752, it was administratively impossible to alter accounting to begin on 1 January.

Runestocks, or clog almanacs

In the days before printing, calendars and perpetual almanacs were carved on wooden staves, known as *runestocks* or runic calendars. Surviving runic calendars may be started at any convenient point. Throughout history, people have been changing the first day of the year to another day. The most familiar is our 1 January, derived from the midwinter solstice: the Norse began the year reckoning there, Medieval Christian reckoning began on Lady Day, (25 March), and the official year in Britain began on that day until 1752. Danish runestocks often began on Old Winter's Day (14 October), reckoned to be the beginning of the winter part of the year. The Celtic year was reckoned from Samhain.

The year can be divided in various ways, as mentioned above: by solar phenomena, the seasons, or, as at present, numerically into fixed months and days. Runestocks of the later type (those which are square in cross-section) aptly divide the year into four, but these are usually not the seasons but the four solar divisions. If we take the equinoxes as the base-line of equal day and night length, then the winter half of the year is that half when the days are shorter than the nights. The summer half, on the contrary, is when the days are longer than the nights. The shortest day, the midwinter solstice, and the longest day, the midsummer solstice, are midway between the equinoxes and form the intermediate markers. Thus the first side of the runestock is at the beginning of the lengthening of the light, the first quarter of the year from the midwinter solstice to the spring equinox. The second side of the almanac is day-lengthening after the equinox as far as the longest day. These two sides comprise the lengthening-day pair, symmetrical around the equinox point. The third side is in declining day-length from the summer solstice to the autumnal equinox, and the fourth declining day-length when nights are longer than days, down to the winter solstice. These two sides are symmetrical around the autumnal equinox-point.

The relationships between increasing day-length and decreasing night, and vice-versa, can be shown as a diagram

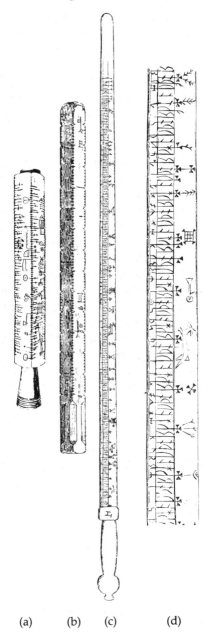

(a)   (b)   (c)   (d)

Fig. 4 Runestocks: (a) and (b) four-sided *clog almanacs*; (c) flat, two-sided stave; (d) detail of a flat stave showing *wend-runes* (written right to left) and day sigils.

of the *Ing* rune, with the two equinoxes as the crossing-points. Likewise, the four sides of the square-section runestock relate to the four directions in the layout of the countryside.

Examination of surviving examples of ancient runestocks shows a profusion of symbols and notation. Of the two kinds of stocks, that is the flat, winter–summer type, and the square, four-quarters staves, the flat are generally simple, being *messe-dag* staves showing only calendar festivals in their sequence. Primestaves or square runestocks are usually far more complex, having the 7-day sequence of the old 28-day month, the Golden Number, various notations for certain solar and lunar phenomena, and other glyphs, generally derived from the archaic *Rune-Hoard*. The names of such staves are many, depending on both country and usages. In England, they are known as *clog almanacs*, derived from an old word for a piece of wood. In Danish, they are *rimstock*, from the ancient word *rimur*, a calendar; and in Norse countries, *prim*, *primestaves* or *messe-dag* staves. Technically, there are different types of stave, depending on their use, *messe-dag* staves are the simplest, containing only the days, with appropriate runes marking festive days. *Primestaves* contain a means for calculating the changes of the moon, in addition to the days of the week. *Rimstocks* use the characters of Wulfila's Gothic alphabet for the seven day-letters, carved along the runestave. Swedish and Norwegian examples bear the first seven staves of the runic *Futhark*: *Frey*, *Ur*, *Thor*, *Os*, *Reid*, *Kaun* and *Hagl*. Of course, these letters do not represent specific days of the week, for if 1 January is a Monday in one year, then it will be a Tuesday the next (or a Wednesday if it is a leap year), and so on. In addition, the runes were used to denote the 19 symbols required for the lunar/solar cycle known as the Golden Number. As the late Norse rune row had only 16 characters, three additional ones—compound bind-runes—were used: *Aurlaugr*, *Twimaudur* and *Belgtzhor*. The accompanying text from Dr Plot's work shows the characters and their names (Fig. 5).

Pagan and Christian calendars ran side-by-side for many centuries, as shown by the use of runes, with their magical addition. In 1689, the physician and antiquary Olaf Rudbeck met a man in the market-place at Uppsala who had a runestock which showed when the January (*Disting*) full moon fell each year. That year, Rudbeck was told, was *Aun*,

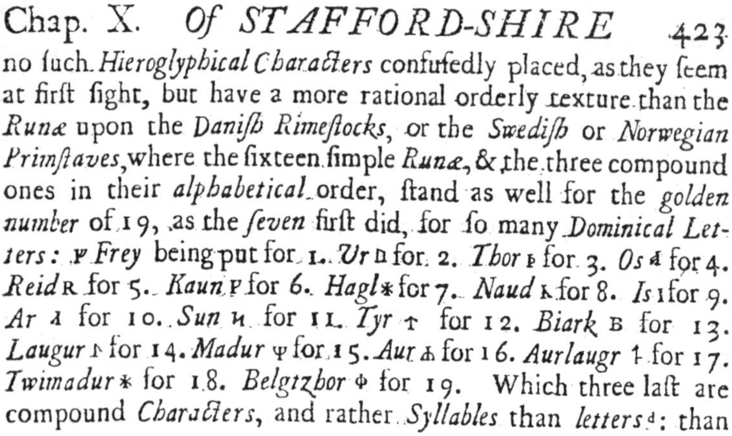

Chap. X.   *Of STAFFORD-SHIRE*   423.

no fuch *Hieroglyphical Characters* confufedly placed, as they feem at firft fight, but have a more rational orderly texture than the *Runæ* upon the *Danifh Rimeftocks*, or the *Swedifh* or *Norwegian Primftaves*, where the fixteen fimple *Runæ*, & the three compound ones in their *alphabetical* order, ftand as well for the *golden number* of 19, as the *feven* firft did, for fo many *Dominical Letters:* ⼂ *Frey* being put for 1. *Ur* n for 2. *Thor* ʙ for 3. *Os* ᚨ for 4. *Reid* ʀ for 5. *Kaun* ⼂ for 6. *Hagl* ⁎ for 7. *Naud* ᚴ for 8. *Is* ı for 9. *Ar* ᚬ for 10. *Sun* ⼂ for 11. *Tyr* ⼂ for 12. *Biark* ʙ for 13. *Laugur* ⼂ for 14. *Madur* ψ for 15. *Aur* ᚼ for 16. *Aurlaugr* ⼂ for 17. *Twimadur* ⁎ for 18. *Belgtzbor* φ for 19.   Which three laft are compound *Characters*, and rather *Syllables* than *letters*⁴: than

Fig. 5 The Scandinavian runes, as used on wooden almanacs. (Extract from Dr Robert Plot's *The Natural History of Stafford-Shire*, London, 1686.)

the beginning of a new calendar cycle. Aun was a legendary Swedish king, reputed to have lived for 300 years, during whose lifetime the moon took a day's journey backwards. The stave's owner informed Rudbeck that the same thing was happening in 1689. Every 310 years, the exact correspondence between the full moons of the festivals, and the days of the solar year recorded on the runestock, goes out of alignment by one day, and has to be re-calibrated by direct observation of the heavens. In 1689, the cycle was out, because the *Disting* moon fell on St Paul's Day rather than on 26 January. The man was delighted to have made this observation, because it enabled him to tell at which point on the runestock he was, as he had inherited the stock, uncalibrated, from his great-grandfather.

The knowledge of such systems of time-measurement, which encompassed periods of three centuries and longer, was current among people who would be considered uneducated and therefore unintelligent in modern terms. Yet these peasants were able to make precise observations of their immediate environment, and to relate it in a way which we, 300 years (an Aun cycle) later, can do only with much intellectual study and effort. Redbeck's informant's runestock was marked with a half-moon symbol for the day on which the *Disting* full moon fell, calculated from a year when the first day of the solar year, that is, one day after the winter solstice, and the lunar year's *Yule Day*, fell on the same day.

In addition to the runic notation used for the seven-day and 19-year cycles is a system of numbers known as *stave numbers*, the old numerical notation of northern Europe. There are several versions of this, having an upright stem onto which various strokes are cut, usually with a cross-stroke for ten. The last stave number on runestocks is 19, but, conventionally used is the symbol for 20. This is the *score*, the old northern system of counting, the number of completion and return.

If all of these notations appear rather complex and obscure, it is only because nowadays we take an accurate calendar for granted, immediately verifiable through the modern mass media. Making accurate calendars and the calibration of time is not something for the average person today, and even in the past, it was the preserve of wise men and women. Runestocks, however, are a vast store of almost-lost knowledge, far more than an outmoded system of calculation. Within any system of notation and encapsulation of information, a deeper reality is encoded for those who can find it. Like modern computer programs, with their own internal logic systems, ancient notation is a form of deep language which contains within it the essence of the modes of thought of its inventors and users. The runic system from which runestocks are derived was primarily magical in function, a kind of magic which acts at all levels in the material as well as the non-material worlds. And although the runestocks which survive are of a late date, their construction and usage attests to their being continuations of the ethos and praxis of the Northern Tradition.

The Eight Festivals of the Year

Combined with the equinoxes and solstices of the solar year, the four so-called *Fire Festivals* of the vegetation year make the eight celebrations of the country calendar, observed by all followers of nature religions. They are known as Fire Festivals because each of them has a fire observance, but equally, there are other times when holy lights, bonfires or *need-fires* are kindled, so the name 'Fire Festival' can be misleading. It is a very ancient name, however. The tenth century Christian Archbishop of Cashel, Ireland, stated that in his time, four great fires were lighted up on the four great festivals of the Druids, namely in February, May, August and November. These are the four Fire Festivals celebrated by adherents of the Elder Faith today.

The four quarters of the May Year are marked according to Druidic custom when the declination of the sun is 16° 20' north or south of the equinoctial line, viewed from the Druidic omphalos four times in the yearly cycle. This makes the four dates of the festivals 4 February, 6 May, 8 August, and 8 November. The February date marks the end of winter and the beginning of spring, the May date the end of spring and the beginning of summer, the August date, the end of summer and the beginning of autumn, and the November date the end of autumn and the beginning of winter. The days celebrated today are slightly different from this, being at the beginning of the respective months. Including the equinoxes and solstices, the following are the Eight Festivals: Yule, Imbolc, vernal equinox, Beltane, midsummer solstice, Lughnassadh, autumnal equinox, and Samhain.

Yule

As our common calendar begins near to the winter solstice, that is a good place to commence. The modern observances of midwinter, sometimes still referred to as Yuletide, are held as a number of separate celebrations on different days, each of which have special traditions reflecting their quality. These begin with the actual solstice on 21 December, starting with the *Mother Night* after sunset on 20 December. The Mother Night is one of the major festivals of Asatrú, sacred to Odin, Ing and Erda, with the liturgical colour of green. The Yule festivities, begun at the solstice, continue with Christmas Eve, Christmas Day and Boxing Day, take in New Year's Eve and New Year's Day (still known in Scotland by the Pagan solar name of Hogmanay, after Hogmagog, Gogmagog or Ogmios), and end at Twelfth Night, when the final trappings of Yuletide—the decorations—are removed. The major event of the feast of Yule is literally the feast, where all manner of food and drink is taken in profusion. It is the major sacred meal of the year, carrying on the Pagan tradition of the holy feast, which was held at the *hof*, a consecrated farmhouse hall which served a whole district.

Clearly, the observance of the solstice is the original purpose of this extended season of festivities, altered and added to by changes in the calendar over the centuries, when the observance, tied to a calendar day, has become out of step with solar phenomena. Effectively, the midwinter festival observes the lowest point of the sun in the sky at midday and the most southerly sunrise and sunset in the year. It is the shortest day, when the sun's vigour seems to be almost extinguished, but, even at its lowest point, it contains within it the promise of day-length again becoming longer.

Because of this, the Roman name of the festival was *Sol Invictus* (the Undefeated Sun). Symbolically, Yule is the day of the rebirth of the sun, and, in various religions of Mediterranean and non-European origin, the chief god has been born at this time. The birthdays of Dionysus, Mithras and Jesus are celebrated on 25 December, the old date of the winter solstice, and all are associated with concepts of rebirth and eternal life.

The name Yule (Anglo-Saxon *Geola*) itself means *Yoke of the Year*, the balance-point across the lowest ebb of sunlight. According to an old Bardic source, couched in the 'question and answer' mode of teaching, the name *Iau* (Yule = Yoke) is given as the name of the supreme deity—

> Because the yoke is the measuring-rod of country and nation in virtue of the authority of law, and is in possession of every head of family under the mark of the lord of the territory ... now God is the measuring-rod of all truth, all justice and goodness; therefore he is the yoke on all, and all are under it, and woe to him who shall violate it.

The traditional sigil of Yule is an enclosure containing dots, symbolizing the seed in the ground, or people in shelter. In the 24-rune circle, it is marked by the rune ♦ , *Jer*, which has the meaning of *season* or *completion*.

Imbolc

The festival of Imbolc or Oimelc is held on 1 February in the modern calendar. In traditional time-reckoning, this is from sunset on 31 January until sunset on 1 February. Imbolc is the festival of the waxing light, paradoxically the coldest time of year, but also the time when day-length begins getting noticeably longer. This is noted in the old country weather-lore rhyme 'As the light grows longer, The cold grows stronger' which commemorates this seeming paradox. Imbolc symbolizes the first stirring of the buried seed within the

earth, indications of the potential of spring, and as such
heralds the arrival of the spring quarter of the year which
runs until May Day. It is a time of renewal, symbolic of cleansing and rebirth.

The festival of Imbolc is also called Brigantia, after the virgin
goddess Bride whose festival was celebrated in Celtic lands
on this day with bonfires and blazing brands. The celebration
was absorbed by the Christian religion, becoming the festival
of the Purification of the Virgin, known as Candlemas from
the observance of lighting candles at midnight in symbolism
of purification. In Ireland, the worship of the Virgin at
Candlemas is manifested as St Bride's day, celebrating St
Brigid, the continuation of the Pagan mother-goddess in her
aspect as the Virgin. And throughout the year, whenever a
woman dons white to be married, she becomes the *Bride*, the
personification of the goddess. At Imbolc, Bride is a threefold
goddess whose attributes are the power of healing, fire-craft,
and poetry. In her threefold aspect, she has been celebrated
as the *Mothers*.

At Imbolc, the goddess is transformed from her aged,
winter aspect as the Hag, veiled in black, carrying her black
rod of barrenness as Hela, guardian of the mysteries of death
and the Underworld. She is transformed into the Virgin
Bride, a manifestation of the solar goddess, Sól, springing
from seeming death into life. In Asatrú, she is Birgit, consort
of Ullr.

The traditional sigil of Imbolc is a five-branched stave,
signifying the upraised hand with spread fingers.

The vernal equinox

The vernal equinox or Ostara, 21–23 March, is the transition-
point between the dark and light halves of the year. At the
equinox, the sun rises due east and sets due west, giving exactly 12 hours of daylight. Although, today, the vernal
equinox is always hailed by the media as being 'the first day
of spring', it is in fact the mid-point of the traditional season
of spring, which runs from Imbolc to Beltane. It is the time of
conception, when the light triumphs over darkness. The
Church celebrates 25 March as the Annunciation, the time
when, in Pagan religions, the Bride married at Imbolc con-
ceives the child to be born at midwinter. In Norfolk, it was
traditional to eat a plum pudding known as the *Harvest*

Strengthener at the spring equinox. The Asatrú festival of the vernal equinox is Summer Finding, sacred to Thor, with a liturgical colour of red. Freyr and Freyja are also honoured here.

The traditional sigil for the spring equinox is a circle with two sprouting 'horns'.

Beltane

The god of Beltane is the solar-fire deity who has gone under the names of Balor, Bel, Belenos and Balder, and his festival announces the arrival of the summer half of the year. The god Bragi and the goddess Iduna are also celebrated now. Beltane commences at sunset on 30 April. This time, known as May Eve in Britain and *Walpurgisnacht* in German-speaking countries, is a time of magic, when the Beltane fires are lit. It is the time when people jump through the smoke and flames to purify themselves for the incoming summer season, and to generate fertility. The Beltane fire, composed of the wood of nine different types of tree, is lit on a specially-prepared sacred grid. This is laid out by drawing a square on the ground and dividing it into nine smaller squares. The eight outer squares are dug out with a spade and removed as turves, but the ninth is left at the centre. This *need-fire* is kindled upon this central square by turning an oaken spindle in an oak log socket—the ancient way of generating fire. In former times, all fires in the locality were extinguished on May Eve, and then re-lit from the village's Beltane Fire, which, burning at the centre of the nine-square grid, was the central hearth of the community. Such a local sacred hearth symbolizes the central divine fire whose sparks we all carry. Beltane hills such as Tan-y-bryn (Fire Hill) in Carmarthenshire; Tullybelton (Beltane Hill) in Perthshire; and the village of Belton, near Great Yarmouth, Norfolk, recall sacred sites for the annual bale-fire. The tradition of eating the May-cake, a cake of oatmeal bearing nine knobs in the grid pattern of the Beltane square, is observed on May Eve.

The day part of Beltane ceremonies has a different character. The fires have already been re-lit from the central hearth, and the festivities of the May-pole can take place. The May-pole, made from the wood of the birch, tree of purification, is danced around in imitation of the twirling of the spindle used in the creation of fire at the May Eve kindling of the

Beltane fire. The merry-making of rural working people on May Day was continued in other forms with the expansion of towns in the Industrial Revolution, and slowly transformed itself into the socialist Labour Day celebrated in many countries today. The blossom, bunting, flags, garlands and May bushes which bedecked houses and carts in the countryside were transformed into the urban May Day banners of Trade Unions and political movements.

The traditional sigil for Beltane is the northern *Tree of Life* with six side-branches.

Midsummer solstice—Litha

The midsummer solstice, in Anglo-Saxon, *Litha*, is the high point of the year, the longest day when the sun is at its highest point in the sky and when sunrise and sunset are at their most northerly points on the horizon. In Asatrú, it is sacred to the god Balder, whose liturgical colour is white. Thor and his consort Sif are also remembered now. It is the mid-point of the season of summer, which runs from Beltane to Lughnassadh. In medieval times, it was commemorated as the feast of St John the Baptist, when bonfires were lit on the highest points in the district, celebrating the highest point of the sun. Bonfires should be kindled on the windward side of buildings, gardens or fields to be protected, so that the sanctified smoke can waft over them (but not so close that they catch fire!). At this time, flaming sun-wheels may be burnt, burning brands swung in circles at the ends of chains, and blazing tar-barrels run down slopes or through streets. Blazing torches can be carried, sunwise, around buildings, gardens or fields to ensure good fortune. Making an important festival in the Northern Tradition, midsummer continues to be a time of fairs and festivals. The great Midsummer Fair held at Cambridge on Midsummer Common is one of the largest in England and a flourishing continuation of these celebrations. Until it was suppressed in 1985, the Stonehenge Festival had been held there at midsummer for 14 years, and was set to become a fully-established reinstatement of the fair formerly held there.

The traditional sigil for Midsummer is an open curve.

Lughnassadh—Lammas

Lughnassadh, otherwise known as Lammas, is the festival of

the First Harvest, held on 1 August, with its eve from sunset on 31 July. Lughnassadh is the beginning of the season of autumn, and is the traditional time for great fairs. It is named after the Celtic god of wisdom and illumination, Lugh, the Celtic equivalent of some aspects of Odin, and is a celebration of the cutting of the first corn harvest and the baking of the first loaf from the new year's crop. Some Asatrú groups celebrate a two-day festival here, with 31 August sacred to Loki and Sigyn, and 1 August sacred to Odin and Frigg. As *Hlafmasse* (the Anglo-Saxon 'Loaf Mass)', it is a key time in the Mystery of John Barleycorn (see Chapter VI).

The traditional sigil for Lammas is a semicircle bisected by a line.

Autumnal equinox

Occurring around 21 September, the autumnal equinox or Mabon is the time of the Second Harvest, the mid-point of the season of autumn, the transition-day between the light half and the dark half of the year. As with the vernal equinox, sunrise is due east and sunset due west. From now on, until midwinter, darkness is the ascendant.

The traditional sigil for this equinox is of a stylized dying plant. In Asatrú, it is the festival of Winter Finding, sacred to Frey, with a liturgical colour of yellow. Balder and Nanna are also commemorated then.

Samhain

Samhain, 1 November, is the transition-point between the seasons of autumn and winter, the Third Harvest when in times gone by all animals not required for work or as breeding stock were slaughtered, and their meat was smoked or salted as winter supplies. Traditionally, Samhain is the Festival of the Dead, the time when we remember our ancestors, whose lives, though now past, are part of that unbroken stream of life of which we are the current representatives. Without their former existence in the past, we would not be. It is at this time that we in turn hail our descendants, those who will come in centuries hence, but whom we will never see or know. Samhain is better known in English-speaking countries from the observances of its eve, known by its Christianized name as Allhallows' Eve, popularly, Hallowe'en, observed after dark on 31 October. In a debased way, the Hallowe'en trappings of plastic skeletons and witches' hats are a continuation of a solemn festival of remembrance of death and the departed. This link with the dead at Samhain is expressed by the custom of divination on the eve, when various methods are used in order to obtain answers to pressing questions about what the coming year might hold. Hallowe'en masks, though made of artificial materials today, continue the old tradition of *guising*, originally a shamanic practice of temporarily taking on the qualities of an otherworldly being. Guising is a custom formerly observed also at Yule, and remaining in the multiple appearances of Santa Claus. Some Asatrú groups remember the dark side of things at this festival in the shape of the demonic beings Sollblindi-Fafnir and Hela, goddess of the Underworld.

Like Yule, Samhain was once a longer festival. In Celtic tradition, Samhain Day itself was the fourth or middle day of a week's celebrations. It has given rise to a number of festivals around the same date. The Asatrú observance of Winter Saturday and Winter Sunday is the nearest weekend to Samhain. In Britain, the observance of Guy Fawkes' Night, when an effigy of a seventeenth-century would-be regicide is burnt ceremonially. The direct link between Guy Fawkes' Night, 5 November, and Samhain is that the attempt on the life of King James I was timed to take place at the State Opening of Parliament which, each year, is held in ' early November, carrying on the tradition of the beginning of the Celtic royal new year at Samhain. The bonfire, still the central part of 'Firework Night', is a continuance of the old Fire Festival in celebration of the ·end of harvest when effigies were incinerated which represented the ills and sadnesses of the year just passed. Remembrance Day, 11 November, chosen originally to commemorate the slain of the First World War, is around this time, and the sentiments expressed there are closer to Samhain than the Christian festival of Martinmas upon which it falls. Even that has now been altered, as a hindrance to commerce, to the nearest Sunday.

The traditional sigil for Samhain is a knot of protection.

The stations of the mystic year

The complete cycle of the harvest year—the *Mysteries of John Barleycorn*—relates the time of day to the various parts of the eternal cycle of life. Each of the important events is a *station* of the year, and generally corresponds with one of the eight festivals. Because stations correspond with a time of day, the daily cycle can be taken as a framework on which to base a cycle of corresponding meditational activities or sacred devotions. The correspondences are as follows—

Time	Festival	Station	Event
16.30		1	Death/rebirth—parent plant brings forth the seed and then dies
18.00	Equinox	2	Calling—ripening of fruit and harvest
21.00	Samhain	3	Awakening—letting go: the seed falls to earth
00.00	Yule	4	Enlightenment—rebirth of the light in the darkness
06.00	Equinox	5	Reconciliation—apparently dead, the seed comes to life again
09.00	Beltane	6	Mystical union—plant in full growth in harmony with the environment
12.00	Midsummer	7	Sanctification—flower opens and is fertilized
15.00	Lughnassadh	8	Completion

Divine Beings and Qualities

The most popular form of worship in the Northern Tradition today is known as *Asatrú* or *Odinism*. As with the Hindu, native American, African and Shinto traditions, Asatrú in particular and the Northern Tradition in general sees the divine world as inhabited by numerous deities, each of them manifestations of transcendental divinity. These deities have various attributes, and one may meditate upon these qualities and see them present all around us in nature and in human society. The names of the deities have altered over the years, and it is by their qualities that they should be known, as some have several alternative names. The list of deities worshipped in Britain, especially, is very long. During the Roman occupation, Roman, Greek, Egyptian, Persian, and Babylonian deities were added to indigenous British ones, and elements of them entered into indigenous worship and tradition. In medieval times, cults of foreign local saints were imported by Christianity, and merged with older versions of the same essence. And since the nineteenth century, Buddhism, Hinduism and other oriental faiths have taken a permanent place in this country.

Unlike many other branches of the Northern Tradition, Asatrú has its own holy books, the *Eddas*, written down in the Christian era, yet retaining the authentic knowledge of Pagan times. The *Hávamál* is a code of rules and conduct, there is a creation myth, and, as with all scripture, many didactic tales of gods and heroes. The *Lay of Grimnir*, for example, records the names and attributes of the northern goddesses. The explanation is given as a dialogue between a seeker after the truth, Ganglieri, and the gods in disguised form. This is the section on the goddesses, which explains the specialized attributes and powers of each of the deities. They can be viewed as divine entities in their own right, or as aspects of the

Fig. 6 Twelfth-century wall-painting of Frigg, riding her distaff, in Schleswig Cathedral, Germany.

female principle, whose names are words of power to be used in appropriate formulaic calls:

> Ganglieri then asked 'What goddesses are there?' *High One* replied: 'The foremost is Frigg, most magnificent. Säga is another: she lives at Sökkvabekk. The third is Eir: she is the best of healers. The fourth is Gefjon: she is a virgin, and women who die unmarried serve her. The fifth is Fulla: also a virgin. She carries Frigg's casket and shoes and knows her secrets. Freyja is as distinguished as Frigg. The seventh is Sjöfn: she turns people, men and women, to love. The eighth is Lofn: She is so gentle and good that she brings together men and women for whom marriage is forbidden or impossible. The ninth is Vär: she hears vows and contracts and takes her vengeance on vow-breakers. The tenth is Vör: her wisdom is such that nothing can be hidden from her. The eleventh is Syn: she guards the hall doorway, and shuts it against those who are excluded. The twelfth is Hlin: her task is to protect those whom Frigg wishes to rescue from danger. The thirteenth is Snotra: she is wise and gentle. The fourteenth is Gná: she is Frigg's messenger. Sól [the sun goddess] and Bil; Earth, the mother of Thór, and Rind, Váli's mother, are also numbered among the goddesses.'

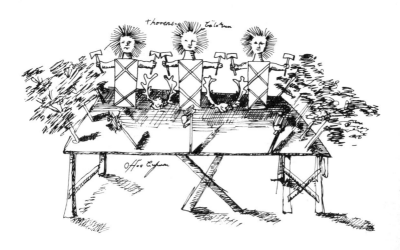

Fig. 7 Altar to Thor, Lappland, 1671.

In addition to these, there are other deities, such as Ostara, the lunar goddess who has given her name to Easter, Skadi, the winter huntress and corresponding alternative names from the Celtic and Baltic traditions.

Similarly, the major male deities of Asatrú are Odin, the god of inspiration, writing, magic, combat and the dead, the shamanistic figure knowing the happenings in the Nine Worlds. His Anglo-Saxon name is Woden, the one-eyed, hooded god. His symbol is the *valknut*, three interlinked equilateral triangles, symbolizing the interpenetration of the three states of being. His consort is Frigg, Queen of the Heavens. Thor is the thunderer, god of farmers and those who work the land; protector of righteousness against iniquity. His symbol is the hammer *Mjöllnir*, and its development, the *fylfot* or swastika. Baldar is an aspect of the solar power, deity of the growing light, and the waxing part of the year, who is symbolically slain each midsummer. His symbol is the mistletoe plant, from which his fatal dart is fashioned, and which is also a symbol of Pagan martyrdom. Höd is the blind god who is fooled into throwing the fatal dart.

Freyr is the male counterpart of the goddess Freyja, the deity of fertility and produce. Heimdall is the guardian-watcher of the gods and custodian of Bifröst, the Rainbow Bridge which links the worlds. His symbol is the horn. Bragi is the husband of Iduna. He is the god of poetry, from whom the word 'brag', meaning 'boast', comes. Mimir is the god of knowledge, wisdom and inspiration. Forseti, son of Balder, is the axe-god, the golden axe being his symbol, whilst Vidar is the son of Odin. Njord is the god of ships, whilst Loki is the trickster-god, a figure which, although disruptive, represents the necessary questioning of authority which must occur if things are to be kept operating in an optimal way, and if progress is to be made. Sub-gods, godlings and giants, the equivalents of many Christian saints, include Wayland the Smith, patron of blacksmiths and metalcraft, fire-giants, frost-giants and other beings who are personifications of qualities found in nature. All of these beings exist under other names in mythological and religious systems all over the world. In Europe, they are found as saints in the Christian calendar, as well as in their own right. Appendix 2 lists the major deities of the northern pantheon and their attributes.

Saints' and holy days

Most of the key dates in the solar calendar are associated with certain saints of the Christian Church. The majority of these saints are said to have been early Christians who were killed because of their beliefs, and who were commemorated as heroes by being revered on a certain day of the year. Even if this is so, it is not the whole story, for the attributes of the more important saints are related directly to the time of year, and clearly have an unbroken continuity with their corresponding pre-Christian deities, sprites and *genii*. This is not surprising, as newer belief-systems have always based themselves upon earlier ones, adopting those parts which were ineradicable, and expressing them in a form appropriate to the new belief. In Europe, it was customary to take over pagan shrines and convert them into churches; the sacred days of the year were also appropriated. The local qualities inherent in the place, expressed in terms of Pagan deities and *genii*, could not be ignored, for it was these qualities which made the sites sacred in the first place. So, for example, high places sacred to deities of light and active protection were rededicated to the archangel, St Michael; shrines of the mother-goddess became churches of St Mary; temples of Helios became churches of St Elias; those of Victory, St Victoria; and so on. Likewise, the qualities intrinsic in certain days because of their relation to the seasonal cycles are an ineradicable part of life. They could not be abolished, and so their re-interpretation in terms of the newer religion became necessary. Thus the tutelary deities of the days were re-Christened, losing none of their old character. In much of northern Europe the cult of saints was severely truncated in the sixteenth century at the Reformation, and most of the days ceased to be observed by the Protestant churches. However, the old country lore, an essential part of the rural year cycle, based on the Elder Faith, retained the knowledge and use of these saints' days as well as those days not marked by notable saints but which are equally important as weather-markers. The major festivals of the rural year are:

New Year's Day (1 January) — The celebrations of New Year begin on New Year's Eve, culminating at midnight, the time when the old year ends and the new one begins. A traditional rhyme for this time is a spell for the removal of all the bad things which happened in the old year and their replacement with good things:

> Ring out the old,
> Ring in the new,
> Ring out the false,
> Ring in the true.

The Kalends of January (3 January) — This is not a notable saint's day, being dedicated to St Geneviève in some calendars. However, country lore holds it to be an important weather-marker:

> If January Kalends be summerly gay,
> 'Twill be wintery weather till the Kalends of May.

Twelfth Night/Epiphany (6 January) — Twelfth Night, after sunset on 5 January, is the eve of the last day of the Yule festival, the time when the debris of Yule is cleared away, and preparation for the return to work begins. In the Julian calendar (Old Style) this is Old Christmas Day—Old Yule—when the days are longer by a cock's stride than at midwinter.

St Distaff's Day (7 January) — This day, named after a sanctified tool rather than an individual, was the day when women resumed their work of spinning after the Yule festival. It is sacred to the goddess Frigg, consort of Odin and an aspect of the Great Mother goddess, whose iconography depicts her riding on a distaff rather than a broomstick (Fig. 6). However, the areas of life covered by Frigg's tutelage are not all work, and this is reflected by the old country rhyme:

> Partly work and partly play,
> Ye must on Saint Distaff's Day:

Old New Year's Day (13 January) — New Year's observances such as wassailing apple trees are still carried out in some places on Old New Year's Day (Old Style), as it is considered that this is the right time in the natural cycle to conduct the rite.

Charming of the Plough (17 January) — This is a festival in modern Asatrú which is a fixed date version of Plough Monday, the male counterpart of St Distaff's Day.

St Paul's Day (25 January) — This day is a key marker in the old runic calender, the day of the *Disting* full moon. Traditionally, celebration of St Paul's Day begins on Paul's Eve. It is a weather-marker, when the state of the weather on that day is said to mirror that of the coming summer:

> If St Paul's Day be fair and clear,
> It do betide a happy year.
> But if it chance to snow or rain,
> Then will be dear all kinds of grain.
> If clouds or mists do dark the sky,
> Great store of birds and beasts will die.
> And if the winds do fly aloft;
> Then wars shall vex the kingdom oft.

Candlemas/Imbolc/Brigantia (2 February) — See above.

St Dorothea's Day (6 February) — This is another weather-marker, for it is said that St Dorothea's Day brings snow.

St Valentine's Day (14 February) — St Valentine's Day is the continuation of the Pagan traditions of both ancient Rome and northern Europe, its dedicatory name being a version of the Norse deity Vali, the archer-god, son of Odin. The dedication of the day was transferred to one of two St Valentines, about whom little is known, and who appear to be a southern European version of Cupid. As with all of the ancient festivals, the divinatory part of the celebration was performed at the beginning of the day according to traditional reckoning—after sunset on 13 February, *Valentine's Eve*. Girls would decorate their pillows with five bay leaves, one for each corner and one in the middle, in order to dream of their lover and husband-to-be. St Valentine's is associated with a purification custom, which involves carrying an arch of brambles, the plant of spirit banishing.

St Winnal's Day (3 March) — St Winnal was a Breton saint who has 50 different known spellings for his name, including Gunwal, Guénolé and Winwaloe. His legend, however, is of control over the sea's tides and the weather, and his day is associated with storms. It is clear that Winnal is a transference from the Pagan deity of wind, tide and weather, Ægir.

All Fools' Day (1 April) — The custom of playing tricks and practical jokes on people, making them into April Fools, is part of the trickster tradition of the Northern Tradition. In every stable society, in order that things should not become too entrenched, there are periods when misrule is permitted for a short time. The Northern trickster god Loki is patron of 1 April. He is a figure who causes trouble yet who can also carry out tasks that others are incapable of. In medieval times, it was often only the jester who could tell the king that something was wrong in his rule; today, satire performs a similar function. Unlike many festivals, All Fools' Day does not commence on the eve, and only operates until midday.

Miura Anjin (14 April) — This is a festival of Ostara, commemorated in Asatrú.

St George's Day (23 April) — Around this day is the remnant of an old festival of fertility, a week before the May Day ceremonies. St George's Day is the traditional day for parades of dragons, hobby-horses and giant effigies through the streets. St George is a version of the northern hero Sigurd the Dragon-slayer, the Siegfried of Wagner's opera.

St Mark's Day (25 April) — The Eve of St Mark (after sunset on 24 April) is a night for divination, foretelling the future. Fasting from sunset, a young woman wishing to see her future lover should make and bake a cake containing an eggshell-ful of salt, wheatmeal and barley-meal. Then open the door. Lover should come in and turn the cake. Also St Thomas's Eve (after sunset on 20 December).

May Day/Beltane (1 May) — See above.

8 June — This is another weather marker:

> If on the eighth of June it rain,
> It foretells a wet harvest mensain.

St Vitus' Day (14 June) — St Vitus' Day is a weather-marker, possibly a Christian version of the day of Vidar, son of Odin:

> If St Vitus' Day be rainy weather,
> It will rain for thirty days together.

St John the Baptist's Day (24 June) — This is the festival of midsummer, like Christmas, now slightly out of place owing to the precession of the equinoxes and the consequent drift of the calendar with regard to solar phenomena. St John's Eve, after sunset on 23 June, was a time of meditation, awaiting the northernmost sunrise. The Druidic observance of midsummer sunrise at Stonehenge each year is one of the few remnants of a very widespread practice in northern Europe of hailing the sun at midsummer/St John's Day. Midsummer bonfires are lit at high points, generally on bare rock surfaces, celebrating the apex of the solar light. These locations are often places of ancient sun-observation.

St Swithin's Day (15 July) — St Swithin's Day is still recognized by most people as the day they do not want it to rain. According to tradition, if it rains on St Swithin's Day, then it will continue to rain for the next 40 days. It is the day from which it is permissible to eat the new crop of apples (if there are any!).

Sleipnir (26 July) — The festival of life in Asatrú commemorates Odin's steed, Sleipnir.

St Mary's Day (15 August) — St Mary, the continuation of the Great Mother goddess in her fertile aspect, is evoked today to ensure a good vintage:

> On St Mary's Day, sunshine,
> Brings much good wine.

St Bartholomew's day (24 August) — Bartholomew's Day is another weather-marker, foretelling the forthcoming autumn:

> If Bartlemy's Day be fair and clear,
> Hope for a prosperous autumn this year.

It is the eve of the Asatrú festival of *The Discovery of the Runes*.

The Discovery of the Runes (25 August) — Commemorates Odin's self-sacrifice to access knowledge.

St Matthew's Day (21 September) — Like St Mary's Day, Matthew's is associated with the grape harvest:

> Matthew's Day, bright and clear,

Brings good wine in the next year.

Michaelmas (29 September) — Michaelmas is the Christian festival of St Michael, chief of the angels, equivalent to rulers of benevolent supernatural warriors in other traditions. In the Northern Tradition, he parallels Heimdall, watcher of the gods and leader of the 432,000 *Einherjar*, or warriors of the gods. Michaelmas is another weather-mark day. An East Anglian adage says 'Harvest comes as long before Michaelmas as dog roses bloom before Midsummer'. The sweets known as *Taffy on a Goose* (sweetened dough in the form of a man riding on a goose) were sold in Norwich until the Second World War put an end to the custom.

Old Winter's Day (14 October) — This is the beginning of the winter part of the year in the old northern calendar, recorded on the wooden almanacs known as *runestocks* or *primestaves*.

St Audrey's Day (17 October) — Time of the famous fair at St Ives, Huntingdonshire, where St Audrey's trinkets ('Tawdry') were sold. The Asatrú festival of Hengest, commemorating the Saxon settlement of Britain.

All Saints' Day (1 November) — This is the festival of Samhain. See above.

All Souls' Day (2 November) — As a continuation of the festival of Samhain, All Souls' begins at sunset on 1 November, when it was customary to light bonfires known as *Tinley Fires* (*Teanlas* or *Tindles*). All Souls' Day was celebrated with festivities which were the continuance of the celebration of the festival of Woden (Odin) as god of the dead. These included the parading of the Hodening or Wild Horse and other guising including mummers' plays, symbolically re-enacting the mysteries of life, death and rebirth. *Soulcakes* are traditionally eaten on All Souls' Day.

Martinmas (11 November) — The feast of St Martin, otherwise known as Martinmas or Hollantide, is the marker of the full onset of wintertime. In former times, it was the day on which hiring fairs were held, where workers could sign up with new masters in the hope of better employment. In Asatrú, it is the festival of the Einherjar, the slain warriors who guard the gods. As a weather-marker, Martinmas often occurs in a period of fine weather known as 'St Martin's Little Summer'. In East Anglia, the following rhyme predicts what will happen in the coming winter:

> If ducks do slide at Hollantide,
> At Christmas they will swim.
> If ducks do swim at Hollantide,
> At Christmas they will slide.
> Winter is on his way
> At St Martin's Day.

St Clement's Day (23 November) — St Clement's Day was the first day of winter in the Old Style calendar. St Clement, as patron saint of Blacksmiths, is the continuation of the Saxon and Norse godling Wayland the Smith. Wayland-Clement was the protector of smiths, and at the customary feast for blacksmiths held at the Wealden village of Burwash, 'Old Clem' was believed to stand over the tavern door. Ancient churches dedicated to St Clement are found close to navigable rivers in places which had Danish settlements. Among the more notable are St Clement Dane's in the Strand in London, St Clement's, Bridge Street, Cambridge, and St Clement's in Aarhus, Denmark, perhaps the sites of erstwhile shrines to Wayland.

St Nicholas's Day (6 December) — St Nicholas is Santa Claus, who in Britain is now more commonly associated with the period around Yuletide. Since the Reformation, the attributes of this saint, themselves a continuation of Pagan tradition, have become merged with the holly-crowned Father Christmas of Yuletide. Father Christmas is an aspect of Thor, traditionally depicted riding a goat and carrying a wassail bowl. On the eve of St Nicholas (after sunset on 5 December), children put out carrots, hay and straw, supposedly for his horse, to be exchanged for presents in the night.

St Lucy's Day (13 December) — The marker of 'Little Yule', a feast of lights which is the real origin of *Lucy*, making it a celebration of the Holy Light. In Denmark, Lucy's Eve is a night for divination of the identity of future husbands. St Lucy is clearly a Pagan goddess of light assimilated into later festivities.

St Thomas's Day (21 December) — This is the actual solsticial day, the real Pagan Yule, a time when the poor and the needy are given money or presents. The eve is a time when dreams may give a glimpse of what is to come in the forthcoming year. In former times, it was customary that those who had been left out could ask for money, a practice known after the saint's day as 'Thomasing' or 'mumping'. In Austria, this is the eve when buildings are spiritually cleansed with holy water and incense.

Christmas Day (25 December) — This is an alternative date for Yule, being an important solar festival in Mediterranean religions, with the births of Mithras, Dionysus and Jesus celebrated then.

St Stephen's Day (26 December) — This is the day when in many parts of Britain the custom of wren hunting was conducted. The people of a village would go out, hunt and capture a wren, the smallest bird. When it had been trapped, it was put into a lantern or a specially-made 'wren house', and then paraded around the village. Often, it was killed, a reversal of the prohibition on killing wrens at other times of the year. The wren was then hung on a holly branch and was borne to its funeral by the *Wren Boys* or *Droluns*. This custom is believed to be a continuation of the Druidic practice of using the song of the wren in divination.

Holy Innocents' Day (28 December) — This is considered to be the unluckiest day of the year, and no work is to be started then, or it will end in disaster. The Tay Bridge disaster, when a passenger train fell into the Firth of Tay with great loss of life, occurred on the 28 December 1879, and was attributed to this day.

Lunar festivals

The Christian calendar preserves a series of Pagan lunar festivals in springtime, though the moon plays no part at any other time of year. By far the most important lunar-derived festival of the year is Easter, the continuation of the lunar spring festival of the goddess Eostre or Ostara. Being held on a specific day, and not a calendar date, it is 'movable', taking place on the first Sunday after the first full moon after the vernal equinox. Two weeks after Easter is Hocktide, then Ascension Day, and finally Whitsun, the last lunar festival of the winter solisticial year.

At Whitsun, which is no longer observed as a popular festival in Britain, owing to official alteration of the Bank Holiday system, there are traditions of bedecking houses with branches of oak. In churchyards and other sacred locations in the landscape, bowers made from tree branches were set up as the focal points of Whitsun merry-making. Ale, brewed especially for the occasion, and cakes were consumed, and there was Morris dancing, dancing on the roofs of church towers, and around labyrinths.

Lucky and unlucky days

The cyclic quality of time is recognized strongly in the Northern Tradition. Just as the seasons and festivals come and go, and return again, so the light gives way to darkness, and light comes once again. Good times are followed by bad times, and so on. Each day of the year is part of several cycles, and certain days are considered to be bringers of good of bad luck. Good luck is associated with correct observance of certain feast days, but in addition to each Friday the Thirteenth, there are the following unlucky dates:

January 1, 2, 4, 5, 10, 15, 17, 29
February 8, 10, 17, 26*, 27*, 28*
March 16, 17, 20
April 7*, 8*, 10*, 16, 20*, 21
May 3*, 6*, 7, 15, 20
June 4, 8, 10*, 22*
July 15, 21
August 1*, 19, 20, 29*, 30*
September 2*, 4*, 6, 7, 21*, 23*
October 4*, 6, 16*, 24*
November 5*, 6*, 15, 20, 29*, 30*
December 6, 7, 9, 15*, 22*, 28

These dates are considered very unlucky; they are days upon which it was considered perilous to fall ill, to start a journey, to commence any work, or to be married, apart from those marked with the asterisk* which are unlucky days also, but not so bad as to prevent action.

Greater cycles—the seven ages of the world

As with the cycles of hours, tides and days, weeks and months, the years are also parts of greater cycles. The sacred number nine is the key to this greater cycle. An ancient poem records the traditional durations of each of the cycles:

Three wattles are the life of a hound	9 years
Three hounds are the life of a steed	27 years
Three steeds are the life of a man	81 years
Three men are the life of an eagle	243 years
Three eagles are the life of a yew	729 years

The life of a yew is one age, and there are seven ages from the creation of the world until its doom, the end of the greater cycle, 5,103 years in all.

The directions and the winds

Because of the light of day, astronomical phenomena and seasonal weather, the directions have their own special qualities. This can be seen in traditional beliefs and customs. The three roots of the Cosmic Tree, Yggdrassil, represent the three quarters of east, south and west, with the tree itself, abode of the gods, to the north, the direction of sanctity in the Northern Tradition. Because of this, entrances of traditional buildings do not usually face north. An old Irish saying states: 'The front of everything is to the south', and the majority of ancient British earthen barrows have their entrances to the east or south, and, millennia later the east and south quarters were still favoured for the front of buildings. Even today in Cambridge, the Backs, that area of gardens and riverside walks so favoured by student and tourist alike, is to the west of the town centre and the river, the fronts of the colleges being to the east. Few colleges face west, and none have northward entrances. Churches, too, favour the south and west for entrances, except in urban situations where it is impossible.

When travelling on foot across country, it is better to keep to south-facing slopes. It was customary for pilgrims to travel along the south side of ridges, and the old Pilgrim's Way through Surrey and Kent to Canterbury shows this. But this tradition is much older than the Christian veneration of St Thomas á Becket, for it is an essential part of the lore of directions in the Northern Tradition.

The direction of the wind is an important factor not only with regard to the weather but also on a more esoteric level. Just as each direction has a quality related to its *sele*—the time and tide of the day and the year, so each direction and its wind have qualities which subtly affect people and animals. The time when the winds are blowing—the *sele of the winds*—is important in interpretation. For example, an old adage describes the prosperity of a forthcoming year from the direction of the wind on New Year's Eve:

> If New Year's Eve night wind bloweth *south*,
> It betokeneth warmth and growth.
> If *west*, much milk, and fish in the sea;
> If *north*, much cold, and storms there will be;
> If *east*, the trees will bear much fruit;
> If *north-east*, flee it, man and brute.

Like the wheel of the runes, the order of the four directions of this traditional rhyme begins with the south, and ends with the east. The final *north-east* is the joker in the pack, the harmful outsider.

Another piece of East Anglian lore attributes the bringing of the best weather to the west wind:

> When the wind is in the *south*,
> 'Tis in the rain's mouth;
> When the wind's in the *west*,
> The weather's at its best.
> When the wind is in the *east*,
> 'Tis neither good for man nor beast.

But in winter:

> The *west* wind always brings wet weather,
> The *east* wind wet and cold together;
> The *south* wind surely brings the rain,
> The *north* wind blows it back again.

The guardians of the directions

The Northern Tradition has four supernatural beasts which act as guardians of the directions. They are detailed in a legend about the Norwegian king Harald Gormsson. He wished to attack Iceland, so he sent his personal wizard there, who did *hamfarir*, travelling in the assumed shape of a

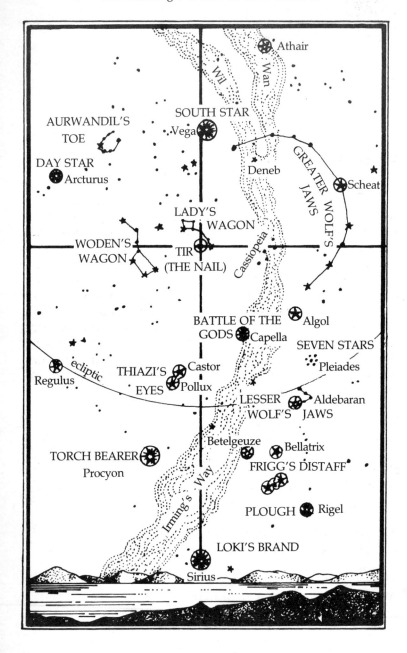

Fig. 8 Map of the northern constellations and star-names.

whale. When the wizard reached Iceland, he was repulsed magically by four guardian beings. He encountered a dragon at Vopnafjord on the north-east coast of the island, a huge bird at Eyjafjord in the west, a powerful bull at Breidifjord in the south-east, and a rock-giant brandishing an iron staff at Reykjanes Peninsula to the south. These are the four direction-guardians which can be invoked in protective workings.

The stars and orientation

The Northern Tradition does not use the same constellations as modern astronomy and astrology. The customary constellations and their names are derived from Babylonian and Egyptian sources, with Greek and Arab additions and modifications. The Northern Tradition constellations are strictly of the northern sky, and relate to northern mythology. Most of the old names are known, only a few of them being lost. Most of the named stars and constellations are in the winter half of the sky (in summer, the further one goes northwards, the shorter and lighter the nights become making the stars less and less necessary for navigation and orientation). The traditional constellations and star-names of the North are as follows (with their customary equivalents in brackets):

The Lode Star (32 Camelopardis)
Also known as *Tir*, sacred star of Tîwaz/Tyr. This was the Pole Star in *c.* 800 CE, the present Polaris, the Nail or Nowl (Navel) attaining that status *c.* 1400 CE. The Nowl is one of the '15 stars' of medieval astronomy. Other members of the '15 stars' are marked with an asterisk(*).

*The Day Star** (Arcturus, α Boötis)
A time-marker by night, otherwise known as the *Bear Star*.

*The South Star** (Vega, α Lyræ)
A time-marker by night, used for geomantic orientation and a navigational aid.

*The Torch** (Algol, β Persei)

*The Torch Bearer** (Procyon, α Canis Minor)

Near Irmin Street (the Milky Way), precursor of

Loki's Brand* (Sirius, α Canis Major)
At the base of the Milky Way.

The Plough (Rigel)

Woden's Wagon (Ursa Major)

Our Lady's Wagon (Ursa Minor)
Vehicle of Frigg, the Great Mother.

Frigg's Distaff (Belt of Orion)

The Boars' Throng* (Pleiades, or the Seven Stars)
From the northern martial arts *Svinfylking* warriors' wedge-shaped battle formation, with the *Lesser Wolf's Jaws*, facing the *Battle of the Gods* complex.

The Battle of the Gods (Auriga and Capella*)
Including the goats of Thor's chariot.

The Greater Wolf's Jaws (Andromeda, part of the Milky Way, the semicircle of stars through Pegasus to Cygnus, including Deneb Algedi*)
The open jaws face the pole of the sky, the Fenris-Wolf threatening the Cosmic Axis, Yggdrassil.

The Lesser Wolf's Jaws (Hyades and Aldebaran*)
Lying directly on the ecliptic, intercepting the sun's path. These are violent and troublesome stars, associated with storms.

Thiazi's Eyes (Castor and Pollux)
The eyes of a giant thrown into the sky by Thor as an eternal commemoration of his deeds.

Orwandil's Toe (Corona Borealis, or the main star, Alphecca*
The toe of the giant Orwandil or Wandil cast into the sky by Thor.

Irmin Street, Iring's Way, Walsingham Way, Bifröst or The Bridge of the Gods (*the Milky Way*).

The two streams of saliva falling from the *Greater Wolf's Jaws* are *Wil* and *Wan*.

The remaining stars and asterisms of the *Fifteen Stars* are known by their southern European/Arabic names: Algorab, Antares, Deneb Algedi, Regulus and Spica.

The constellations of the Northern Tradition are markers of the seasons, and have connections with seasonal rites and legends. At the end of autumn, the Torch Bearer heralds the approach of Loki's Brand onto the Bridge of the Gods, where the Battle of the Gods is taking place. At midwinter midnight, Loki's Brand stands at the southern end or Irmin Street (the Milky Way), with the Greater Wolf's Jaws and Orwandil's Toe opposite each other as vernal and autumnal constellations.

The stars have always been used in orientation, in which their symbolic qualities play an important part. For example, the traditional way of sowing parsley in the Fens of East Anglia is to plant the seed in drills running due north–south. The way of obtaining the correct orientation is to sow at night, taking bearings from the constellation of Woden's Wagon and the *Nowl* (Pole Star). In this way, the qualities of the iron contained in the herb are said to be released by the rays of the moon. Navigation by the stars at night can be accomplished on land or at sea by gaining orientation in the same way. In navigation, the rising-points of notable stars and constellations like Frigg's Distaff (due east) were used as markers until the advent of the magnetic compass *c.* 1150 CE. The legendary names of the stars relate the qualities of time, direction, and space, to cosmic myth—a holistic universal view which is much at odds with modern materialism, yet which is a truer model of the image of human beings.

II

Natural Lore

Consider what are the true ends of knowledge, and they seek it not
either for pleasure of mind, or for contention, or for superiority to
others, or for profit, or for fame, or power, or any of these inferior
things; but for the benefits and use of life.

Francis Bacon

Everything in nature has its own unique qualities, which can
be recognized by those willing to find out. Above all other
things in the Northern Tradition is a profound reverence for
the Earth, seen as the Earth Mother goddess. This idea is the
same in all variants of the faith, even though the goddess may
be called *Gaia, Freyja, Cerridwen, The Lady* or something else.
This personification of the Earth, seeing it as a sacred being
rather than an enormous inanimate rock, is the fundamental
world-view. As an extension of this, all aspects of the natural
world should be revered, as should places of power within it:
locations where the gods are present. Sacred places in the
landscape are recognized by their special qualities as places
where, by meditation, prayer, ritual and ceremony, one may
gain access to states of enlightenment. This world picture, so
different and at odds with the materialist one assumed in
most schooling, is the approach one must take when approaching sacred rocks, holy wells, stone circles and similar
places of power. Their power is something which cannot be
experienced by materialistic means. It is only through the
holistic vision of the totality of existence, both material and
non-material, that the entire circle can be comprehended.
These are things which can only be explained partially by
language. A true understanding comes from a fusion of the
analytical and intuitive faculties of consciousness.

Sacred Materials

Stones

Hagstones — A stone with a natural hole in it is known as a *hagstone*. These are usually flints whose fossil inclusions have been worn away by running water and hence are manifestations of the power of water in its *force* aspect. Even the most fluid of materials can penetrate the hardest if sufficient time is available. In customary usage, hagstones or *hol(e)ystones* are hung on a flax string above a bed to prevent bad dreams and psychic attack. They are also animal protectors, hung in stables to prevent similar disturbances of horses, where they also served as pre-industrial technical instrumentation. When hung on a flax string in the stable, a line was drawn on the wall on a middling day at the point where the stone hangs. Then, as the weather changes, atmospheric humidity will cause the flax to alter in length, and the stone will rise above or fall below the line. In the days before the invention of the barometer, the hagstone was held to be sacred to Woden's consort, Frigg, the Queen of Heaven who rules over the seasons.

Irish stones are healing stones used in England, having been brought from Ireland for the purpose. In legend, the stones of Stonehenge, exceptional for their medicinal qualities were transported by the wizard Merlin from Ireland. Irish Stones have an inherent healing power, being touched to a wound or diseased part of the body, but they lose their power if they touch English soil. Irish stones are also used as charms to repel toads, frogs and snakes from entering a house, a power also ascribed to soil brought from snakeless Ireland.

Kit-cat stones are naturally conical, black stones which are thought to possess healing powers. Their conical form echoes the 'cone of power' generated by certain magical procedures, and is seen as a solidified manifestation of this geometric shape. Their conical form is short, and they should not be confused with *thunderbolts* (see below).

Fossils as charms — Many fossils have long been considered to have luck-bringing properties. In former times, before it was known that they were the petrified remains of extinct organisms, it was thought that they were the products of the *vis plastica*, the creative or plastic force in the depths of the Earth. Whatever their theorized origin, they have been used in magic, and today that use is as valid as it ever was.

Snake stones — There are a number of common fossil charms. The most notable, because of their spiral form, and their not inconsiderable size, are *ammonites*. These are the fossilized remains of extinct cephalopod molluscs, distant relations of modern genera like the pearly nautilus and the octopus. The name *ammonite*, used today both colloquially and scientifically, comes from the association of these fossils with the Mediterranean deity Jupiter Ammon, the horns of whose sacred rams are echoed in the fossil's spirals. These were known as *Cornu Ammonis*, the Horns of Ammon, or *snakestones*, connected with the god Thor. In parts of England, before they became more valuable in an untouched state, ammonities were carved with the head of a snake, making them an image of the World Serpent, Jörmungand, whom Thor attempts, in vain, to catch. Snakestones are still the emblem of the Yorkshire port of Whitby, being placed on its coat of arms, granted in 1935. Many Whitby snakestones are composed of the black stone known as jet, prized for its protective qualities. In Scotland, ammonites have the alternative name of *crampstones*, for they once had a use in curing cattle of the cramps, by washing the affected part of the cow in water in which an ammonite had been steeped for some hours. Ammonites are also protective when built into houses and other buildings. There are notable examples near Avebury in Wiltshire. Copies of ammonites exist on several eighteenth century buildings in Lewes and Brighton in Sussex, and on a nineteenth century building at Bexley, Kent.

Adderstones are fossil echinoids, relatives of modern sea-urchins and starfish. These were considered to be powerful antidotes for venomous snakebite, and possession of one ensured success in disputes and battle. According to legend, these stones orginated as frothy balls exuded at midsummer by vast assemblies of intertwined snakes. Such a ball would be tossed into the air and, if caught before it hit the ground, it could be used for magical purposes. As a remedy, adderstones are ground up and used for the treatment of indigestion.

Fairy loaves — The fossil echinoid *Micraster*, or *fairy loaf*, is heart-shaped, and if kept in a house, it is said that the household will never go short of bread.

Shepherds' crowns. Another fossil echinoid, *Echinocorys*, which has a crown or helmet shape, is the *Shepherd's crown*, prized as a lucky charm.

Screwstones are the internal mould fossils of various types of organism. The most screw-like are the so-called *Portland screws*, used as protective charms. Outside the Isle of Portland, the most common screwstones are the moulds of the stems of crinoids or sea-lilies. These are in fact columns composed of discs, which are strung together to form a protective necklace or as a rosary. Large screwstones are useful magical protectors when built into the wall of a house.

Starstones or *asteriae* are the fossilized remains of corals or crinoid stems. These are pentagonal fossils, with the feathery impression of a five-pointed star upon them. Being a naturally-produced pentagram, starstones have always had a magical function, and are much prized today.

Toadstones — The stones which were believed to be jewels originating in the heads of toads, but which in true origin are the teeth of fossil fish, were prized as a cure for poisoning and epilepsy. Also known as *bufonites*, these stones have been set into rings and lockets, or worn as pendants. They are said to change colour, or sweat a strange liquid, if the wearer is under psychic attack, or if any drink near them is poisonous. Toadstones are mentioned by Shakespeare in *As You Like It*, where Duke Frederick says:

> Sweet are the uses of adversity,
> Which, like the toad, ugly and venomous,
> Wears yet a precious jewel in his head.

Useless non-ore-bearing stone found in mines is also called *toadstone*, from the German *tod Stein*, 'dead stone'. These toadstones are worthless, financially and magically.

Tonguestones — Again, like toadstones, *tonguestones* are the teeth of extinct fish, in this case, sharks. They are said to resemble the human tongue, and to fall to earth from the moon during eclipses. Magically, their function is primarly to ward off the Evil Eye, and also to prevent rheumatism and the cramps.

Thunderbolts — Stones known as *thunderbolts*, again, like snakestones, sacred to Thor, are usually the pointed, internal guards of fossil belemnites, the remains or another extinct mollusc. These were assumed to be the thunderbolts cast down from the Upperworld at various times during thunderstorms. In addition to being thunderbolts, belemnites have also been seen as candles belonging to the *little people*, and in Swedish they are called *vätteljus* — gnomes' candles. As medicinal objects, they have been used to treat sore eyes and rheumatism in both people and horses. As with snakestones, the water in which *thunderbolts* have been steeped is the curative agent.

Crystals

Crystals appear as 'frozen light', the most perfect natural manifestation of the geometry which underlies the physical universe. Various crystals have been used in the Northern Tradition, but all of them have been considered to be crammed with solidified light, manifesting the power of supernatural beings and a superabundance of energy. The seven systems of crystalline structure are ascribed correspondences with the planetary deities: the cubic system is ruled by Saeter/Saturn; tetragonal (quadratic), Thor/Thunor, Jupiter; orthorhombic, Tyr/Tîwaz, Mars; monoclinic, Sól, the sun; triclinic, Frigg/Freyja, Venus; trigonal (rhombohedric), Odin/Woden, Mercury; and hexagonal, Ostara, the moon.

Fairy stones are twinned crystals of staurolite, forming the cross shape of the rune *Gyfu*, meaning the gift from (or to), the gods.

Sun stones are also known as *Solarsteinn*, and are crystals of Iceland spar, a transparent calcite which has the optical property of bending light in two ways, so if a mark is etched on the surface and presented to the light, the mark appears double. These crystals were used by Viking navigators to find the sun for navigation on overcast days, and were highly prized

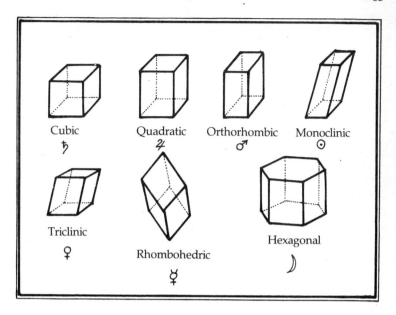

Fig. 9 Planetary correspondences of the crystalline systems.

manifestations of the goddess Sól.

Crystalline salt — Salt is the great preservative, both physically and magically, and so large salt crystals, sacred to Seater, have always been considered potent charms against harm. As perfect cubes, they are an image of perfection which underlies building lore and the mason's craft.

Precious stones are rare crystals of value. As with all materials, precious stones have correspondences. A series of 12 of the best known jewels are ascribed to the 12 months of the year, the days of the week and the corresponding deities:

Stone	Day	Deity	Zodiacal sign
Diamond	Tuesday	Tîwaz	Aries
Sapphire	Friday	Frigg	Taurus
Emerald	Wednesday	Odin	Gemini
Agate	Monday	Mani	Cancer
Ruby	Sunday	Sól	Leo
Sardonyx	Wednesday	Odin	Virgo
Chrysolite	Friday	Frigg	Libra

Stone	Day	Deity	Zodiacal sign
Opal	Tuesday	Tîwaz	Scorpio
Topaz	Thursday	Thor	Capricorn
Amethyst	Saturday	Seater	Aquarius
Bloodstone	Thursday	Thor	Pisces
Turquoise	Thursday	Thor	Sagittarius

Because of these and other correspondences, it is possible to make jewellery which reflects the innate powers of the deities and times through the medium of crystals and their surrounding metals.

Metals

Few metals are encountered in nature as the pure, uncombined metal. Apart from nuggets and inclusions in special places, metals must be extracted from the metalliferous ore by smelting. In former times, this was done locally by experts whose craft was partly technical, partly magical. Metals extracted in this way had been produced according to certain rituals, and were therefore sacred, possessing qualities additional to the normal chemical and physical characteristics of the metal. According to tradition, each metal is dedicated to its corresponding deity, day of the week and planet, times and qualities which are especially appropriate for using that metal.

Silver is ruled by the moon in her aspect as Ostara. It is the best conductor of electricity, with the atomic weight of 108, one tenth of the moon's radius in miles (1,080). Silver's day correspondence is Monday and it brings good fortune in connection with dreams and merchandise. Silver rings are thought to be preventative of cramp, and in former times the silver was often set with a piece of copper on the inside, linking the powers of the moon with that of Venus (Mani and Frigg).

Iron — Because of its hardness and ease of working, iron is one of the most useful metals. It is also magnetic, showing an affinity with the magnetic field of the Earth, and for these reasons it has been thought especially magically powerful. In the days before electromagnetically produced magnets, they were created by hammering iron in the smithy in a north–south orientation. This is one of the mysteries of the craft of the smith, the godling Wayland, Christianized as St Clement. According to folklore, an iron bar placed across a barrel will stop the beer souring, especially during thunderstorms, and iron used in walls or under thresholds will ward off harmful sprites and attacking magic. It is customary to drive iron nails into trees, door-posts, high-seat pillars and dragon-posts of timber-framed buildings, cradles, the beds of women in childbirth and other places needing extra protection. Iron objects, such as scissors, have been buried under the threshold of houses, and iron is the active metal of magically-protective and luck-bringing horseshoes, which are held up by iron nails. In its protective aspect, it is ruled by the warrior-sky-god Tîwaz/Tyr, corresponding with the planet Mars, whose symbol is the iron sword, an important magical tool in its own right. The day corresponding with iron is thus Tuesday.

Quicksilver is a unique metal because it is liquid at temperatures conducive to life. It is the sacred metal of Woden/Odin, and bears the name of the planetary deity Mercury. It is the only metal which has no use as a tool, but which has proved invaluable in scientific instruments such as barometers and thermometers. Scientific knowledge is ruled by the wisdom of Odin, but quicksilver is traditionally associated with loss, fear and debt. The day of quicksilver is Wednesday.

Tin is the metal of Thor, bringing riches, honour and one's desires. Its day is Thursday. In his Christianized form as the patron saint of Cornwall, St Piran, he is the discoverer of the metal, whose silver streams ran from the black stones placed in a fire. Tin is thus the metal of surprise transformation, from the black, seemingly useless ore to the refined, silvery, useful metal.

Copper is ruled by Frigg, corresponding with the planet Venus, and the day Friday. Its powers bring love and friendship. As a ring or bracelet, copper has been worn to prevent rheumatism and cramp.

Lead is the metal of Seater, the deity of Saturday, sometimes identified with the trickster-god Loki. Like quicksilver, it is a highly poisonous heavy metal, customarily associated with the dead and used for wrapping the dead. Lead is also the metal of votive offerings, and as such is a metal of protection and supporter of doctrine.

Gold is the metal of the sun and the solar goddess Sól, whose day is Sunday. Naturally, its signification is money, fortune and hope. Its incorruptible nature makes it a symbol of eternal life, hope and truth.

Lore of the Living World

Birdlore

Birds have always been associated with spiritual powers. Shamans and deities have been said to use birds as messengers, or as physical forms in which to travel. From the ravens of Odin to the dove of the Christian Holy Spirit, the bird has been transporter of spiritual virtue. The behaviour of birds, creatures of the air, is in total harmony with the winds and weather. Because of this, since the earliest times birds have been observed as indicators of how the weather is developing. To see seagulls dipping their heads in the sea, for example, is a sure sign to East Anglian fishermen that a gale is imminent. Birdlore rhymes often refer to the weather:

> If the cock goes crowing to bed,
> He'll certainly rise with a watery head,
> When black snails cross your path,
> The black cloud much moisture hath,
> When the peacock loudly bawls,
> Soon we'll have both rain and squalls,
> When rooks fly sporting high in the air,
> That shows the windy storms are near.

Similarly, soothsayers and augurs have observed the number and flight patterns of birds in order to presage future events. In the Northern Tradition, there is lore associated with most common birds. The following covers the more major and characteristic examples:

Cock — If one hears a cock crow in the afternoon, a visitor is imminent, but if it should crow at night, it is ominous, portending trouble or a death. If a hen should crow, then supernatural influences are at work. The cock is an indicator of the weather, crowing at sunset being held to indicate that a wet morning would follow. Weathercocks on churches, windmills, outbuildings and even hayricks are another aspect of weather lore, indicating the direction of the wind, and the attendant weather and spiritual states which it brings.

Crow — The crow is not a fortunate bird in the Northern Tradition; it is a foreteller of bad news. A crow at the window indicates that news of a death is imminent.

Linnet — The linnet is named after its love of eating the seeds of the flax plant, from which linen is produced. Flax was one of the gifts of the goddess Frigg to humans, and the linnet is the sacred bird of the goddess Hlin, one of the goddess-servants or lesser attributes of the goddess.

Magpie — Magpies are a bird of omen. There are many different variants of the rhyme below, but most of them encapsulate the mystery of life and death within them.

> I saw seven magpies in a tree,
> Six for you, and one for me,
> One for sorrow, two for mirth,
> Three for a wedding, four for a birth,
> Five for silver, six for gold,
> Seven for a secret never to be told.

Peacock — The peacock is connected with weather lore, its calling seen as a foreteller of rain and squalls. Even today it is not unusual to see straw peacocks on the roof-ridges of thatched houses as a magical protection against the worst effects of storms.

Raven — The raven is the sacred bird of the Celtic god-king Bran, whose head was buried at Bryn Gwyn, the White Mount, in what is now the Tower of London. Ravens are still kept at the Tower, because legend has it that should they leave, then the Tower, and with it London, would be destroyed. The raven is also the sacred bird of the god Odin, whose two ravens, Hugin and Munin, are the shaman's attendants. The Vikings, in common with all warriors, used luck-flags, and theirs was the *Raven Banner*, a flag bearing the Black Raven of Odin. Raven banners were made with great ceremony, usually being sewn by the daughters of great warriors or kings. Ravens bring luck to the house where they nest. It is decidedly unlucky to kill one.

Robin — The robin is considered to be a protective bird, and in autumn, certain behaviour of the bird is a sign of a severe winter on the way.

Yellowhammer — There is a country prohibition on killing the yellowhammer in May (for the 'Devil's blood' is in it). Although the lore surrounding this is lost now, it appears that this bird may have been sacred to the Pagan deities of the merry month of May, calling for the prohibition.

The lore of trees

Every tree has its own special physical and magical qualities, and the Northern Tradition recognizes this, prescribing the appropriate wood for its corresponding purpose. The following list gives the physical, symbolic and magical functions of all of the common indigenous northern European trees.

Alder (*Alnus glutinosa*) — The Alder's connection with and resistance to water ensured its use in piles driven into rivers for bridge foundations, or under buildings constructed on wet ground. The foundations of whole cities, like Amsterdam, were made of alder, and so it has the symbolism of foundation. As it was a footing for buildings, so for humans, for it was the favoured wood for clogs. It was also favoured for making whistles and flutes. When burnt, it charcoal was favoured for gunpowder-making, and as the complementary to fire, the corresponding rune of the alder is *Is*.

Apple (*Malus* spp.) — The apple tree bears a fruit which is the symbol of eternal life, its fivefold symmetry reflecting the *Golden Section* of sacred geometry and number. It is the holy tree of the Isle of Avalon, and the Norse goddess of eternal youth, Iduna. Because of the special conditions needed for growing apples, orchards have long been considered sacred ground. This requirement survived until recently in the charters of the *Free Miners* of the Forest of Dean and Cornwall, which allowed them to mine for mineral ore on any land except the King's highway, churchyards and in orchards — three classes of sacred ground. In Herefordshire, it was customary that if someone wished to enclose common land, then he had to plant an apple tree there first. The lord of the manor then had some of the fruit each year to preserve his rights over the enclosed land.

If the sun shines through the trees on midwinter morning (or its transferred festival, Christmas), then there will be a good crop in the forthcoming year, and prosperity for the orchard's owner. At midwinter, apple trees are wassailed to remove any unwanted sprites and ensure a good crop, producing the sacred drink, cider, in the next season (see Chapter 6). Its corresponding rune is *Ing*, fertility and limitless expansion.

Ash (*Fraxinus excelsior*) — The Ash or *ashentree* is vitally important in the Northern Tradition, for it is the tree which forms the cosmic axis, Yggdrassil. The ash was also one of the two ancestors of the human race, for in the Norse creation-myth, the first man, Askr, was made from an ash tree. His wife, Embla, was an elm. The idea that humans were descended from trees was widespread in ancient Europe. In Greece, certain families were said to have been descended from the spirit of the ash tree.

It was good for divination and charms, for its bud forms the lunar crescent, linking it with the mutable qualities of the lunar deity Mani. Because the ash is a sacred divinatory tree, an image of the World Tree, Yggdrassil, and Odin's spear, *Gungnir*, it will bring bad luck to cut ash without good reason. The wood of ash is good for fence-posts and the handles of tools and weapons. In Ireland and Wales, the slats of coracles are made of ash, as were the wands of Druids. Ash wood has been favoured for the spiral wands beloved of northern European wizards and cunning men. Ash 'courts the flash', being prone to lightning-strikes, and so is considered a good conductor of magical force, especially when cut at the summer solstice. The spear of Odin, *Gungnir*, symbolized by *Gar*, the 33rd rune in the Northumbrian system, is an ash stave, the portable version of the cosmic axial tree Yggdrassil. As the immobile Cosmic Axis, ash has protective qualities against ill-wishers, and to cut it for that purpose is acceptable. In Lincolnshire, where the ash is known as *heder*, cunning men use it to defeat the effects of female ill-wishers. Likewise, snakes, the lesser-world serpents, are said to be warded off by ash, and to carry an ash wand or talisman will protect one against snake-bite. Scottish herdsmen use ash staves for driving their cattle, because of the protective attributes of the wood.

The broomstick of the traditional besom is made of ash wood. In Norse tradition, the sacred high-seat pillars of the *Hof*, the King's or Lord's Hall in which religious feasts were celebrated, were made of ash. In more recent times, the lintels over the rear door of the Romany *vardo* (caravan) was made of ash for magical reasons. Finally, in healing, the ash used to be split and children suffering from rickets or rupture passed through it three or nine times. The split was then bound up and, if it healed, the belief was that the child's infirmity would heal also. Such trees were guarded and rarely felled, lest an effected cure be undone.

Unlike most trees, the wood of the ash will burn when green without sputtering. The smoke of ash wood is a benevolent incense, and it was traditional to give newborn babies their first bath by an ash fire. The sap issuing from this burning ash wood was considered a beneficial medicine for babies, welcoming them into the world. The leaves of the ash tree are also lucky, especially those with an even number of divisions on each side (the 'even ash'). Like four-leafed clovers, these are uncommon, but if one is found, it should be picked with the following charm:

Even Ash, I do thee pluck,
Hoping thus to meet good luck,
If no good luck I get from thee,
I shall wish thee on the tree.

The 'even ash' should be worn in a hat, as a buttonhole, or carried in the pocket. The runic correspondences of the ash are *As*, *Gyfu*, *Hægl* and *Eh*.

Aspen (*Populus tremula*)—aspen is a wood of protection; one of its uses was as a physical or magical shield. Like the hazel, these shields can be divinatory or mnemonic in function. *Mete-wands*, measuring rods of aspen, were used as the measure of a corpse when the coffin was being made. Also known as the 'shivertree', the aspen is reputed to have the power to heal fevers or 'the ague'. The method of effecting a cure is to take a lock of one's hair, pin it to the aspen trunk and utter the formula:

Aspen tree, Aspen tree, I pray thee
To shake and shiver instead of me,

then to return home in complete silence.
Another technique is to insert the patient's nail-parings into a
small hole bored into the tree trunk, and to fill in the hole. If
the bark grows over the hole again, then the patient will
never again suffer the illness.

A lesser tree, with mainly medicinal uses, the aspen has the
runic correspondence of *Peorth*.

Bay (*Laurus nobilis*) — The bay is a tree of preservation, sacred
to the Celtic god Maponos, and the corresponding deity of
medicine and healing, Nodens. Its leaves are also useful in
cooking. Planted by a house door, the tree wards off
pestilences. It is used frequently today in tubs as ornament
and residual magical protection for urban restaurants and
shops. Sometimes it is bedecked with ribbons, now considered ornamental and customary, but still with the magical
effect of an offering to the plant-sprite. Bay is said never to be
struck by lightning, and a leaf placed under the pillow at
night will induce pleasant and informative dreams. The bay's
runic correspondence is *Sigel*.

Beech (*Fagus sylvaticas*) — The beech has been used in antiquity for making writing tablets, for the inscription of
knowledge, and is hence a tree of wisdom. As with growing
knowledge, which separates from and later re-joins to
strengthen its original source, the beech has exceptional
qualities of ingrowth, where branches amalgamate with each
other, or with the branches of other trees. Beech flowers in
May and produces its nuts, beechmast, in October, covering
the fruitful half of the year. Its runic correspondence is *Nyd*.

Birch (*Betula pendula*) — The birch was the earliest tree to
recolonize the land after the ice sheets retreated and is seen as
a symbol of rebirth, springtime and purification. It is the tree
which forms the first letter of the ogham script, and the rune
Beorc, sacred to the mother-goddess. Birch is the customary
tree of May-poles, being bedecked with red and white ribbons. To set up birch brances in or on a house brings good
fortune and averts malevolent influences. At Yuletide, it is
stripped of its white bark and burnt as the Yule log. As a Yule

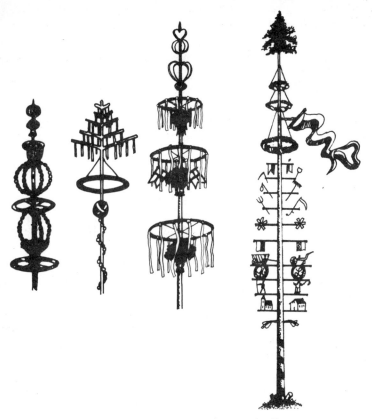

Fig. 10 May-poles and May garlands.

log, the birch must be handled only after appropriate personal purifications, including thorough washing of the hands. One of the holy cities of Sweden in Pagan times was Birka, 'place of the birches.'

In craft tradition, the resilient but hard wood of the birch found favour for making babies' cradles, appropriate both for the nascent quality of the tree and the magical protection afforded by the wood. The birch's abilities to drive away evil continued until recently in the use of 'the birch' as a form of corporal punishment, when a flogging with the twigs of the plant were held to drive away the evil spirits or thoughts from the miscreant. In addition to *Beorc*, the runic ascription of the birch is to the second rune, *Ur*.

Blackthorn (*Prunus spinosa*) — The blackthorn is one of the most magical of plants. A hardy and thorny shrub, it is the British native plum, supplying the fruit known as the sloe, which ripens in September and October, and which is a component of the alcoholic beverage sloe gin, considered by many to have medicinal and magical properties. In growth, blackthorn suckers freely to produce impenetrable thickets, so it creates a physical barrier which operates also on a psychic level. The blackthorn is a source of staves, sticks and slivers, having powers of magical protection against all forms of psychic harm. It is the favoured stick of hereditary wise women throughout southern Britain, being used for blasting—the projection of protective energy. It is ascribed as one of the aspects of the rune *Thorn*.

Bramble (*Rubus fruticosa*) — The bramble or blackberry is a thorny plant, and as such, is protective. A bramble bush growing in the form of an arch is considered a sacred plant, and to crawl under it from east to west, i.e. *diesal*, will rid one of certain ills, including skin ailments. Bramble leaves are a remedy for scalds, burns and inflammations of the skin. Nine leaves are floated in water from a holy well, and then each leaf is drawn in turn over the affected part, whilst the practitioner says the following charm three times per leaf:

> Three angels came from out the east,
> One bought fire and two brought frost,
> Out fire, and in frost,
> Out fire, and in frost.

Thorny bramble branches are also used for making *sprite flails* (see Chapter 4). Its runic corresponence is *Thorn*.

Elder (*Sambucus nigra*) — Known also as lady elder, elderntree or bourtree in England, the elder is a fairy tree *par excellence*. In German, its name *Hollunder* has connections with the Underworld and Hela, the goddess of death, personified as Frau Ellen or Ellhorn, Sacred to the Lithuanian god Puschkeit, elder pith was fashioned into images that were weighted so that they would come up again when pushed down. In Poland, it is customary to bury sins under elder trees, where they would not do harm, but be gradually absorbed and eliminated by the trees' power. Elder twigs can be woven into a garland for wearing around the head on May Eve, when the wearer will be able to see supernatural beings. Elder whistles have a magical function, and should be used with caution lest that which is summoned is unwanted. Elder was hung in front of stables to ward off harmful sprites and lightning, and when planted in front of an entrance serves to conciliate them, and to promote vigour and fertility in the livestock. Its runic ascription is to *Feoh*, the first rune, meaning cattle and mobile wealth, so in this aspect it is protective. It is considered fatally unlucky to burn the wood of the elder tree, and to bring it indoors at all is believed to bode ill-fortune. Use of the wood itself has various prohibitions. It is not to be used as a switch for driving animals to market, nor to chastise children. Elder should be kept well away from babies' cradles, and in the kitchen it is not to be used as skewers in poultry cookery. The fruit of the elder, however, is useful. Elderberry is used for jam and jelly as well as being fermented to produce elderberry wine, a potent sacramental drink.

Elm (*Ulmus* spp.) — In the Norse legend, Embla, an elm, was the first woman. The elm's wood has been used for the manufacture of coffins, representing the death aspect of the Earth Mother goddess. There are various species of elm: English elm (*Ulmus procera*); smooth-leaved elm (*Ulmus minor*), and the Wych elm (*Ulmus glabra*), less susceptible to the scourge of Dutch elm disease. Its runic ascription is to *Gyfu*.

Fairy tree (*ash/oak/thorn amalgam*) — The name 'fairy tree' is given to natural amalgams of trees, usually hedgerow standards, where ingrowth has occurred between an ash, oak and thorn. In Ireland, such trees are held to possess special character, where the special qualities of the trees, place and *genius loci* create a magical power.

Hawthorn (*Cratœgus* spp.) — Hawthorn is one of the plants sacred to the various thunder gods of the North — Thor, Taranis, Perkunas etc., and is the main aspect of the rune *Thorn*. When planted as a hedge, it creates not merely a good physical barrier, with its resistant thorn-bearing branches, but also acts as a psychic shield. For this reason, the thorn hedge was the preferred boundary around sacred enclosures in pre-Christian times, leading to its second runic ascription, to the stave *Ethel*. It is also one of the major fairy trees, and to sit under a hawthorn bush on certain days—May Day, Mid-summer's Day and Samhain—is to run the risk of being enchanted or 'fetched away'. It is also very bad luck to cut down a hawthorn, and there are many country tales of supernatural retribution being vented on those who have done so.

There are three separate species of hawthorn, each of which has slightly differing characteristics. The common hawthorn (*Cratægus monogyna*), also known as whitethorn or the may tree, produces in May the brilliant white or pink blossom that appears all over the shrub. Customarily it is a marker of the onset of the summer half of the year, recalled in the country adage:

Ne'er cast a clout,
'Til May be out.

This means, do not change from your winter clothes until the blossom of the hawthorn has come out. The Midland hawthorn (*Cratægus lævigata*) flowers a week before the May tree, and is mainly a hedgerow plant. The third type of hawthorn is the Glastonbury thorn (*Cratægus monogyna* 'Præcox'), which flowers at the winter solstice. Magically, hawthorn in general is the plant of the rune *Thorn*, which stands for active protection when upright and passive protection when reversed. As a protection, hawthorn twigs were held to have exceptional power if gathered on Ascension Day, a continuation of the Pagan lunar calendar of the North. However, they must be gathered by a person other than the user.

Hazel (*Corylus avellana*) — Hazel is the tree of wisdom. It is associated with divination, especially with regard to the use of its forked twigs in dowsing. A wand of hazel was also said to guarantee the carrier a fair hearing in difficult circumstances, and were thus used by the Druids as a symbol of authority. In the Viking period, Norse open-air courts were surrounded by a palisade of hazel staves linked by ropes delimiting the area of sacred jurisdiction. This boundary was known as the *vébond*, a magical as well as physical barrier. Hazel is also the best wood for making ceremonial and magical shields. The Celtic ogham device known as *Fionn's shield* is a representation of the magical hazel shields of ancient wise men, upon which were written their personal mnemonic devices, for hazel is the tree of the Celtic poets. The fruit, hazel nuts, are symbols of fertility and wisdom.

Holly (*Ilex aquifolium*) — Holly is the sacred tree of the Celtic god Taranis, equivalent of Thunor and Thor of Saxon/Norse belief. He is the Holly Giant of Yule, who carries a club of the wood. It is a lightning suppressor, and the material from which sacred staves and cudgels can be made. It is ascribed to the rune *Man*. Holly blossom acts as a magical protection to prevent the entry of harmful people or forces into the house when fixed to the door sill and door handles. Door handles and sills can also be made of the wood for added protection. These protect against malevolent forces, the Evil Eye, especially the wood from trees which have suffered ingrowth of branches. Holly is most associated with Yuletide, when it is a favoured decoration both of the house and of the pudding. The favourite Christmas carol about the sacred trees of Yuletide, which contains much traditional lore, says:

> The holly and the ivy,
> When they are both full grown.
> Of all the trees that are in the Wood,
> The holly bears the crown.

In Yuletide custom, the holly is considered to be male and the ivy female. After Yule, a holly sprig kept in the house will also protect it from lightning for the coming year.

Ivy (*Hedera helix*) — Ivy is believed to strangle trees, and is thus the bringer of death, yet it is a broadleafed evergreen, retaining its leaves in winter when others are absent. These attributes give the ivy the dual death/life significance, and its association with Yuletide, the time of death and birth. Great and ancient ivy vines resemble the serpent which chews ceaselessly at the base of the world tree, Yggdrassill. The enormous ivy vines which formerly existed at the magical cave known as St Beatushöhle, near Interlaken in Switzerland, were the inspiration for Goethe's ideas on metamorphosis which in turn inspired Rudolf Steiner's Anthroposophy. Growing on the wall of a house, ivy protects the inhabitants against psychic attack. As a cure for corns, ivy leaves are soaked in vinegar and then bandaged to the corn. The juice of ivy leaves, snuffed up the nostrils, is said to prevent a runny nose during colds. Food or drink taken from an ivy-wood bowl was formerly considered a cure for whooping-cough. Ivy's runic correspondence is *Ing*.

Juniper (*Juniperus communis*) — The juniper or savin is a plant of preservation against harm. In Scotland, Juniper twigs are used as a sure way of warding off the Evil Eye. Charcoal made from juniper wood (savin charcoal) has a special quality of rapid burning which made it a favourite for gunpowermakers. When burnt, juniper smoke is a powerful anti-demonic incense. Its runic ascription is *Sigel*.

Linden (*Tilia platyphyllos*) — The linden or lime tree is a mark tree, one connected with the dispensation of justice — the 'law tree' of the *Edda*, and the gallows tree. In Berlin, the famous boulevard called *Unter den Linden*, 'Beneath the Linden Trees', was once the royal sacred highway of the Kaisers of Germany. Linden trees grow in many towns and villages in Austria, Germany, the Netherlands and Switzerland, as the *Dorflinde* — the 'village linden tree'. These trees are grown at geomantically important points such as major road junctions, in market-places and in front of town halls; places of public gathering and celebration. The classic *Dorflinde* has been pruned and trained to make it a central trunk supporting two or three disc-like arrays of branches. This artificial modification makes the linden into a represen-tation of the Cosmic Axis linking the Underworld through this world to the Upperworld. The linden's runic cor-respondence is *As*.

Maple (*Acer campestre*) — Maple is the traditional wood from which the *wassailing bowls* used at midwinter were turned on the lathe. Although it is not a long-lived tree itself, the maple is connected with a charm to ensure longevity. To gain a long life, a young child should be passed through the branches of a maple tree. Its runic correspondence is *Man*.

Mistletoe (*Viscum album*) — Although not biologically a tree, mistletoe has always been considered as one of the sacred trees, one of special qualities, because it does not have roots in the ground but grows semi-parasitically upon the branches of other trees, most commonly the sacred apple and oak. Ac-cording to Norse legend, a dart of mistletoe killed the white god, Balder. It was a very important sacramental plant in Druidic tradition, for the white berries are supposed to resemble the droplets of semen of the sky-god. At Samhain, the Archdruid cut the mistletoe with a golden sickle. As it fell from the tree, the mistletoe was caught in white cloth held by virgins. It was then consecrated and distributed to the people to use as charms over their house doors. The Christmas custom of kissing under the mistletoe is a continuation of this Druidic sacred rite. But because of the Druidical connection, mistletoe was forbidden to be used in church decoration, except in York Minster, in a city where many Pagan traditions were carried on in churches until the Reformation. At York, each Christmas, a branch of mistletoe was brought into the Minster by the clergy and laid on the High Altar, at which 'A public liberty, pardon and freedom to all sorts of inferior and even wicked people at the gates of the City to the four corners of the Earth' was pronounced. The runic ascription of mistletoe is *Sigel*.

Oak (*Quercus robur*) — The oak has always been held in great regard as the major sacred tree of Europe, venerated as the holy tree of the sky-god, whether the Zeus of the Greeks, Jupiter of the Romans, or Perkunas, Thor, Thunor or Taranis of the North. Sacred to the thunder god in all his guises, the oak is said to ward against lightning, though itself is very prone to being hit. Oak sprigs or pieces of lightning-struck oak have been used as house protection against lightning. Because of its structural strength, oak was favoured as the main load-bearing members in timber-framed buildings, and also for ship-building. As a protective tree, doors, especially, should be made of oak, as were the practical shields of warriors. The acorn is the sacred fruit of the oak, being the literal meaning of the Northumbrian rune *Ac*. It is the symbol of potential; 'Great oaks from little acorns grow'. Acorns kept in a house were believed to assist in protecting it from lightning-strikes, and the traditional design for the bobbin at the end of a cord on a pull-down window blind is the acorn. The acorn, too, is the protector of the staircase, and it was traditional to carve acorns on the main bannister posts.

It was long considered not merely unlucky but actually blasphemous to cut down an oak, especially one which bore mistletoe, or which grew at a sacred place of power. There are many records of misfortunes befalling those who cut special

oaks. One such tale involves a mistletoe-bearing oak at Nor-
wood which was cut down in 1657 during the proscription-
breaking times of the Commonwealth. The man who felled
the tree broke his leg, and everyone else connected with the
work suffered bad luck. Even the London apothecaries who
bought the mistletoe suffered. Oak trees at geomantically important locations were common in former times, and many
place-names, such as Selly Oak, attest to their local
significance, long after the originals have fallen. Like the
mandrake, the oak is reputed to give off loud groans when
uprooted or felled, 'as if it were the *Genius* of the Oake lamen-
ting', according to Aubrey.

The oak is the tree of midsummer, so at the festival of Yule,
at the opposite end of the year, its wood is burnt as the Yule
log. In order to be effective, it should be kindled from the
charcoal of the previous year's log and ritually burned as a
substitute fire for the sun at its lowest point on the eve of the
solstice, and kept burning afterwards for as long as possible.
The oak is said to last for 900 years, three Aun cycles of the old
northern calendar, the magic number nine, one hundredfold:

> An oak is three hundred years growing,
> Three hundred years blowing,
> And three hundred years decaying.

As a major tree, the oak has several runes ascribed to it: *Rad*,
Jer, *Tyr* and *Eh*.

Pine (*Pinus sylvestris*) — The pine or deal is the tree of illumination, being the meaning of the rune *Cen*, and as such
represents the torch of knowledge. Its resin makes a pungent
incense, and its cones, deal apples, carry within their structure the sacred geometry of the Fibonacci Series. The magical
wand sacred to the fertility-god Freyr has a deal apple at its
end, signifying the generative power.

Poplar (*Populus canescens*) — Poplar was used for making the
shafts of arrows, and thus has divinatory qualities which
have also caused it to be made into divinatory shields. Its
runic parallel is *Eoh*.

Rowan (*Sorbus aucuparia*) — The rowan or mountain ash is
primarily a tree of house protection, being planted by the

garden gate or near the door to ward off unwelcome psychic visitations. In Norse tradition, it was the tree which saved Thor from being swept away in an Underworld river. Rowan wands have been used as dowsing rods for finding metals rather than the hazel rods of water-divination, and amulets carved on rowan wood have been made as proof against drowning. In Lincolnshire, the rowan, otherwise known as the berry ash, or *sheder*, is used to deflect the spells of malevolent male magicians. On quarter days, rowan wands should be placed over the lintels of house doors to ensure good fortune for the following quarter. Tied in a cross with red thread, rowan twigs removed from the tree without the use of a knife are used to protect stables and byres and, by association, garages. In combination with birch, and put over a doorway on May morning, rowan gives protection for the whole year, but must be removed and replaced with new twigs at the next Maytide. These crosses are also used to protect freshly-planted seed-beds. A necklace of the berries is considered a strong protection against medical harm. The wood of rowan can be used for the crossbeam of a chimney breast in traditional cottages and for magically-protective *speer-posts* (sometimes wrongly called 'witch-posts'). In former times, the tackle of water-mills, whipstocks, churn-staves, plough-pins, and pegs of tethers to shackle cattle were all made from rowan. Its runic correspondence is *Nyd*.

Service tree (*Sorbus torminalis*) — This tree, related to the apple, hawthorn and rowan, is a tree of protection against wild things, and its wood can be used for wands and talismans. Its runic correspondence is *Eolh*.

Spindle tree (*Euonymous europæus*) — This tree, with its smooth grey bark, is one of the trees whose wood is connected with the rotation of the Cosmic Axis, and is thus a tree of the Heavenly Queen, Frigg in the Norse tradition. In former times, its wood was used for making spindles for wool-spinning and butchers' skewers. It is uncommon now, because it was deliberately exterminated because of its connection with parasites which overwinter on the tree. Its runic correspondence is the Northumbrian rune *Gar*.

Spruce (*Picea abies*) — The spruce is the Yule-tree, which represents the eternal Cosmic Axis and all that is implied by

its permanence. The Yule-tree is evergreen, carrying life
through the low ebb of the year at midwinter. It is adorned
with lights and silver spheres which represent the stars and
planets. Its runic correspondence is *Dag*.

Wayfaring tree (*Viburnum lantana*) — Related to the elder, this
tree, which is generally restricted to southern England, is one
of protection, useful for making travellers' talismans. The
corresponding rune is *Rad*.

Willow (*Salix* spp.) — There are several species of willow,
each of which has its own special characteristics and uses.
The willows divide into several classes. Some willows are
wetland trees, which include the white willow (*Salix alba*) and
the crack willow (*Salix fragilis*). When pollarded, these produce straight poles used for hurdle-making. Another group
of willows are the osiers. The most common are the common
osier (*Salix viminalis*) and the purple osier (*Salix purpurea*). The
osiers create rods used in basket-making, and have many
local varieties, selected over the centuries as the most appropriate and successful for the locality in which they are
grown. These will have their own specific lore and usages,
which may yet be recovered by the diligent searcher.

The willow is symbolic of purification and rebirth, and
staves cut from it will put forth roots and leaves and become
new trees. It is fast growing. An old rhyme says 'The willow
will buy the horse before the oak will buy the saddle'.
Because of its resilience, willow is favoured for making fenc-
ing, for supporting thatch, as the wattles in wattle-and-daub
wall infill in timber-framed houses, and as switches used in
the ceremony of 'beating-the-bounds'. Ceremonially, rods of
willow are the eight *ifins* of the Celtic ogham alphabet variant
known as *pine ogham*, with the phonetic value of æ. They are
used in the ceremony of the Haxey Hood, enacted in Lincolnshire, where 13 willow wands are bound together with 13
withies.

The great sallow or goat willow (*Salix caprea*) and the grey
sallow or common willow (*Salix cinerea*) are broad-leaved,
shade-tolerant woodland plants whose catkin-bearing shoots
are the 'pussy willows' used for decoration by the churches
on Palm Sunday in continuation of pre-Christian festivals in
honour of Freyja. In the Northern Tradition, this tree is
sacred to the goddess Freyja, whose totemic animal is the

cat—'pussy'. All willows are ascribed to the rune *Lagu*.

Whortleberry (*Vaccinium myrtillus*) — A protective plant whose twigs are used in the Scandinavian ceremony of Little Yule (13 December), a festival of lights which is the precursor of Yule itself. This festival is associated with the star known in the Northern Tradition as the Torch-Bearer (Procyon), the precursor of Loki's Brand (Sirius), the marker of midwinter. Its rune is *Cen*.

Witch hazel (*Hamamelis* spp.) — Although a native plant of North America and Asia, the properties of the witch hazel have been known in Europe for centuries, and have become assimilated into the Northern Tradition as it is practised to-day. Witch hazel is a medicinal product used to arrest bleeding, and also the source of an oil used in perfumery. Its runic correspondence is the Northumbrian rune *Stan*.

Yew (*Taxus baccata*) — The yew is a tree associated with eternal life, being one of the longest-lived of northern European native tree species. Because of this, it was planted in holy places where the ashes or bones of the dead were deposited, and is common in British churchyards today. Ancient plantations of sacred yew trees are recalled in Norse tradition, by Ullr, god of archery and winter, who lived in Ydalir, a sacred yew grove. Yew was used in the Middle Ages for bow making, and is associated with the runes *Eoh*, *Eolh* and the late rune *Yr* (which means *bow*). The yew is a very poisonous tree and in hot weather it gives off a resinous vapour, which shamans have inhaled to gain visions.

Special trees

In addition to the inherent qualities of different species of tree, trees themselves may have a character derived from the place in which they grow. Trees of exceptional size or prominence, and those distorted by the wind, or through growth patterns produced perhaps by the forces of underground water, have always been held in special regard. Such trees have their own names, and have been resorted to by the local people at times of celebration and tribulation as a place where beneficent powers could be contacted. As mentioned above, trees bearing mistletoe are sacred in the Bardic tradition, and

trees bearing the dense tangle of twigs known as a witches'
broom were held to have special properties. Witches'
brooms, massive outgrowths either caused by biochemical
changes stimulated by a parasitic fungus or induced by
mechanical injury, were valued as useful objects for sweeping magic.

In ancient Ireland, there were four special trees, corresponding with the fourfold division of the island. The most important of these was the evergreen oak which grew on the Plain
of Mugna beside the River Barrow in east Leinster. It was
reputed to be 30 ells in girth and 300 ells high, and possess
special properties. The four holy trees of Ireland correspond-
ed with the solar-cycle calendar:

Oak	Mugna	Midsummer
Ash	Dathe	Equinoxes
Ash	Tortu	Equinoxes
Yew	Ross	Midwinter

In Ireland, trees were sacred to the god Bel, Beli, or Bile, the
King of the Otherworld, as the darker aspect of the bright
sky-god Balor. The name Bile means tree, giving the name of
the May festival, Beltane, as tree-fire. In P.S. Dinneen's *Irish-
English Dictionary*, published in London in 1904, the meaning
of the word *Bile* is given as: a mast; a tree, especially one
growing in a hill-fort or beside a holy well; a large tree; a
scion, progenitor or champion.

Herbs

Technically, a herb is a non-woody plant, that is, a broadleafed flowering plant which is not a shrub or tree. Herbs have
three major uses: culinary, medicinal and magical. Herbalism
is a massive and complex subject, and there are many good
books available for those who wish to find out about the
magic and power of these active non-woody plants. Northern European practice finds a use for almost every wild
plant, for most have some medicinal property, discovered
over centuries of observation and experiment by generations
of wise women and men. When used medicinally, herbs and
preparations from them should be taken only under expert
supervision. Many herbs are dangerous when used with in-

sufficient knowledge, especially when taken in large doses or over long periods of time. It is foolish to collect herbs and use them for medicinal purposes without expert advice. If you need herbs, then it is better to grow them yourself than to scour the country for wild plants. Identification of many herbs requires sound botanical knowledge, and many popular guide books have insufficient information for positive identification of unfamiliar plants. Also, many herbs growing wild today will have been in contact with various harmful products. Herbs growing on derelict land may be growing on spoil tips containing wastes such as heavy metals and other industrial pollutants. In the country, they may have been exposed to pesticide and fertilizer residues, and by roadsides, they will have accumulated quantities of internal combustion engine exhaust products such as lead and benzopyrene. Herbs should never be collected from sites such as these, and that restricts the areas available, making growing your own or buying herbs a safer option.

The mystic mandrake

Botanically, the mandrake or mandragora is a member of the Solanaceae which contains several poisonous species including the deadly nightshade. Its botanical name is *Mandragora officianarum* L., and the plant is indigenous to the lands around the Mediterranean Sea, its northernmost range being at Mount Vicentia on the southern side of the Venetian Alps. The mandrake was introduced into England around the tenth century. It is mentioned in the Anglo-Saxon Archbishop Ælfric's *Vocabulary*, where it is called the 'earth-apple'.

The Mandrake has a curiously-shaped root, from which both its name and ascribed properties are derived, for this root is often humanoid in form. In Ancient Greece, the followers of Pythagoras called it the 'Anthropomorphic Plant.' Because it was believed that the mandrake brought death on those who dug or pulled it up, ingenious methods were devised to avoid this danger. Theophrastus, who wrote the first Greek *History of Plants* around 230 BC, described many techniques of gathering medicinal plants, including the mandrake. These techniques are the earliest recorded in Europe, and parallel almost exactly the methods used in northern Europe. Whether or not they are the origin of them is not important; they are long-established methods which have stood the test of time. One of the most important prescriptions of Theophrastus is that when gathering certain active roots the gatherer should stand on the windward side, so that the oils and essences should not fall upon the gatherer. One and a half thousand years later, in his *De proprietationes Rerum*, Bartholomæus Anglicus wrote: 'They that dig mandragora, be busy to beware contrary winds while they dig, and make three circles about with a sword and abide with the digging unto sun going down and trow so as to have the herb with the chief virtues.'

Theophrastus states of the mandrake that 'the leaf mixed with meal is useful for wounds, and the root for erysipelas. When scraped and steeped in vinegar it is also used for gout, for sleeplessness and for love potions. It is administered in wine or vinegar. They cut little balls of it as of radishes and make a string of them, hang them up in the smoke over must'. In the Greek tradition, mandrake was associated with Circe, the sorceress who turned men into swine by her magic potions. The goddess Aphrodite was known as 'Mandragoritis', or 'She of the Mandrake.'

According to tradition, mandrake was gathered in a cermonial manner by the Greeks. Three circles were drawn with a magic sword or knife around the plant, and the operator faced west when it was cut. This precaution was good for other medicinal plants, too. When hellebore was cut, a circle was made three times with a two-edged sword, and the first piece to be cut was held in the air. 'The operator,' wrote Theophrastus, 'must stand towards the east, saying prayers, and he should look out for an eagle both on the right and on the left, for there is danger to those that cut it if the eagle should come near that they should die within the year.' The same sanctions applied with the cutting of the mandrake.

The mandrake is first mentioned in Anglo-Saxon in the *Herbarium* of Apuleius Platonicus, which is said to have been written in the first half of the eleventh century. Apuleius described the mandrake thus:

> This wort which is named Mandragora is great and illustrious of aspect and is beneficial. You will take it in this manner when you come to it, and you recognize it thus that it shines at night altogether like a lamp. When you first see its head, then inscribe it instantly with iron lest it fly from you; its virtue is so great and famous, that it will instantly fly from an unclean man when he

comes to it without an iron, but you will dig the earth earnestly with an ivory staff. And when you see its hands and its feet, then tie it up [with a string]. Then take the other end and tie it to a dog's neck, so that the hound be hungry; next, cast meat before him so that he may not reach it unless he jerk up the wort with him. It is said of this wort that it has such great power, that whatever tugs it up will soon be deceived in the same manner. Therefore, as soon as you see it is jerked up and have possession of it, take it immediately in hand and wring the ooze [juice] out of its leaves into a glass ampulla or pitcher, and when need comes upon you, that you should help anyone with it, then help them in this manner. . . .

The *Bestiary* of Philip de Thaun, written *c.*1121, elaborates upon the problems of mandrake-pulling:

It is gathered by stratagem. Listen in what manner. The man who is to gather it must fly round about it. Must take care that he does not touch it. Then let him take a dog, bound. Let it be tied to it—which has been close shut up and has fasted three days and let it be shown bread and called from afar—the dog will draw it to him—the root will break—it will send forth a cry—the dog will fall dead at the cry which he will hear. Such virtue this herb has, that no one can hear it but he must die and if the man heard it he would directly die. Therefore, he must stop his ears and take care that he hear not the cry, lest he die as the dog will do which shall hear the cry.

Because mandrake is not indigenous to Britain and difficult to cultivate, it has been traditional to substitute the root of the bryony instead. The mandrake root or the bryony substitute was carried by women as a charm to promote fertility, and they were considered bringers of prosperity to their owners, useful in the divination of secret things, and in giving to the lover his or her heart's desire. In Wales, black bryony, with its dark green leaves and red berries, was known as 'charnel food', for it was believed to grow beside the gallows-tree or at crossroads on the graves of witches and suicides. Another Welsh story is that the mandrake or bryony grew from the tears of an innocent man who was executed on the gallows. Like the mandrake, the bryony is supposed to shriek like a human being when pulled up. Welsh tradition asserts that people who uproot a mandrake or bryony will die within the year, expiring with the groaning sounds of the plant itself, or in abject penitence for having pulled the doom-laden plant.

Manifestations of the Earth Spirit

The Northern Tradition sees the planet Earth not as in-

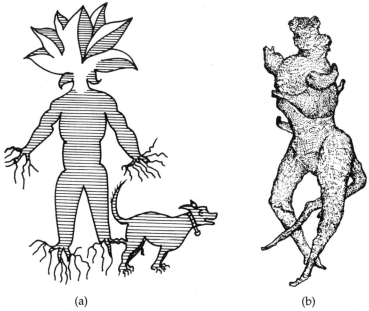

(a) (b)

Fig. 11 (a) The mandrake, with the dog that pulled it out of the ground, from a thirteenth-century drawing; (b) Anthropomorphic bryony root, given to Professor Henry Balfour by an Oxfordshire labourer in 1916.

animate, but alive with spirit, *önd*, which manifests in various forms, corresponding with the fundamental character of the element to which it belongs. The Northern Tradition sees the existence of five elements: Earth, Water, Air, Fire and Ice. These elements traditionally correspond with the major directions: Earth, the Centre; Water, West; Air, East; Fire, South; and Ice, North.

Earth elementals, land wights, yarthkins and the ward

Earth sprites or Earth elementals, whose direction is the Centre, seem to have the most complex hierarchy, and the most names, with many local variants. They are known as elves, brownies, gnomes, fairies, hyter sprites, hobgoblins, trolls, tarans, land wights, oakmen, woodwives, bogy beasts, buccas, the Gentry, portunes, pixies, leprechauns etc. The whole subject of the Earth elemental kingdom is vast, so here I will restrict myself to the most important types of sprites connected with the land, and encountered by those dealing with magical places of power in the landscape.

Landvættir, hyter sprites or land wights are guardian spirits of the land. Icelandic respect for these sprites provided that where fields or fells were hallowed by and for them, no fetid smell should be brought near them, and no living thing should be destroyed there. Their precincts were not to be looked upon with unwashed faces. Figureheads, magical protection against sea-demons, had to be taken off ships within sight of land, so that the land wights should not be assaulted. Places where the land wights have been driven away, desecrated areas, are known as *álfreka*. Sadly, many parts of the Earth are now in this condition.

The *ward* is a spiritual vigil which protects a village or town from internal troubles and external dangers. The sprites of the ward assemble each dusk at a power point in the village, and then go along *fairy paths* to their posts for the night. These sprites are the spiritual analogues of people, living and dead, of the settlement. Their watch-posts are *ward hills*, stones, crosses and holy trees on the roads and paths leading into the settlement. The ward forms a protective ring around the town, keeping out bad winds and harmful beings. Unfortunately, many settlements are now wardless, open to psychic attack and demonic interference.

Yarthkins, on the contrary, are hostile earth spirits, whose disturbance will prove costly in many ways to those foolish enough to risk it. Unlike the land wights, these are not approachable, and must be contained or deflected by remedial geomantic structures such as sprite traps, mirrors, consecrated staves and blocking-stones.

Holy ground

Places which are generators or receptacles of *önd*, where the Earth Spirit manifests itself in many ways, are rarely left in their original condition. All over the world, recognition of their sanctity has taken the form of leaving offerings, or constructing shrines and temples at the place. In the Northern Tradition, there are several classes of sacred site, each with their special qualities and appropriate descriptive name. These range from objects sacred in their own right, like trees, rocks and waterfalls, to full-scale sacred enclosures (*temenoi* or *frithsplots*) with buildings.

As certain trees are themselves sacred in the Norther Tradition, there are individual trees which call for reverence. Many named trees which remain, despite wholesale destruction, are descendents, on the same site, of the sacred trees of old. In addition, there were sacred groves of trees, a few of which still survive, unrecognized by most people, to this day. Sacred images of deities, stood by themselves in the open on holy places of power, like modern memorials commemorating secular heroes. These were called a *wig* or *wih*. A more complex form of sacred shrine was the *træf* or *hørgr*, variously described as a temporary hut erected for a specific ceremony, but often a more permanent tent, tabernacle or pavilion, less permanent than a full-scale wooden or stone temple but nevertheless a major shrine. Finally, there were two types of sacred building: the *hof*, which was an ordinary farm hall, where sacred feasts such as Yule were celebrated; and the *ealh*, the full-scale Pagan temple. Many place-names in northern Europe retain elements which show the former presence of one of these features, e.g. Wigston, Trafford, Wheeley, Ealing, etc. When the Christian religion took over, most of these sites were occupied by Christian places of worship, such as churches and chapels, inside which traces of the Elder Faith in the form of carvings and ceremonial observances still survive.

Ley lines, fairy paths and sacred trackways

Today, the word *ley* or *ley line* has become common knowledge, even when people are not quite sure what precisely a ley is. A number of books, many magazine articles and a few television programmes have tried to investigate the phenomenon from various viewpoints, but more often than not they have been bogged down in basic definitions of what a ley is or is not. Most of the problems come from approaching the matter in a topsy-turvy way, taking theories and speculations about leys and trying to make them fit the landscape, rather than looking at the landscape *first*. This approach comes from a fundamentally urban, literate worldview, whose first experience of landscape lines has been through the pages of a book, most probably by or about Alfred Watkins. In the meaning of ancient straight trackways, the word *ley* was adopted and popularized by Alfred Watkins, a Hereford antiquary who had noticed that many ancient sites in the landscape were located in straight lines with one another. After a visit to Blackwardine, Hereford-

' Alfred Watkins 1855 - 1935 '

Fig. 12 Alfred Watkins (1855–1935), popularizer of the ley line theory:
man of his landscape.

shire, in 1921, he realized from looking at maps that he could
plot various alignments across the country, linking sites of
ancient sanctity. Among these were churches, standing
stones, holy wells, hill-forts, ancient mounds, tree clumps,
earthworks and *straight pieces of old roadway*. These lines, he
believed, were the remains of ancient prehistoric tracks laid
out across the countryside as trade routes.

Watkins thought that leys had been marked originally by
standing stones, earthworks, dew-ponds, fords and clumps
of trees, especially Scots pine. Where churches are found on
leys, he showed that many of these had been placed on the
former sites of stones and earthworks, as it was the custom of
Christian missionaries to take over Pagan sacred places for
their own worship. In this way, the later sites preserved the

location of earlier sacred places. Although Watkins always insisted that his alignments were ancient trackways, later ley hunters suggested that, in addition to tracks, they may have had other powers. At the beginning of the twentieth century, Sir Norman Lockyer showed scientifically what country people had always known, that Stonehenge and other stone circles lined up with the rising and setting positions of the sun, moon and stars, and that in the case of some of them, these lines extended through the countryside, marked by standing stones or earthworks. In 1938, Arthur Lawton, a member of Watkins' Straight Track Club, suggested that they might carry some sort of 'earth energy'. The word *ley* was coined by Watkins in 1921, and then it had a precise meaning. Now, it is applied to many phenomena including lines in the ground which dowsers can detect with rod or pendulum. It is applied to *overground* energy, too, as detected by dowsers, and even to psychical or magical links of various sorts of subtle energy. The words *ley lines*, *energy leys* and *E-leys* are also encountered in 'Earth mysteries' literature, without any existing consensus definition of them. As Watkins coined the word, we ought to respect his usage, and to find alternative words when we talk about straight lines which are not alignments linking ancient sites together in 'a fairy chain' in Watkins' words. Because of this, I use traditional words to describe ancient tracks, straight or otherwise.

Irish tradition preserves the knowledge of 'fairy paths' across the countryside, linking ancient earthworks known as *raths* with other places of power. At certain times of year, people avoid the paths because the inhabitants of the non-material world travel along them. Prohibitions exist against building houses or other structures across these fairy paths. Similar traditions exist in other parts of the world in places where the rural tradition has not been destroyed, such as the ceremonial straight pathways of Peru and Bolivia. The French *Capitularia* of 1677 refers to 'the Pagan trackway' known as *yries*, which may or may not have been straight, but which was marked by bushes upon which rags were tied. Whenever we walk along one of these ancient tracks, we can still feel the magic quality of the countryside with which Watkins so obviously was in tune. Magically, such tracks can be found intuitively, and their straightness or otherwise is only incidental if the presence of *önd* is felt there. These tracks are the fairy paths of many lands, and whether or not they coincide with Watkins' definition of leys, where they have not suffered *álfreka*, they are a vital part of the magical landscape.

Places where trackways, fairy paths or roads meet, pass over sacred ground or cross one another are considered especially powerful, being equivalent to shrines in their own right. They are usually ruled by a specific local power, sprite, genius or deity, either in its own right or as an aspect of a universal deity. Sacred to the gods of flow, commerce, energy and fertility, crossroads have always been the site of ritual and performance, the favoured place for the foundation of new settlements. In ancient Greece and, later, Rome, the crossways was the *locus* of Hermes (Mercury), and often a *Herm* was set up. This structure was a pillar with an effigy of the god's head and genitalia. Frequently, the *Herm* was accompanied by a tree and an altar upon which offerings would be made. A traditional American Blues song recalls this ancient custom of prayer at crossroads:

I went down to the crossroad,
Fell down on my knees,
Down to the crossroad,
Fell down on my knees,
Asked the Lord above for mercy,
Hear me if you please.

Hermes/Mercury is the southern European equivalent of Wotan/Woden/Odin, who is also the deity of the crossroads, and the god of hanged men, among other attributes. Because of this, in former times it was cusomary to set up gallows or gibbets at crossroads, where corpses or pieces of dismembered convicts were hung up as a deterrent to crime. As well as displaying bodies and pieces of butchered humans, the crossroads were used for burying the bodies of those who, for some reason, did not qualify for burial in a Christian graveyard, including witches, suicides and criminals. Traitors, or those on the losing side in civil strife, were one such category. The *Chronicle* of Roger of Wendover, for example, records that King Edward the Confessor ordered the burial of the traitor Godwin, thus: 'Take forth this dog and traitor and bury him in a cross-way, for he is unworthy of Christian sepulture.' Until 1823, English law directed that the body of a suicide was to be buried in a crossroad, and a stake to be driven through it. Other candidates for disposal in this manner were executed witches, heretics, highwaymen, outlaws, Gypsies and others, the presence of whose spirits in consecrated ground was considered undesirable. It was considered that if the body was pinned down with iron or ash spikes the spirit of the executed person would not return to haunt his or her killers. The *önd* would be carried away along the roads and dissipated, rather than powering a vengeful ghost.

The subterranean world—natural and artificial caves

According to tradition, the subterranean kingdom is peopled by certain sprites who are only encountered when disturbed by human activity in the course of exploration or mining. Spirits are known to dwell in natural caves, and all religions have stories of encounters between holy people and the denizens of the subterranean kingdom. These beings are seen as dwellers in the cave rather than Earth spirits. Miners' traditions, however, are full of stories about supernatural encounters, and there are several names of the Earth spirits met with underground. The deep-earth sprites are gathornes and knockers, beings who can bring disaster on miners if not propitiated properly.

Underground structures have an important role to play in initiatory rites and meditation. Cut off from the sights and sounds of the world (and the invisible radiations), the initiate or practitioner can explore the inner realms. In many ways, underground structures are ideal for these practices. They are places where initiations and rituals requiring long and unbroken periods of concentration can be conducted unseen by the prying eyes of the uninitiated. Even today, it is quite risky to enter an underground structure, but in the past, with poor lighting, no rescue services and many species of wild animal which are now extinct in Britain perhaps waiting there for a meal, to go underground was unthinkable to most people. Those who were brave or foolhardy enough to do so and survive were the guardians of arcane knowledge. The legends of Orpheus, Hermod, and other entrants to the subterranean kingdom are mythical accounts of the initiatory rites conducted inside real subterranean places. These underground structures are places of complete darkness, where 'alternative' experiences soon take one over.

As havens of darkness, subterranea are places where it is

impossible not to have an acute awareness of light. The contrast between the darkness and the light so important in many religious systems can be experienced directly when we enter the subterranean kingdom, and many ancient structures were designed deliberately to exploit this clash. The ancient Druids used to observe the overhead passage of the stars from the bottom of shafts dug in the ground, giving rise to the old adage 'Truth lies at the bottom of a well'. The native American Hopi tribe still use similar structures in their observances. The Hopi underground shrine or *kiva* is entered by a vertical shaft which serves as a sighting tube to the heavens. During all-night ceremonies, the various parts of the rite are started or finished at the appropriate time marked by the appearance of certain key stars viewed up the shaft.

Folk-legends attribute paranormal experiences to those who have entered the Underworld, such as a loss of an awareness of the passage of time, hallucinations and meetings with supernatural beings. Modern research on sensory deprivation, the conditions experienced when for some reason one or several of the sense organs are cut off from their normal stimuli, has shown that, after a while, phantom sensory responses are generated. In the case of entering total darkness, hallucinatory images will begin after a few hours, their content being related to the state of mind of the person. Thus a person who believed that a cave was full of troglodytes, demons or wraiths of the dead would experience hallucinations which would take those forms. If the energies present in the underground structure, such as electrostatic, gravitational and magnetic fields, concentrations of radiation and other environmental phenomena act upon the brain, then the unusual sensations would be conditioned by these also. Of if, indeed, there were spirits of the dead or elementals present, then sensory deprivation would permit their perception when under normal conditions they would remain unnoticed.

Deep in the Earth, we are cut off from all solar radiation, cosmic rays and other influences which affect us all continuously on the surface, but underground, we are influenced by the numinous qualities of the Earth, the energies detected by dowsers and sensitives. Sensory deprivation is added to by an awareness of the forces within the Earth, and of any other more supernatural manifestations of the Underworld. In Irish triadic tradition, there were Three Dark Places on Erin, of which Uaim Cruachain (Cruachu's Cave) at Rathcroghan, County Roscommon, is the most telling. In a complex of sacred and secular Iron Age earthworks is a long natural cleft in the rock, part of which has been made into a dry-stone-walled *souterrain* passage. Some of the stones have inscriptions in ogham and, from its traditional associations, it is certain that this was a cave of ritual. Its part-natural, part-artificial nature is typical of magical places of the Northern Tradition. Many of the earth houses, *Souterrains* and *Fogous* in Ireland, Britain and continental Europe, are remarkably complex structures, often incorporating natural features, and cunningly hidden from outsiders. All over the world, natural caves, often in association with springs or subterranean rivers, have been places where prophecy has been accessible. Mother Shipton, the famous *völva* (wise woman), is associated with a cave, and many holy wells where old women would, for a consideration, tell fortunes with the aid of the waters are in or near caves. It has been suggested that the energies created by running water, such as the production of negative ionization in the atmosphere, creates favourable conditions in the human brain to access areas of consciousness which normally are suppressed. These mysterious caves were visited by devout people who saw consulting the oracle as a religious act. When the Christian religion arrived in Europe, the traditions of many such places were just altered a little to fit in with the new doctrine. In some places, such as the Cave of St Beatus, near Interlaken, Switzerland, the Christianization of the Celtic sacred place is recalled as a combat between a saint and a dragon (as this cave is on a major fault line in the Alps, it is a site of great geomantic power; the saint used the cave for his religious devotions, whilst a church was built directly over the largest chamber of the cave, 3,000 feet below).

Although natural caves have their own sacred connections, people have also created artificial subterranea for their initiations or devotions. Being custom-made, these could more readily fit in with the requirements of initiation, and the mythical structure of the Underworld. The creation of an artificial cave or mine is the reverse of the usual process of building construction. It involves the removal of a relatively small amount of material from a large mass to leave a cavity. This is the opposite of the creation of a built structure, which is a space produced indirectly by its enclosure with solid

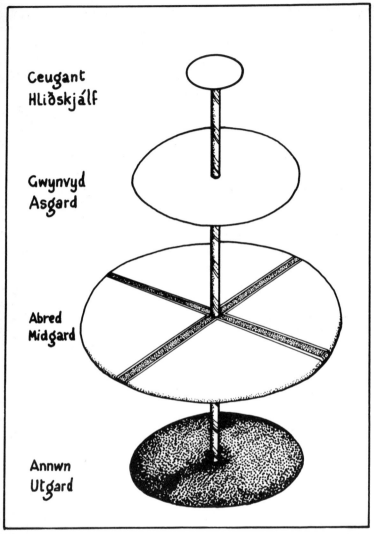

Fig. 13 The Cosmic Axis. This is the world axial tree, Yggdrassil, and the Bardic system of spiritual worlds. At the top, *Ceugant* is the seat of the Highest Power, the Air Throne Hlíðskjálf of Odin. This has the symbolic number 81, the sacred square. It is top of the Cosmic Tree, a crown of 37 oak leaves and 11 acorns. This is *Gwynvyd, the White Land*, and beneath it lies *Asgard*, the abode of the gods and souls who are with the gods. Being the place of light and knowledge, it has the traditional number 9. The earthly plane, *Abred*, is below this, and is the world of matter, with the traditional number 27. Finally, the Abyss, *Annwn*, lies at the foot of the axis, the place of unmanifested, unformed souls and matter.

material put together. Underground structures have many special characteristics that separate them from the conventional built environment. Being cut into the body of the Earth, they are in immediate contact with underground water, but out of contact with the winds, which play such a large part in cooling. Likewise, the structure is not in contact with solar heating, and hence the temperature in underground structures remains remarkably constant throughout the year. Obviously, the disadvantages of subterranean structures include absence of natural lighting and ventilation problems, yet rock-cut houses have been a feature of every land where the geology has permitted their construction. Similarly, subterranean structures for sacred use are found all over the world, ranging from the great rock-cut temples at Ellora in India to the smallest niches cut in cliffsides.

The Underworld's axial links

Psychically subterranea are an image of the lower part of an axis which runs from the Underworld, through the Middleworld in which we live, into an Upperworld. This link is known as the *Cosmic Axis* or *Axis Mundi*. In Britain, this is described in the ancient lore of the Druids known as the Bardic Tradition, collected together by the great Welsh bard Llewellyn Sion of Glamorgan (*c.*1560–1616). Sion recovered many ancient Welsh manuscripts from Raglan Castle which described the beliefs of the Druids. In this tradition, the Cosmic Axis links *four circles of being* arranged on this vertical axis. In effect, only three are accessible to humans and spirits, for the uppermost, *Ceugant,* is the sole abode of the transcendent creator, Hên Ddihenydd, the Allfather. The circle immediately below *Ceugant* is called *Gwynvyd*, the *White Land*, whose name translates as the quality of *Felicity.* Here is the abode of the enlightened—saints, demigods and people who have transcended the reincarnatory cycle of their earthly lives. This is equivalent to *Asgard* in the Norse conception. Below this is the Middleworld, *Abred*, which also has the alternative name of *Adfant*—'the Place with the Turned-Back Rim'—an allusion to the 'flat Earth' idea current in former ages. It is the Middle Earth, *Midgard*, of Norse tradition. Here, good and evil are present in equal quantities. Here there is free will, for in *Abred* every act, within the confines of fate, is one of consent or choice. Whatever one does, one could do differently, and therefore it is appropriate that one should receive punishment or reward according to one's acts or works.

Just as the righteous ascend the axis to the bright Upperworld, those whose lives have been less than perfect descend to the Underworld, *Annwn*. This is a place of re-purification, for the Bardic Tradition asserts that human beings undergo successive reincarnations. This belief is preserved in the ancient Cornish saying, *'Ni fuil an sabras athragad death'*—'There is nothing in death but an alteration of life'. Here, in *Abred*, a series of lives is led in free will, with spiritual progression or retrogression dependent on action. The perpetration of real evil ends in a fall down the Cosmic Axis into the abyss of *Annwn*, the Loveless Place or Land Invisible. This fall is *obryn*—transmigration into a lower form, *Annwn* is a state containing lower, insensate matter and organisms that have not progressed sufficiently yet to enter *Abred*. Eventually, after re-purification, *Abred* is regained. The Celtic legend known as the *Descent Into Annwn* and other myths of entrance into the Underworld to rescue the 'damned' are well known. In these legends, the hero or heroine goes to bargain with the guardians of the abyss for the soul of someone, sometimes successfully, but often not. The features of these legends are similar to those undergone by shamans in their trance journeys, and all of the aspects of the Cosmic Axis can be experienced in this way. This concept of the worlds was reproduced when constructing artificial sacred subterranea, whose features would reproduce for the initiate the surprises, terrors and insights of the subterranean kingdom. To enter such a place might give a foretaste of the Underworld, or a means of accessing the spirits of the departed. Only by entering such a place today can one experience a physical descent into an image of the Underworld.

Water sprites

Water, the source of life, also has its deities and sprites, whose direction by ancient tradition is the West. Water sprites have many names—nixies, kelpies, neckans, undines—which describe various elemental phenomena such as strong currents, whirlpools and tidal bores. Each river or stream of any size has its own Water spirit which is often considered to be the causal factor in human drownings, often be-

Fig. 14 Romano-Gallic image of Sequana, tutelary goddess of the River
    Seine, France. Discovered hidden near the remains of the shrine at the
    river's source.

ing seen as demanding a certain number of human deaths
each year. The news media still speak of a 'death toll' in an ac-
cident, implicitly meaning that the appropriate being has
taken its quota of human lives as a sort of payment so that
others may pass freely. Many rivers have their own
spirits—the Trent has the Eager (the Norse god Ægir); the

Mersey, Belisama; the Ribble, Peg O'Nell; the Tees, Peg Powler; the Seine, Sequana—and so on. One deity's name seems to be the most widespread—Nectan. The sacred River Boyne in Ireland springs from the well of Nechtan. In Germany, the River Neckar is sacred to the deity. In Celtic Britain, the deities called Nudd and Nodens, Christianized as St Neot, are the same Water sprite. Where St Neot or St Nectan is the local saint, there we can expect to find the site of a shrine of a water sprite. At St Nectan's Glen, near Tintagel in Cornwall, a famous waterfall still punches its way through a hole in the rock forming St Nectan's Kieve, a magical spot giving rise to a stream which flows to the sea through Rocky Valley past two ancient classical labyrinths carved on a rockface. Adjoining Dozmary Pool, the final resting-place of Excalibur, King Arthur's sword, was the hermitage of St Neot, with its holy well containing three fish. Nectan, or Neot is the deity of the River Ouse, celebrated at St Neot's Huntingdonshire, where formerly St Neot's Fair was held for three days starting on Lammas Eve (31 July). St Neot is the priest-king sometimes manifested as St Nectan. One East Anglian rhyme calls the spirit Nicky Nye, the local variant of Nectan:

Nicky Nicky Nye,
Pulls you down,
Underneath the water,
Drown, drown, die.

Wherever there is a *mitchpool* (whirlpool) in a river or the sea, this can be seen as a manifestation of the Water sprite, a dangerous place to be. Throughout Europe, spring waters have been seen as the gift of Mother Earth, who sends them up for human benefit, and the deities of wells are an aspect of the Great Mother. Divination and oracles made by drinking the waters of holy wells, or through interpreting the sound of running water, is seen as a means of contacting the will or message of Mother Earth. Waterfalls, places where the 'force' aspect of water is most prevalent inland, are places of power in the landscape. The physical effect of their incessant roaring—*white noise*—and the negative ions liberated into the air by their action have measurable effects on human feelings of well-being, creating an uplifting, soothing atmosphere. Sprites such as Nectan and the Urisk (a half-human, half-goat being) frequent waterfalls and follow humans at night without doing them harm.

The air and the winds

Although scientifically the air we breathe is of known composition (about four-fifths nitrogen and one fifth oxygen, and other gases, with traces of industrial pollutants), traditionally, it has meant a lot more than just a mixture of gases. In everyday modern speech we say 'there's something in the air', or that someone puts on 'airs and graces', and we talk of a disease called malaria, meaning 'bad air'. These idioms show that there is something more to the air than its physical characteristics, and indeed, there are traditions of certain types of air which have an effect upon people and their surroundings. A place can have 'bad air', air which brings sickness, and produces headaches and aches in the nape of the neck. It is believed that the subtle qualities of air can be altered deliberately by black magic as a malevolent on-lay upon a place or person. This is known as *laid air*, which can be countered by protective magic. Finally, the qualities of the time, the influence of the *seals*, the time of day, the runic or planetary hours, is sometimes spoken of as a type of air, *seal air*.

Often certain qualities of air are seen as rule by Air elementals, whose canonical direction is the East. These are given various names: sylphs, gremlins, zephyrs, and, personified as the Winds, the spirits who are present in winds, as sub-elements within them. Just as the direction of a strong wind is tempered by eddies and temporary changes in direction, so these elementals are in relation to the main winds and their direction-qualities. In the European Tradition, there are eight major winds, corresponding with the eight directions. These are known either as the traditional North, South, East, West, etc. winds, or by their Latin names as used by Roman and Renaissance navigators and *locators*. Of these, the four cardinal directions, North—East and North—West play the greatest part in northern European lore.

English	Latin
South	Auster
South-West	Africus
West	Favonius
North-West	Cautus
North	Septentrio
North-East	Aquilo

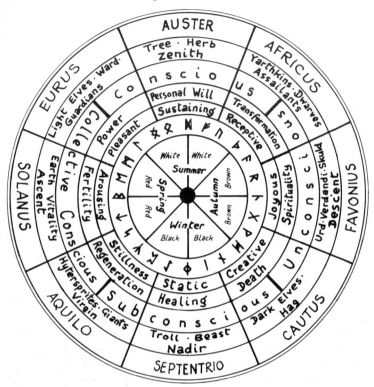

Fig. 15 The *Rose of the Winds*, showing the correspondences between the winds, the qualities of the directions, the runes and the seasons.

English	Latin
East	Solanus
South-East	Eurus

Each of these winds has two auxiliary sub-winds or breezes, one on either side, making the 24-fold division of the circle which corresponds to the hours of the day and the runes of the Elder Futhark. Thus, each wind and breeze has a mystical connection with the qualities of time and of the runes.

The 16 breezes are arranged as follows (their runic correspondences are shown in Fig. 15).

Breeze	Wind		Breeze
Leuconotus	— AUSTER	—	Altanus
Libonotus	— AFRICUS	—	Subvespos

Breeze	Wind	Breeze
Argestes	— FAVONIUS	— Etesias
Circius	— CAUTUS	— Cotus
Thrascias	— SEPTENTRIO	— Gallicus
Supernas	— AQUILO	— Boreas
Carbas	— SOLANUS	— Ornithiæ
Cæcias	— EURUS	— Vultumus

Storms, waterspouts, lightning and weather magic

At any place, wind-storms generally occur around the same time of year, and come from the direction of the prevailing winds. The prevailing wind at any given place is magically related to the quality of the direction from which it blows, according to the Rose of the Winds. Magically, wind-storms are ruled by the fierce wind-giant Hrelsweg from the Eagle's Mount, at the end of the Earth, and each of the wind-directions are sub-elements of his power. Whirlwinds are a spiral manifestation of the wind, and as such are held in special regard. The twisting effect of many magical fields can be found mentioned in many folk-tales and in eyewitness accounts of poltergeist activity. Like whirlpools in bodies of water, the whirlwind and the waterspout are examples of this physical effect in the air. Little whirlwinds are said to be the passage of spirits, as are *dust devils* and similar local microclimatic effects. Waterspouts and hurricanes are relatively uncommon in northern Europe, but when they do occur, as in 1987, they can be devastating. A waterspout is formed when a tight whirlwind takes place over water, drawing it up into a column or pillar, opening out at the top to merge with clouds. A waterspout is an awesome sight, a manifestation of the irresistible power of nature, or the deity in whose form it may be visualized. The common shape of a waterspout resembles the cosmic pillar, Irminsul, for which it may have been a model.

Raising the wind

Calling up the wind has always been part of folk magic. Before the availability of manufactured power sources, the wind was used in milling and transport. Until the end of commercial sailing, Swedish seafarers in the Baltic would build stone labyrinths by the shore to ensure a fair wind. When becalmed, they would row to a nearby island or coastline, construct a labyrinth and conduct ceremonies in it to call up the wind. In some places, whistling in a certain way and direction was held to be effective. Also, *dobbie stones*, stones with natural or artificial hollows in which offerings, such as milk, can be placed, have been used traditionally in rites for raising the wind. The modern tradition of these stones is that they are receptacles for milk for sacred cats, and are sometimes called *cat troughs*. This is a continuation of the earlier practice which added honey to the milk, or substituted brine or ale. Dobbie stones are sometimes stones with natural depressions, and sometimes artificially hollowed out. They are found near the farmhouse door, by field-entraces, and places where paths cross boundaries, such as stiles and gateways.

To call up the appropriate wind, offerings should be placed in the bowl from the corresponding direction from which the required wind should blow. The cupped surface is a reflection of the dome of the heavens, or the skull of the slain primal giant Ymir, and, by the law of correspondences, it is a microcosm of the circle of the horizon or the Rose of the Winds. Dobbie stones, fashioned from the 'bones of the Earth', are thus an image of the skull-cup from which the warriors of the northern martial arts would drink. Offerings like this are in the tradition of *Álf-blót*, an offering to the elves, or local spirits of the land. The sacred cats referred to are spectral or natural, and are the totemic creature of Freyja. Apparitional creatures like the Exmoor Cats, the Surrey Puma and other sightings occasionally reported in the press may well be glimpses of these beings.

Lightning, corposant, will o' the wisp and rainbows

Lightning is a frightening and dangerous phenomenon, being massive electrical discharges between the air and grounded objects. As the sacred emanation of Thor and his equivalents, thunder and lightning has always been considered literally ominous, that is, bringing omens in the domain of Air and Fire elementals. In British folklore, there is a widespread belief that the day of the week on which thunder is heard is significant. One tradition states that if there is thunder on a Monday, a royal child will be put to death; Tuesday, failure of the crops; Wednesday, death of the tillers of the land; and Thursday, the death of women. Thunder on other days has no special ominous meaning. The direction that lightning sinks from view is also significant, recalled by an East Anglian rhyme:

If it sinks from the north,
It will double its wrath;
If it sinks from the south,

Fig. 16 The *corposant—St Elmo's fire*—luminescent on the mast and spars of a sailing galleon. (From a contemporary engraving.)

It will open its mouth;
If it sinks from the west,
It is never at rest;
If it sinks from the east,
It will leave us in peace.

Associated with lightning are the Fire elementals, whose traditional direction is South. These are the salamanders, fire witches, pinkets, corpse candles, will o' the wisps, fireballs, earthlights, balls-of-light or BOLs, and lights often lumped with so-called unidentified flying objects (UFOs). Among unexplained, 'Fortean' or supernatural phenomena, these are the most enigmatic, having spawned more tales and speculations than any others. The East Anglian word for lightning is *spirit*, for example 'spirit lit on the chimney'. There it is seen as an example of *önd* flowing rapidly from above, devastatingly powerful, but without physical form. The more physical, though still tenuous, manifestations are the *corposant* or St Elmo's fire and the will o' the wisp. In the days of sail, the corposant was a awesome sight to seamen. In Dampier's *Voyages*, we read that when it appeared on the very top of the mainmast, or at a yard-arm, it was 'like a star', a small, glittering, light, but when it appeared on the deck, 'it resembles a great glow-worm'. The corposant also grounds itself. Sailors have reported lights creeping or 'travelling' about in the scuppers. On land, 'something white moving along' was often seen in former days at Aldreth Fen, Cambridgeshire. This manifestation was 'as big as a large cat without head or legs'. When poked with a stick, the stick passed through it, and it was often seen in moonlight. Will o' the wisp, known in East Anglia as Will (the Earth, or ground, is known as *Will's Mother's*) is closely allied to the corposant, appearing to react to human activities as if controlled or motivated by some form of intelligence, a luminescent manifestation of *önd*.

Another notable weather phenomenon esoterically associated with fire is the rainbow, created when sunlight shines through droplets of rain which act prismatically to give the illusion of a spectrum in the sky. All over the world, rainbows are symbols of the gods, being seen as a bridge from Heaven to Earth. The colours of the rainbow when brought together as dyed threads have a magically protective function, the seven colours symolizing the seven planetary deities and their powers. The Norse Rainbow Bridge, *Bifröst*, guarded by Heimdall, is just that. At the rainbow's end, of course, is the legendary crock of gold, indicating a divinatory function. Although the likelihood of finding gold by that means is remote, a rainbow's orientation is considered to foretell forthcoming weather:

Rainbow in the *south*, heavy rain and snow,
Rainbow in the *west*, little showers and dew,
Rainbow in the *east*, fair skies and blue.

Ice

Unlike the other four elements, the presence of ice in nature is less prevalent. In most places, outside high mountains or the polar regions, it is the seasonal element of winter-time. Ice is the fifth 'element' in the Northern Tradition, being the static, solid form of water. It is associated with massive, inexorable processes. In form, ice ranges from the delicate, sixfold crystalline patterns of snowflakes (the form of the rune Hægl) to glaciers and continental ice-caps. The elementals of Ice are therefore not the gnomes of Earth or nixies of Water, but giants, slow and massive.

However we look upon these beings, whether as arrays of physical matter and forces acting in a certain way; as the interaction between human consciousness and partially-controllable energy-systems; or as wilful entities, endowed with some kind of power and consciousness, the outcome is the same. By using traditional ways of seeing and thinking, we can gain a rapport with conditions which modern society marginalizes. In the next chapter, we will see the context in which these magical acts and beings operate.

III

The Magic of the North

The Earth is not an inanimate body, but is inhabited by the spirit
which is its life and soul. All created things draw their strength from
the Earth Spirit. This spirit is life, it is nourished by the stars and gives
nourishment to all living things that it shelters in her womb.

Basilius Valentinus

The Unbroken Spiritual Tradition

The spiritual exercises of the Christian tradition are well
known, and widely practised today in many parts of the
world. But it is not commonly known that these are in part
derived from the northern European techniques of earlier
times, modified in line with a different theology. These northern techinques are based upon involvement of the material
world with the realm of the spirit. Underlying the practices are
the fundamental tenets of the Northern Tradition. The Northern Tradition respects the life force. It respects the fundamental polarities of existence, the law of the unity of op-
posites, in a dynamic balance. It does not represent the dominant side of things expunging or attempting to expunge its
opposite. It does not preach human dominance over nature,
nor subservience to it, either. To be in balance with the world
is to be neither its master (which is an impossible delusion)
nor to be at the mercy of things. It is found and renewed in
the cycles of the season. It has natural enjoyments whilst retaining right-mindedness and balance. Ultimately, it is the
right usage of the creative force which exists within nature
and within ourselves, tolerating other visions and versions of
a myriad multifaceted truth. This creative force is neutral; it
has no direction until directed. It is up to the practitioner to
direct it for the maintenance of harmonious balance within

the world, for the good of all and without subverting the free will of others.

With the Northern Tradition, unlike Buddhism, Judaism, Christianity or Hinduism, we are dealing with a tradition whose practices were for many years prohibited and actively suppressed for political reasons. This is because the early Christians were persecuted by Romans emperors, who were Pagan. When the Christian religion became the state church of the Roman Empire, with the claim of universal and ex-clusive truth, it set about persecuting Paganism, which it saw as having persecuted *it* in the past. In Rome, this had been the case, but the spiritual tradition of northern Europe, as in ancient Greece, had been one of free conscience, where everyone was free to worship any deity, including the Chris-tian ones, or to be an atheist. This ethos included a democratic way of decision-making in the community, the equal rights for men and women. Despite Pagan tolerance, the Church was not, and extended its persecution of other faiths outside the Roman Empire into many other parts of the world, including northern Europe.

Because the old ways were part of everyday life in northern Europe, however, the laws and punishments enacted against Paganism were ineffective. This was especially true in the countryside, which was more difficult to police than towns. Pagan artifacts were disguised as Christian ones, or hidden in secret places. Sacred objects were, and still are, hidden away in hidey-holes, brought out only at the right time, handed down in the family and only seen by trusted people. For those who could write, it was too dangerous to write anything down, so many traditions were handed down by word of mouth, to the present day. In this way, the knowledge of the Northern Tradition survived for centuries without the help of a priesthood, for the observance of any tradition in itself is an act of faith.

Any attempt to suppress eternal realities based on the cycle of life must be doomed to failure. Over 1,200 year ago, the *Penitential* of Archbishop Egbert (736–66) stated that people should be punished 'If any exercise divinations and soothsayings or keep vigils at any spring or at any other creature, except at the Church of God. . .'. Nearly three cen-turies later, the *Dooms* of King Cnut (1020–3) stated: 'V: And we earnestly forbid every heathen practice. V;i: It is heathen practice if one worships idols, namely if one worships heathen gods and the sun or the moon, fire or flood, wells or stones or any kind of forest trees. . . .' Few took any notice of these and other laws, though many were punished for ignoring them. The *Capitularia Regum Francorum*, published at Paris in 1677, has a list of rural practices then in use, but forbidden in France by the Church, as they had been for 1,200 years. Among them were ceremonies for the deceased, known as *dadsissas*, and ceremonies at their tombs. The ceremonies of Mercury and Jupiter were forbidden, along with sacrifices made to any other divinity. This included the observance of the festivals of Mercury or Jupiter (worship on Wednesday and Thursday, the two holiest days of the Northern Tradition, sacred to Odin and Thor). Observance of *Vince Luna*, an eclipse of the moon, was also out.

Fig. 17 The wayside shrines of natural religion were Christianized by the addition of a cross, as in this engraving. But the practices of the Elder Faith continued at them unabated. (From J.G. Heck's *Iconographic Encyclopædia of Science, Literature and Art, 1851.*)

It is clear that, as in many other places, the substitution of a Christian deity for a Pagan just meant that the original one was worshipped in the guise of the later. In seventeenth century France, the Mother goddess was petitioned in the form 'of that which good people call St Mary'. Doubtless she still is. Attempts were made to prevent worship at 'the irregular places which they cherish for their ceremonies', which included 'watersprings as the sites of sacrifice', processions through churches and 'the Pagan trackway, which they name *Yries*, marked with rags or with shoes'. The construction of small huts known as sanctuaries (equivalent to northern *hørgr*) was noted. The prohibition included 'the

ceremonies of the woodland, known as *Nimidas'*, and rites
performed upon stones. The moats surrounding houses in
the country, prevalent also in eastern England, were suspect
as important in the rites of the Old Religion.

In the seventeenth century, the making of images was prohibited. The *Capitularia* notes especially images made of flour
sprinkled on the ground (step patterns and the like); images
made from rags; 'the image which they carry through the
fields'; and 'the wooden feet or hands used in heathen
ritual'. Kindling the 'fire made by rubbing wood, that is, *nod-
fyr'* [need-fire] was a serious offence. Consecrations with
chanting or calls was frowned upon, as was divination and
prophecy. Augury from the dung of birds, horses, cattle, or
from their sneezing, was mentioned specifically, as was the
interpretation of stormy weather, and the use of things
similar to horn and snail-shells [spirals, whose form expresses the mathematics underlying all life and growth].
Even 'the heathen practice of gazing into a hearth or an amor-
phous mass' [of embers] was forbidden. Traditional
talismans, phylacteries and 'things bound' were also prohibited. Finally, 'those believing that because women praise
the moon, they can drew the hearts of men towards the
Pagans' were condemned.

List of these sorts of practices can be found in almost every
country where the Church attempted, invariably without
success, to suppress indigenous religious observance.
Wherever they exist, they consistently refer to the same
classes of sites, and the same practices which are observed today, if one knows where to look for them.

Devotional Exercises, Útiseta and Other Techniques of Meditation

Surviving folk traditions in parts of northern Europe, written
records in ancient sagas and more modern accounts record
the precise details of these techniques. The devotional tradition includes singing, praise, repetition of calls and the name
of the deity being worshipped, images and rituals. Devotion
is simple. It does not require elaborate ritual. The recognition
of a sacred place by an offering of flowers, or a candle, is
enough. The re-establishment of ancient sacred places, and
the recognition of other, new, ones, is an important means of

refurbishing a hierarchy of sacredness which has fallen into a measure of disrepair.

The spiritual exercise tradition involves 'sittings-out', postural exercises, and, most of all, inner discipline. There is no need for images and elaborate ritual. Knowledge comes from within, illuminating the outer world. *Útiseta* or *sitting out* is an important technique, where a person 'sits out' under the stars to hear inner voices and commune with the universe. Spiritual exercises such as *Útiseta* are practices designed to bring the aspirant into communion with ultimate reality. Such states are not attained easily. One must have purity of intention: that the powers one has or is attempting to acquire will be used only for one's personal needs, subverting the free will of no other person, or for the benefit of all people. Generally, such spiritual exercises should only be undertaken in a state of purification, after appropriate rituals of cleansing and protection, and in a state of physical cleanliness, involving ablutions and the wearing of clean clothes.

Suitable locations for sitting out are high places of ancient sanctity, preferably those away from populated areas. Unfortunately, interference is almost guaranteed at sites near cities, no matter what the time of day or night. Solitary, wild places, especially those known to be sites of ancient numinous quality, geomantic places of power, where the flow of *önd* is appropriately strong, are ideal. This is best at a high point, and in earlier times the burial-mounds of royalty and warrior-heroes were chosen. Today, ancient artifical mounds, either geomantic mark-points, traditional holy hills or burial-mounds, which have been made deliberately at places of power where *önd* is strong, are equally useful, but, as with any powerful technique, it should be approached carefully and gradually.

Techniques

The spiritual exercises of the Northern Tradition have a number of elements. They can be broken down into five basic parts:

1 Sitting in a definite posture — The body must be in a relaxed yet alert position. There are two ways of sitting. One is with legs crossed, such as may be seen in ancient represen-

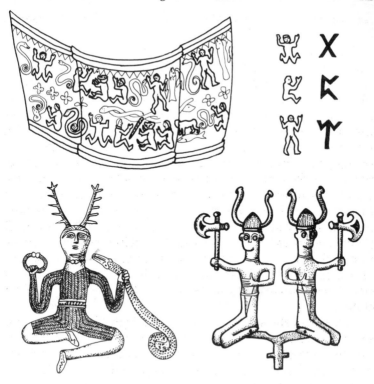

Fig. 18 Posture magic. *Top*: part of the Gallehus Horn without runes, with figures in various meditational postures (Danish). *Bottom left*: Cernunnos, the horned god, in *útiseta* posture, from the Gundestrup Cauldron (Dano-Celtic). *Bottom right*: axe-gods (=Forseti), bronze figures found at Grevens Vaeng, 1778. All of these items date from around the year 500 CE.

tations of the gods, such as Cernunnos. This goes under the German name of *Keltensitz*, although it is known from all of the northern countries. The second is sitting with the legs under the body, as if kneeling, again a posture seen in ancient sacred images. There is also the tradition of standing, assuming runic postures (*stödhur*) appropriate to the meditation being undertaken (see Fig. 18).

2 Regulation of breathing — This involves quiet, deep, regular breathing. When the breath is under control, a state of serenity is readily accomplished. One of our own aspects of *önd*, the breath, is our own immediately controllable part of the universal life of the cosmos.

3 Banishment of unwanted thoughts — This is perhaps the
most difficult part. Attention is first withdrawn from external
objects and other distractions. The eyes are closed, and mental images seen there suppressed. Bodily sensations will fade
and become almost unnoticed. When these first three
elements have been mastered, then the ground is prepared
for the final two, which are the use of concentration, and
making the call.

4 Concentration — Banishment of unwanted thoughts and
images can be accomplished by concentrating the mind upon
some definite thing. The visualization of the symbol of a
cosmic image is usual. This may be something especially important to the meditator, such as the World Tree, Yggdrassil,
a deity's sacred tool or weapon like *Mjöllnir*, the Hammer of
Thor, or of a particular rune. Meditators should find a symbol
which most appeals, and dwell upon it in their meditation
until it becomes part of their consciousness.

5 The call — The sacramental energy present in words is
known throughout the world's sacred technologies. The Hindu *mantra* is the nearest type of sacred sentence to that of the
Northern Tradition. In the Northern Tradition, the *call* is the
sacred sound which parallels the mantra. It is full of consciousness, based upon the runes, a mass of radiant energy
when called by a practitioner. The call may be the name of a
deity, or a sacred formula, broken down into its runic
phonetics, and repeated during meditation whilst the appropriate rune, deity or sacred object is visualized. The call
expresses a particular aspect of sacred reality with which the
meditator has the most affinity.

The seer's journey — Seer's journeys may take one of two
forms: journeying inwards, or as a physical pilgrimage to a
place of mantic power.
    The physical seer's journey is an actual pilgrimage, involv-
ing travelling a prescribed route along sacred paths,
trackways and roads to a holy site, visiting other, wayside,
sacred places on the way. Journeying seership can be accomplished by several means, that most appropriate to
oneself being discovered by experiment. Exploring a wild

area until one finds a good location for sitting out is one method. Another, once popular in Scotland, is being wrapped in a cow's hide or blanket, with only the head free, and lying all night by a holy well or waterfall to experience visions. The ancient Greek Pagan master Pythagoras, after being ritually cleansed, slept in the skin of a black sheep by a river to gain knowledge, and much of our knowledge of geometry, still used today, came in this way.

The inward seer's journey is similar to what is modernly termed *pathworking*, travelling through inner landscapes. In the Northern Tradition, this is accomplished through the images of scriptural stories from the *Edda* or the *Sagas*, such as Hermod's ride to the Underworld, or Thor's journey into Utgard. The re-enactment of an archetypal journey, either physically, or in the mind, re-creates qualities and insights which cannot be put into words.

When the exercise is finished, whatever it is, there should be a re-awakening, a re-entering of the 'normal' world. This is done in the reverse order from the methods used to being meditation, consciously ordering each part of the body in turn to start functioning again. The body, as well as the mind, should feel revitalized after the exercise.

Mounds, platforms, earth houses and chambered cairns

Although most practitioners cannot have their own place to sit out, or their own subterranean structure, it is traditional to perform meditation at such places. Often, the functions of mound and earth house were combined, with subterranean passages under tumuli. Many of the prehistoric 'passage graves' or chambered cairns are likely to have been of this nature, with only a secondary use for burials. The platform on top of the mound was an important part of the practice of *útiseta*. It is one of the items which comprised the essential paraphernalia of a Norse *völva* (wise woman), and its use is known from many parts of northern Europe. In the twelfth century, it was forbidden in Norway by a 'Great Law' enacted against practices of which the Church disapproved. In Holland, it continued openly until the late seventeenth century, when it succumbed to the *Heidenjachten*, Heathen Hunts, organized by the Church to kill Gypsies and indigenous Pagans.

In his book *Korte Beschryvinge van Eenige Verborgene Anti-quiteten*, published in 1660, Johan Picardt wrote about these Frisian wise women, known as *witte wijven*. Until his time, they lived in the Dutch provinces of Drenthe and West Friesland, practising their craft of healing, divination and magic for anyone who came to see them. The *witta wijven* lived in special shamanic lodges, or earth houses. These structures were built in the last years of a technical tradition dating back for 5,000 years. Each lodge was a hollow earth mound entered by steps cut in the mound's side. On top was a wooden platform, to which access was gained by a chimney from inside the lodge. These platforms, bedecked with staves, skulls and magic items, were used for sitting out. Outside the earth house, skulls, bones and other magical paraphernalia were erected on posts as protection against intrusion, both human and supernatural. Wherever it was us-

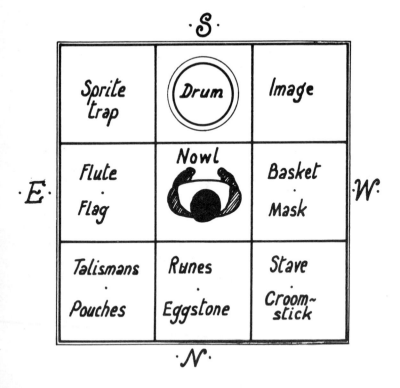

Fig. 19 Location of sacred objects within the grid of nine used in *útiseta*.

ed, the basic form of the platform was a grid structure, the nine-square pattern especially, reflecting the sacred number nine. In the nine-square pattern, a square was divided into three along each of its sides, and the points joined with lines. This created a grid of nine small squares. This is the first 'square number' which completely encloses a square within a square, and in magical terms, it provides a completely protected square at the centre of a larger square. The layout of sacred items which can surround the sitter-out is shown in Figure 19.

The ancient chambered cairns and so-called *passage graves* of ancient northern Europe have local folk traditions which combine sacred rites and solar observances. These are the forerunners of the shamanic lodges of the *witta wijven*. Although technically above ground, having been built up on the surface rather than dug into the earth, these vast stone-built chambers have all of the key features of subterranean shamanic lodges. Although many hundreds of such sites exist in northern Europe, important accessible examples of such constructions include the West Kennet long barrow near Silbury Hill in Wiltshire, New Grange in Ireland and Maeshowe, Orkney. The function of these structures was not primarily one of burial, for the long approach passages which lead to the internal chambers are aligned precisely upon sunrise, or sometimes sunset, on important days in the Celtic calendar.

The technical ability required for locating and designing these structures was of a very high order, reconciling many complex variable features into a functional instrument of ancient wisdom. The great chambered mound at Maeshowe, Orkney, is a fine example which illustrates the main features of such places. Situated near the Loch of Harray, outwardly it is an earth mound about 115 feet in diameter and 24 feet high (35 m × 7.5 m). Internally, it contains several chambers located at the end of an approach passage 54 feet (16.5 m) in length. The main chamber is made from closely-fitted, levelled megalithic stones of such high quality workmanship that the jointing has been compared with that of the Great Pyramid, which was built some centuries after Maeshowe.

The passageway acts like a telescope aligned upon a prominently-situated standing stone 924 yards (844 m) from the entrance to the howe. This alignment precisely marks a solsticial sunrise, linking the structure not only with the landscape in which it is situated, but also with cycles of the heavens. Another megalith to the west, called the Watchstone, marked the equinoxes. Far from being a tomb, Maeshowe was an underground observatory used in the distant past for the monitoring of the calendar, a practice inseparable from the religion of the era. When we use the ancient techniques today, like our forebears, we should strive for the greatest possible harmony with all of the variable factors of time and space. Places such as this are still accumulators of *önd*, as anyone can discover for themselves.

Seidr—völvas and warlocks

In the Northern Tradition, several different classes of practitioner are known from a variety of sources and, under different names or none, are recognizable today among traditional and hereditary practitioners. In ancient Iceland, wise women were known as *völva* or *fjölkunnig kona*, whilst a wizard or cunning man was called *fjölkunnigr madr*. The art of the wise was generally known as *fjölkyngi*, which translates as *'much knowledge'*, or *fródleikr*, 'wisdom' or 'learning.' In the Northern Tradition, *Seiðr* is a means of oracular divination, which was not used for healing as in Lappish, Inuit and Siberian shamanism. This form of magic enabled the *völva* to have a rapport with animals, to travel astrally by their means, or even to assume their shape and qualities. Assuming animal form or other disguise was known as *hamrammr* or 'shape-shifting.' Rapport with animals depended on the type of practitioner: martial arts masters communed with ravens, starlings, geese, bears, wolves or wild swine; wise women with cats and birds according to the deities to which they afforded devotion. Goddesses and gods are often depicted with the animal with which they have rapport. An eleventh century wall painting in Slesvig Cathedral, which was built during the period of dual faith shortly after the official conversion of Denmark to Christianity, shows the goddess Frigg, the female shamanic counterpart to Odin. She is riding on a large light-coloured striped cat which is probably meant to be a Siberian tiger.

There were other words to describe practitioners, depending on the country in which they operated. The Pagan wise women expelled by Filimer, King of the Goths, from the territories under his control, were known as *haliarunos*, a word

Fig. 20 Freyja riding her cat or Siberian tiger. Wall-painting at Schleswig, contemporary with that in Fig. 6, and probably by the same artist.

inferring the use of the runes. A *þhul* (*þulr*), was a shamanically-inspired poet, orator or sage. In the Anglo-Saxon poem *Beowulf*, Unferth has the same title, *Thyle*. The word is connected with *Thule*, a place-name element meaning 'the place where people are forced to turn back'. To bring his hard-won knowledge to the human world, the seer must return from the other worlds.

The Scots dialect word *warlock*, meaning a cunning man or male white witch, is rarely used today except pejoratively. Because dictionary definitions have given it meanings like 'liar', it has fallen from use, but it is clear that in reality it relates to the power to shut in or enclose, i.e. a person with the capability of making binding spells. This is found in the Norse tale *Eiríks Saga Rauða*. The story is set in Greenland, some years after the Christian religion was imposed. A *völva* conducting a ceremony asks the assembly that a song called

Varðlokkur should be sung to enable the continuation of the ceremony. No-one knows it, except a girl on a visit from Iceland. She is Christian, but has been taught it by her nurse. Reluctant at first to sing the *Varðlokkur*, knowing it to be Pagan, eventually she is cajoled into singing, and the ceremony is completed without interference. The power of the warlock, then, is to *ward* off evil spirits and to *lock* or bind them up. Another old Scots dialect word with magical connotations is *fret*. The modern usage of this word is 'worry', but originally this was worry in the form of a seer's foreboding.

Magical abilities

Among the magical abilities of the northern practitioners, teleportation, invisibility, shape-shifting and superhuman strength are reported. A whole terminology exists, describing subtle differences of quality. For example, people in possession of second sight, that is with insights into the spirit-world, were known as *ófreskir*. Those capable of seeing into the future, being 'far-sighted', were *framsynn*; shape-shifting was *bregda sér*; and the seemingly supernatural strength of the martial arts as *rammaukin*. In the *Vatnsdoela Saga*, Heid the wise woman predicted that Ingimund and his band would settle in a land as yet undiscovered, west over sea. Heid told Ingimund that his *hlutr*, a sacred image of Freyr which had disappeared from his purse, would be found again when he dug the post-holes for his hall in the new land. Ingimund did not want to go to the new land, Iceland, but instead sent two Finnish magicians there to find his teleported *hlutr*. Some time later, the Finns returned to Ingimund in Norway, having found the image but been unable to recover it. So they directed Ingimund to the place, a dale between two woods, Vatnsdal, where Ingimund founded the hall call *Hof*.

Many of the early saints of the Celtic Church possessed and continued the traditional practices of the Elder Faith, performing acts of magic and extrasensory perception. In Adamnan's *Life of Saint Columba*, for example, is a catalogue of miraculous happenings whose character is identical to those performed by wise men and women of the Northern Tradition. One such example took place when Abbot Cainnech sailed from Iona, but left his staff behind. It was taken to Columba's oratory, and left with him 'at prayer'. When Cainnech landed in Ireland, he knelt to pray, and beside him was his staff, teleported there by 'the divine power' used by Columba.

The Northern Martial Arts Tradition

The Northern Tradition, forged in the hardship of the ice and snow of Ice-Age Europe, was originally one of continuous struggle against overwhelming odds. This required self-reliance and, if necessary, a willingness to die selflessly for family and comrades, calling upon those reserves of superhuman strength which lie within all of us. To be capable of these feats of will, strict training in self-control comparable to that used in the oriental martial arts was required. This was manifested in the warrior tradition, which later passed into Chivalry and finally succumbed to the formation of standing armies, and technology in the form of firearms. The hero-traditions in Arthurian literature and the German and Norse sagas show us that there were two main cults within the warrior tradition—that of the wolf and the bear, with a lesser, but regal, cult of the wild boar. These are best known from the Norse warrior groups known as the Berserkers and the Ûlfhednar.

Beserkers, Ûlfhednar and Svínfylking warriors

> They . . . went without mailcoats, were frantic as dogs or wolves; they bit their shields and were as strong as bears or boars; they slew men, but neither fire nor iron could hurt them. This is called 'running berserk'. . .
>
> *Ynglinga Saga*

Today, the phrase 'going berserk' is used when someone flies into a great rage and attacks people or things at random, using seemingly superhuman strength. Originally, 'to go berserk' meant to go into battle wearing a bear-skin 'shirt'. The wearing of the bear-skin shirt was the mark of the *Berserker*, a practitioner of the martial arts who went without normal chain-mail armour, yet who was so strong and ferocious that he was feared by his opponents. The bear-skin shirt was a symbol that the Berserker could draw upon *bear's strength*, that superhuman power manifested in the eastern martial arts as the channelling of *ki*, the *önd* of the Northern Tradition. *Bear's strength* was a technique taught by northern

martial arts masters. They would demonstrate their channelling of *önd* by the connected feat of *bear's warmth*, where they
sat scantily clothed or naked in the winter snow, yet did not
feel the cold or suffer from it. It appears that the Berserkers
were devotees of the widespread European warrior-cult of
the bear. This was personified in the goddess Artio or Ar-
tiona, one of whose shrines was near the modern Swiss
capital of Bern, founded by a medieval warrior after a supernatural bear appeared to him there. The power of the bear
was gained at the Berserker's initiation. *Hrolfs Saga Kraki* tells
us that, among the tests, the would-be Berserker had to kill
the image of a beast set up in the royal hall, then to drink its
blood, when the power of the beast would be assimilated
with the warrior's power. One of the Viking Age Swedish
helmet-panels illustrated here shows such an event (Fig. 21).

The Berserks were ascribed with the power of *hamrammr* or
shape-shifting. This could be direct, by acting upon and alter-

Fig. 21 Helmet-panels with scenes from the northern martial arts, showing Berserkers, Ûlfheðnar and Svínfylking warriors, as well as the binding of the Fenris-Wolf by the god Tyr. From Torslunda, Öland, Sweden
and dating from the sixth century.

ing the perception of others, or an out-of-the-body experience. It is clear that the Berserker was a practitioner of a
specialized form of shamanic martial arts which involved not
only the control and channelling of *önd*, but also psychic
manipulation. Sometimes, this involved combat in the astral
body. One famous Berserker, Bothvar Bjarki, champion of
King Hrolf of Denmark, fought in the king's army in the form
of a bear, whilst this human body lay in a trance as if sleeping
back at his quarters. Because of their martial prowess,
Berserkers were present as key fighting men in the armies of
pre-Christian Norse kings. Harald Fairhair, a Norwegian
king in the ninth century, had Berserkers as his personal
bodyguard.

The Ûlfhednar wore wolfskins (wolf-shirts, *vargstakkar*)
over coats of mail, and, unlike the Berserkers, who fought as
squads, entered combat singly as guerrilla fighters. There
were also the Ûlfhamir, the wolf-shirts, who are believed to
have fought, like the Berserkers, without armour. An Ûlfhednar is shown on a die from Torslunda on the Baltic island of
Ölund. This die was a former on which the craftsman hammered the metal plates used magically to protect and adorn
helmets. It shows a man wearing a horned helmet and carrying two staves. Next to him is an Ûlfhednar, a wolf-headed
man, armed with a spear. In Britain, there is a carving on the
eleventh-century church at Kilpeck in Herefordshire which
may be a late rendering of the tradition. It is a wolf-mask with
a human head looking out in a carving on the outside of the
church, probably a stone copy of the usable masks hung up
on Pagan temples, used in time of ceremony or war. Similar
masks are used by modern shamans, acting as spirit receptacles when not worn. One of the by-names of Odin, *Grim*,
means 'the masked one' and the old Norse warriors wore a
literally grim visage when going about their business.

The boar-warriors had the wild swine as their totemic
beast. Their technique was to fight in the formation known as
Svínfylking, the 'Boar's Head', which was a wedge with two
champions known as the *rani* (snout) at the front. The boar-
warriors were masters of disguise and escape, having an in-
timate knowledge of terrain. Like the Berserkers and Ûlfhednar, the boar-warriors used the superhuman strength of the
boar as the basis of their martial arts.

The techniques of the Berserkers and Ûlfhednar were
fraught with dangers, especially for the uninitiated. An ex-

ample is recorded in the *Volsunga Saga*. In the forest, the heroes Sigmund and Sinfyotl came across two men fast asleep wearing magic golden rings. Suspended above them were two wolfskins, which they removed every fifth day, putting them on again by means of the rings. Sigmund and his son put on wolfskins, and agreed to follow certain rules when they fought: 'They spoke in wolf-language, both understood that speech. . . They made an agreement that each of them would be able to take on seven men, but no more. If outnumbered, he must call out in wolf-language. . .' The two Volsungs donned the wolfskins, but then, uncontrollably, became wolves and killed people until they finally succeeded in removing the skins, and burnt them. The wolf-language is a form of *call* like the *Kiai* of oriental martial arts, which has the effect of momentarily lowering the blood-pressure of opponents, allowing the warrior to strike. The chilling sounds are conjured up in the old Norse writing known as *Hrafnsmál*: 'The Berserks bayed. . . the Úlfheðnar howled. . .'

·The tradition of wolf-warriors is not just Nordic. In Radnor, the daughter of a Celtic Welsh prince waged war against her enemies in the form of a wolf. Across the water, a thirteenth-century Irish book, *The Wonders of Ireland*, states: 'There are certain men in the Celtic race who have a marvellous power which comes to them from their forebears: for by an evil craft they can at will change themselves into the shape of wolves with sharp tearing teeth.'

Feats of arms ascribed to members of these warrior clans, and also to others bearing names of wolf and bear, are legendary. In Arthurian literature, the beginning of Malory's *Le Morte d'Arthur* furnishes us with a wolf-clan warrior, for Uther Pendragon's assistant knight is Ulfius. This, or another, later becomes King Arthur's chamberlain. The greatest Anglo-Saxon poem is about a wolf-cult warrior; *Beowulf* is a compound name composed of that of the Saxon fertility-god, *Beow*, and the wolf. Sacred names are very much part of the magical tradition, and the names of warriors, as in the native American tradition, are based upon the warrior-clan to which the man belonged, and his own prowess. Accounts of heroes like the Saxon champion Ordulph or King Arthur (Artos = bear) demonstrate that the practitioners of the Western martial arts were more than enraged maniacs. These stories tell us that these warriors were men who had undergone physical and spiritual training comparable with the better-known martial arts of the Orient, and were capable of the extraordinary feats associated with high adepts of craft. Ordulph kicked in the oaken gates of the city of Exeter with one blow: the *Hávamál* tells of the fifth rune enabling the warrior to halt an arrow in flight. Both are techniques known today in oriental martial arts, and it is clear that they were known and practised in the northern martial arts too. Until the late Middle Ages, there was no warrior who was not also a practitioner of magic. Magic used in battle is referred to in the *Hardar Saga*, where the *Herfjottur* (*war fetter*) is enacted, a binding spell, bringing on paralysis or loss of power in the enemy. As late as the fifteenth century, English kings had attendant magicians, such as the famous Friar Bungay, who magically altered the weather so that his master won battles.

Önd: the Power of Geomancy, Magic and the Martial Arts

According to traditions from all parts of the world, there is a force or conglomerate of forces or energies which sustain all being. It has as many names as there are languages and belief-systems. It is the *prana* of the Hindu system; the *pneuma* of the Pagan Greeks; the *universal plastic medium* of the alchemists; the *animal magnetism* of Mesmer; the *odyle* of Von Reichenbach; the *vril* of Theosophy; the *orgone* of Wilhelm Reich and the *ch'i* or *qi* of Chinese geomancy and martial arts. It is the *önd* of the Northern Tradition. Everything in the universe possesses *önd*. This *önd* can be viewed as a spirit, special character, or impersonal power. It is an active essence which belongs both to the material and the magical domains. In plants, *önd* gives medicinal powers; in foodstuffs it is the essence which makes children grow and gives us the energy to keep alive. In living plants, it is the resident soul. This soul can be lost, degenerate or be stolen, and consecration rituals are designed to prevent this. (For example, the soul of the earth, in the individual field or garden, is protected by the *Four Holes* Ritual). When analysed by scientific methods, *önd* is that quality of matter known as energy. However, it is not just a medium for the transference of energy by chemical, magnetic, electrical and other means, but it is also the formative patterns of geometry and flow present in all material things and processes.

In the landscape, this energy is drawn down from the sky to high points, from whence it flows in the manner of water or air, its direction, flow and form being determined by the patterns of the land. In some places, it accumulates and becomes stagnant; in others, it flows away too rapidly. Where it is concentrated in special ways, here are the places of power in the landscape, places where *önd* may be manifested in many possible ways. It may appear as Earth spirits (*landvættir* or land wights); hytersprites; yarthkins etc., each having beneficial or harmful effects upon human activities conducted there. Geomants, magicians, traditional hunters and farmers have always had a subtle rapport with the landscape and the qualities inherent in it , and the most accomplished of them have prospered accordingly. Similarly, this energy is present in the human organism, and practitioners of the crafts of meditation, healing, spiritual enlightenment and the martial arts use techniques which direct and enhance this power. Being at a place of power and performing the correct procedures to draw the *önd* into the body enhances the individual's performance as well as harmonizing it with the subtle energies of the world.

In the Northern Tradition, a personified aspect of *önd* is *Hamingja*, the controllable energy through which shape-shifting and other skills are accomplished, personalized as a guardian sprite. Occasionally this energy is visible emanating from the hands of practitioners of the healing or the martial arts. In the eighteenth century, one of Franz Anton Mesmer's patients told him: 'At each pass you direct towards me, I see a little column of fiery dust which comes from the end of your fingers and seems to incorporate itself in me, then, when you isolate me, I seem surrounded by an atmosphere of this fiery dust.' The energies dealt with by present-day practitioners of the martial arts were studied scientifically in China in the 1970s. *Wu Style Taijiquan* by Wang Peisheng and Zeng Weiqi, published in Beijing in 1981, tells of scientific work on this energy. It mentions how Chinese scientists using modern instruments succeeded in finding out first in 1978 that the *qi* emitted from the palm centre of a *qigong* master is a kind of far infra-red radiation. Again, in 1979 it was demonstrated that the *qi* emitted from fingertips of another *qigong* master was a current of fine particles with electrical charge—a kind of 'fiery dust'.

Such manifestations are known from holy people in all of
the world's religious traditions. In his book, *De Beatificatione et
Canonizatione*. P. Lambertini quotes Pope Benedict XIV: 'It
seems to be a fact that there are natural flames which at times
visibly encircle the human head, and also that from a man's
whole person fire may occasionally radiate naturally, not,
however, like a flame which streams upwards, but rather in
the form of sparks which are given off all round; further, that
some people become resplendent with a blaze of light,
though this is not inherent in themselves, but attaches rather
to their clothes, or to the staff or to the spear which they are
carrying.'

The haloes shown around the heads of deities and saints
are depictions of this power. Externally, lightning and the
corposant are closely allied to this. Similar energy emissions
have been found at stone circles by researchers of the British
'Earth Mysteries' group known as 'The Dragon Project.' But
even though scientific studies of such things are still in their
infancy, practitioners of these crafts can use them without
knowing *what* they are, in the same way that we see colour
without knowing what wavelength of the electromagnetic
spectrum we are perceiving.

Sacred Names and Runic Kingship

In magical terms, a person's name is of great importance,
determining his or her destiny. Today, every practitioner of
the runes and Northern Tradition magic has his or her own
magical name, based upon the name and power of a rune or
totemic animal or plant. Cult warriors of the North had
names which expressed their associated power, and so, in a
subtly different way, did kings. Many kings of pre-Christian
times had runic names, being embodiments of the aspect of
önd represented by the rune. The second King of Kent
(488–512 CE) was named Æsc, the name of the 'god-rune' and
the Cosmic Tree, and after him, subsequent kings of the na-
tion were known as *Æscings*, with the runic meaning of
'becoming a god'. Many other Saxon, Anglian and Jutish
kings in England bore names with numinous runic power:
Ethelbert, Ethelric, Ethelred, (*Ethel*, ᚷ); *Kenric, (Cen,* ᚲ);
Osred, Osric, Oswald, (*Os*, ᚾ); Sigeric (*Sigel*, ᛁ), etc.
Also among the names of these kings were some connected
with the warrior cults. In Mercia there was Wulfhere

(656–675), Cenwulf (794–819), Beornwulf (821–823), Bertulf (838–852) and Ceolwulf, last king of Mercia (crowned 874) who lost to the Danish invaders in 877. The kingdom of East Anglia had King Aldulf (664–713), while Northumbria boasted Heodwulf (572-3), Freodwulf (573–580), Ceolwulf (729–737), Oswulf (757–759), Erdulf (crowned 794, deposed 806, restored 808, died 809).

Only the kingdoms of Mercia, East Anglia and Northumbria had rulers with 'wolf' names, even if we include Ludecan (Mercia, 823–825). Of bear-cult names we have the Mercian monarch Beornred (755) and Beornwulf, mentioned before; the East Anglian king Beonna (749–758, who ruled jointly with Ethelred, then alone until 761); and possibly Beorhtric of Wessex (784–800). Later monarchs, under the influence of the Christian religion, did not use runic or totemic power-names, and the tradition lapsed.

Runelore: Origins

The runes are one of the fundamental elements of the Northern Tradition. More than just an alphabet for recording and transmitting information, the runes are a system of sacred knowledge, and eternal expression of universal laws. Runic is the oldest known sacred writing system of northern Europe, involving something far deeper and more complex than just a sort of writing. The name *rune* itself has the meaning of *mystery*, or *secret*, the same as the old English word *rown* and the modern German word *raunen*, to whisper. So, according to their name, the runes are secret wisdom, whispered lore, hidden counsel, the Great Mystery of existence.

Runes have a threefold nature, in keeping with the triadic structure of Northern Tradition teaching. First, at their most basic level, they are ideographic characters, representing things in stylized pictorial form, which is processed and understood by the right-hand side of the brain. This includes their geometric form. Secondly, they are phonetic, enabling them to be used for writing names or transmitting information like any alphabet. This function is processed and understood by the left-hand side of the brain. Finally, there is the conceptual level, the symbolic content of the rune, its deeper meaning and mystery.

The runes began thousands of years ago in the last Ice Age as the first rock-scribings, which later developed into ideographic representations of physical things and abstract notions. But it was much later that these figures became the runes as we know them. According to legend, it was when Odin was hung upon the World Tree for nine days and nine nights, and underwent torments, that the true nature of the runes was revealed to him. In the *Hávamál*, a poem from the northern European scriptures, Odin tells of this shamanic ordeal:

> I know that I hung on the windswept tree
> For nine days and nine nights,
> Wounded by a spear,
> And given to Odin,
> Myself to myself,
> On that tree
> Which no man knows
> From what roots it grows,
> They gave me no bread
> Nor drinking horn.
> I looked down,
> I picked up the runes,
> Screaming, I took them.
> Then I fell back.

The ascent and descent of the shaman Odin through the nine worlds penetrated by the World Axis tree Yggdrassill, 'the Hazel-wand of the World', the 'Tree of Measure', a process fraught with danger and agonies, accessed otherwise unattainable insights. Symbolically, Odin's shamanic ordeal was the flash of realization that joined the workings of the right and left hemispheres of the brain together in the runes. Historically, this moment occurred when the ancient sigils of the Rune Hoard were merged with the phonetic North Italic (Etruscan) alphabet to create the triadic runes we use today. This act of singular, transcendent genius, was truly the mead of inspiration.

In pre-Christian northern Europe, the runes were used by scribes, diviners, wise men and women for everything from fortune-telling to memorial inscriptions. But whatever they were used for, they had a basic religious and magical meaning. The Christian Church, prohibiting everything which did not fit its ideology, eventually succeeded in driving the runes underground. In seventeenth century Iceland, for example, it was an offence punishable by burning alive to possess runes!

Despite this persecution, for several centuries, runelore was hidden or partly forgotten, preserved in ancient writings, on runestones and surviving ancient talismans and almanacs. Of course, knowledge of the runes has never died. It continued in hidden forms in folk tradition, magical formulae, heraldry, vernacular architecture, folk-art and hereditary magical practice. But since the last century, a public reinstatement of runic knowledge has taken place, and new information and insights gained from a practical use of the runes. This has been accelerated since the beginning of a new cycle in 1979, with a quantum leap in interest and understanding, which is growing year by year.

Runelore: Meanings and Use

There are a number of related runic systems in existence. The most popular is the oldest, a system with 24 runes or *staves*, known as the *Elder Futhark*. Futhark is the runic equivalent of the word *alphabet*, being derived from the first six letters of the rune-row.

The runic staves have a specific order which relates to the year-sequence and the corresponding directions. Of course, as with any magical system of great depth, there are alternative correspondences, but the one described here is the most basic.

The 24 runes are:

1   *Feoh* — Cattle, wealth
2   *Ur* — Ox (Aurochs), primal strength
3   *Thorn* — Thorn, protection
4   *As* — God, divine power
5   *Rad* — Riding, wheel, motion
6   *Cen* — Pine, torch, illumination
7   *Gyfu* — Gift of the gods, talent/burden
8   *Wyn* — Joy, prosperity
9   *Hægl* — Hail, formative causation
10 *Nyd* — Need, necessity
11 *Is* — Ice, static force
12 *Jer* — Season, completion
13 *Eoh* — Yew tree, bow, defence
14 *Peorth* — Dice cup, the dance of fate
15 *Eolh* — Elk, defensive power
16 *Sigel* — Sun, brightness, victory

17 *Tyr* — The god Tyr, sword, power
18 *Beorc* — Birch tree, regeneration, purification
19 *Eh* — Horse, transformation
20 *Man* — Human Being, intermediary between heaven
    and earth
21 *Lagu* — Water, life-energy
22 *Ing* — The god Ing, limitless expansion and protection
23 *Odil* — Homestead, possession
24 *Dag* — Day, the bright light of high noon

Fig. 22 The 24-character *Elder Futhark*, with phonetic equivalents.

There are alternative spellings of many of the runes, for instance, *Odil* and *Ethel*, or *Ansur* and *As*. These do not change
the inner meaning of the runes any more than calling a dog
Hund or *chien* changes the creature described. Also, some
rune users transpose the final two characters, *Odil* and *Dag*.
Of course, this makes no difference in divination, where the
individual order does not matter except in the final reading.
There is also the Anglo-Saxon system, an extension of the
Elder Futhark, with 29 runes; and an extension of that, the
longest rune-row, the Northumbrian, which has 33
characters. Scandinavian runes, although derived from the
Elder Futhark , have only 16 characters. This is sometimes
known as the *Younger Futhark*, and there are several, related,
versions of it. A late system of the runes, the *Dotted Runes*,
like the Elder Futhark, has 24 characters, but arrived at as a re-

expansion of the 16 Scandinavian runes. The meanings of some of these runes are different from the Elder Futhark, and the order is the same as the Roman alphabet. In German-speaking countries, the *Armanen* system of 18 runes is often used. These, based on the Younger Futhark, were revealed to the Austrian magician Guido von List while he lay with bandaged eyes after a cataract operation in 1902. Since 1960, some runic practitioners, especially in the United States, have added a blank card or stone to runic divination, following in the footsteps of other Americans who added the 'Joker' to the card pack in the last century. The name *Wyrd*, Fate, has been given to this non-rune, an attempt to bring into rune-casting an equivalent of the Tarot 'Fool'. The 'rune' *Wyrd* is interpreted as the unavoidable.

The runes can be a lifetime's work in themselves, and once one begins to study and use them, then almost every day will bring new parallels and insights. For a full use of Northern Tradition magic, however, a working knowlegde of the runes is necessary. There are several useful books available for those who wish to make the runes a major part of their study. They are listed in the Select Bibliography. For divinatory purposes, rune cards and rune stones are available from specialist bookshops and 'occult' suppliers. In general, the scope and powers of the runes are best described in the old Norse work, *Hávamál*, the saying of the High One—Odin;

I learned nine lays of power from the famous son
Of Bolthorn, Bestla's father, And a drink I had
Of the precious mead poured from Othrerir.
Then I began to be fruitful and to grow and thrive.
Word sought word after word in me:
Lay sought lay after lay in me.

You will find runes and ingenious staves—
Very great staves, very strong staves—
Which a mighty thule painted, and great gods made,
And the prophet of the gods carved.

Odin among Æsir, but Dain for elves
And Dvalin for dwarves,
Asvidr for giants:
Some I carved myself.

Do you know how to carve them?
Do you know how to read them?
Do you know how to paint them?

Do you know how to test them?
Do you know how to pray with them?
Do you know how to sacrifice with them?
Do you know how to send with them?
Do you know how to offer with them?

It is better not to pray at all than to sacrifice too much—
a gift always looks for something in return.

It is better not to send than to offer too much—
So Thundr carved before the birth of nations
At that point he began when he came back.

I know those lays which no lord's wife knows,
Nor any man's son.
Help one is called and it will help you
Against sorrows and trials and every grief there is.
I know the second, which those sons of men need
Who wish to live as healers.

I know the third: If my need grows dire
For shackles on my deadly foes, I dull the blades
Of my enemies—neither weapons nor tricks will work for them.

I know this, the fourth: If warriors lock up
My shoulder-limbs, I call thus,
And I can go: the shackles spring from my feet,
And the handcuffs from my wrists.

I know this, the fifth:
If I see an arrow shot in battle,
Shot deadly straight, None flies so hard I cannot stop it
If I catch sight of it.

I know this, the sixth: If a thane does magic on me on the
Fresh roots of a sapling,
He who calls down curses on me
Those same misfortunes will consume *him*, rather than me.

I know this, the seventh:
If I see a high hall burning around bench—comrades,
None burns so fiercely that I cannot save them;
I know the spell to call.

I know this, the eighth:
Which is useful for everyone to learn,
Whose hate grows for the sons of a war-lord;
I can soon change that.

I know this, the ninth;
If I need to keep my ship afloat,
I can still the wind, smooth the waves,
And lull the sea to sleep.

I know this, the tenth:
If I see hedge-riders flying on high,
I work it so that they go apart
From their own skins, and their own souls.

I know this, the eleventh:
If I must lead old comrades into battle,
I call beneath their shields, and they go in strength,
Safe to war, safe from war, safe wherever they are.

I know this, the twelfth:
If in a tree, high up, I see a corpse swinging from a noose,
Then I carve and I colour the runes,
So that the man comes down and talks with me.

I know this, the thirteenth:
If I should throw water on a young noble,
He will not fall, no matter if he goes to war—
The hero will not fall beneath swords.

I know this, the fourteenth:
If I should preach the gods at the troops' parade,
I will know how to distinguish all Æsir and elves;
Few of the unwise know how.

I know this, the fifteenth,
Which the dwarf Thjothrerir
Called before Delling's doors.
He called power to Æsir and strength elves,
And foresight to Hropta-Tyr.

I know this, the sixteenth;
If I wish to have all the wise woman's fun and games,
I steal the heart of a white-armed maiden
And I turn all her thoughts.

I know this, the seventeenth:
So that the maiden will not want to avoid me.

Loddfafnir, you will take a long time to learn
These lays, though they will do you good if you do,
Be serviceable if you grasp them,
Useful if you have them.

I know this, the eighteenth,
Which never will I teach Maiden or Man's wife
(It is better to understand everything alone—the end follows),
Except that woman who folds me in her arms,
Or perhaps my sister.

Now are the *Hávamál* sung in Hávi's Hall,
Vital to the sons of men, useless to giants' sons.
Hale he sang, hale he who understands.
May he who understands them use them well,
Hale to those who have listened.

Fig. 23 Danish runestone. The central lines represent the Cosmic Tree,
Yggdrassil, and the runes are read from the base of the tree to the top,
then downwards on the right-hand panel, and upwards again on the
left. The small 'x's are punctuation and consecration marks.

Number Magic

The Northern Tradition has a complete and coherent
number-lore which underlies magical practice, which is simple in use and obvious in meaning once you start using it.
Odd numbers are considered better or more lucky than even
ones, with practical applications in everyday life. In cooking,

pastry will be heavy if rolled or turned an even number of times. Likewise, a nail should be hammered an odd number of times. Hens' eggs should be set in odd numbers, 13 being the best, a geometrical arrangement of one in the centre surrounded by six others, and six more placed in the gaps between the outer six. Parcels can be packed in a similar way, making the 'baker's dozen' of any round or ovoid objects. Charms should be repeated either three times, or nine. A powerful call is 'By the Power of Three Times Three'.

The Northern Tradition teaches the threefold structure of all things: the *triads* of Welsh tradition are a formalized version of a system which was widespread thoughout northern Europe. The threefold system is based upon the sequential nature of all things, which have a beginning, a span in the middle and an end. These are all versions of the fundamental triad of being: formation, preservation and destruction. Thus, Allfather (1), the initiator, produced (2), the diad, primal motion, *önd* or energy, which in turn produced the first number (3), creation itself. Thus basic beliefs and traditions are expressed in *Triads*. For example, the *Three Foundations of Bardism* are peace, love and justice, which may be accomplished by three *triads*: (1) Worshipping the gods, doing no evil, and exercising fortitude: (2) Seeking truth, clinging to justice and performing mercy; and (3) Being faithful to Natural Law, having concern for the welfare of humanity, and bearing with fortitude the accidents of life.

Traditional lore is expressed in triadic form, for it is easy to remember, and makes its point immediately. The *Laws* of the British king Dunvallo Molmutius, laid down in the fifth century BC, were triadic, ensuring 'Security of life and person, security of possessions and dwelling, and the security of national rights'. In ancient Britain, the *Three Ornaments of the State* were the learned scholar, the ingenious artist and the just judge, while the *Three Corruptions* were pride, superfluity and indolence. Bad things as well as good ones come in threes. It is a common belief today that if one thing is broken, then two others will follow shortly; this is general with any misfortune.

Four is a lucky number, the four-leaved clover being a physical manifestation of this fourfold. Ofen, the fourth is the odd one out. the necessary completion and recapitulation of a triad. Thus the triad of birth–maturity–old age is completed by death, and the phases of the moon—first quarter, full

moon and last quarter—completed by the darkness of the
new moon.

Number-lore has survived in almost unrecognized ways in
folk-lore, rhymes and riddles, as can be seen from the
number five. The bean riddle, seemingly a meaningless play
of numbers, is, in fact, a mnemonic for remembering the
sacred decade.

Q: How many beans make five?
A: Two beans and a bean, a bean and a half and half a bean.

It must be remembered that each bean is composed of two
parts, and it is these which are the units for the *tetractys*, the
equilateral triangle formed from ten units:

half a bean	○
a bean	○ ○
a bean-and-a-half	○ ○ ○
two beans	○ ○ ○ ○

Seven is a very magical number. The seven planetary
deities, the days of the week, the seven colours of the rainbow, the seven ages of human beings, and the seven ages of
the world are all well known. A seventh son of a seventh son
has the power of *framsynn*, far-sightedness. Seven
horseshoes on a house are a powerful charm against evil.
Two of the major Northern Tradition constellations, the
Boars' Throng and Woden's Wagon, have had the alternative
name of the Seven Stars, and even today this is a popular
name for public houses.

Eight is the number of completion and return; there is the
eightfold division of the circle and in natural measure. As a
time period, eight years is important in the Northern Tradition. Every eight years, the great national sacred festivals of
Sweden and Denmark were celebrated. In mythology,
Siegfried served King Gibich for eight years, the Swan
Maidens spent eight winters with Wayland and his brothers,
and Loki lived at the Earth's centre for eight years. Release
came only with the dawn of the ninth.

Nine is *par excellence* the magic number of the North, being
the power of three times three. Nine nights make up eight full

days, the period that Odin hung on the World Ash to gain the knowledge of the runes for human use. Nine years is the period of the ascent of the moon northwards, to be followed by the same period southwards, the whole being the complete solar–lunar cycle. A powerful protective sigil is a single spot surrounded by eight others, nine in all, emblematical of the number of completion, and all that it stands for. Nine is the first square which produces a geometrical figure which totally encloses the first square, and for that reason it is used in protective magic. As an array of dots, it forms the rhombus figure of the rune *Ing*, limitless expansion.

Ten is another sort of number of completion. It is the basic number for modern numerical notation, based on the number of digits on two hands. It is the number of the *tetractys*, the summation of the formula $1 + 2 + 3 + 4$.

Thirteen is the archetypal unlucky number said to derive from the disruption wrought by Loki to the 12 chief gods. The number is universally unlucky in European tradition, and there are similar stories from other cultures to account for its misfortune.

Eighteen is the number of the 'round figure' solar-lunar Saros cycle (18.6 years), encompassing twice nine. It is the number of lays in the *Hávamál* runic explanation, and the 'eighteenth rune' is a kenning for a great mystery.

In traditional counting, 20, the score, is the completion of a cycle in the same way that 10 is in modern numerical counting. It is the beginning of the next cycle. Even today the French language still counts by scores, when other modern languages have long abandoned the custom. The word *score* has the meaning of a scratch or furrow, the customary mark made when one had counted to 20.

Just as 'By the power of three times three', is a charm to empower a working, so an alternative, invoking the power of three times seven, can be used:

Three times seven
Are twenty one:
And you'll know better
For time to come.

Several traditional riddles and games retain magical number lore, much of it now unrecognized. The children's riddle:

As I was going to St Ives,
I met a man with seven wives.
Every wife had seven sacks,
In every sack were seven cats.
Every cat had seven kits.
Kits, cats, sacks and wives,
How many going to St Ives?

The answer to this is one, as they were coming *from* the Huntingdonshire fair town. However, the numerical sequence implicit in the rhyme is of great interest to magical numerologists. There is another numerical sequence which is sometimes encountered on old *clog almanacks* or *primestaves*, the ancient calendars used in the north of Europe before the invention of printing. It is usually shown as a series of crosses and upright lines, drawn between two parallels, and goes by the name of *St Peter's Game* or the local variation of it—*Sankt Päders Lek* in Swedish and *Pietarinleikki* in Finnish. Clearly the sequence is pre-Christian in origin, but, as with many ancient origin-myths, the sequence was given a Christian angle during the Middle Ages. According to the story, which is an explanatory legend of a magical number-sequence, St Peter was on board a ship on which there were 30 crew and passengers. Apart from Peter, there were 15 Jewish and 15 Christian passengers. The 15 pieces on either side are reminiscent of the 30 playing pieces in the board game *Backgammon* and its forerunner, *Tables*. A storm blew up, and Peter decided that the only way that a shipwreck could be avoided would be if half the ship's complement (excluding himself, of course) were thrown overboard. The fair (or magical) way of choosing the victims was put forward by someone that every ninth person out of the 30 should go, leaving only 16 on board. In order to rig the event so that all of the Christians were saved, he arranged the people in a certain sequence, and then threw every ninth one into the sea to drown. Apart from the unpleasant anti-semitic element in the story, this St Peter's tale is of great interest, for it involves determining an appropriate sequence of dividing 30 into two equal parts by counting in nines, which is XXXXIIIIIXXIXXXIXIIXXIIIXIIXXI (45213112231221).

There are several connections between this sequence, the calendar, board games and the labyrinth design. A common name for stone labyrinths in Finland is *pietarinleikki*, and there may be some deeper numerical connection between the sequence and the design of some forms of stone labyrinth. The closeness of 30 to the lunar month cycle means that the sequence can be used to perform different acts of corresponding days, magically linked to the ninefold. The entire number counted adds up to 465 units, almost the number of weeks in nine years. Traditional mathematical sequences such as this are still relatively uninvestigated, having survived as folk stories and riddles. They are an as yet untapped resource of magical knowledge.

Natural Measure

Natural measure is the system of measurement used in Europe between the Iron Age and the medieval period. It has roots in the oldest-known system of measurement, and survives today in the mile and its traditional sub-multiples. As a system, it is based upon direct measurement, with practical applications for craftspeople, agriculture, trade and cooking. It is related directly to the characteristics of the material being dealth with, and easy division, rather than upon mathematics. Far from being random or unwieldy, as people who deal with figures on paper rather than real objects or materials have often claimed, natural measure is based upon an interlinked systems of measures, each with their own symbolic numerical structure but compatible with one another, and, where necessary, divisible by all of the main divisors.

In natural measure, as in the *airts* of direction, the eightfold division is paramount. The eightfold division of weight, length and capacity is related to the geometrical properties of the square rather than to intellectually later and more left-brain concepts such as number. The division of a linear object by halving it, then halving it again and so on, produces divisions $2 \times \frac{1}{2}$; $4 \times \frac{1}{4}$; $8 \times \frac{1}{8}$, etc., and, commonly, traditional measures have been based upon this progression. The use of the sacred number three, giving three successive divisions, produces eighths, the basis of the 3–8 link present in natural measure. This eightfold system relates the division of objects to the division of the world and time (see Chapter 1).

The English mile, as used today in Britain, Eire and the United States, is a multiple of the most ancient and consistently conserved measure of them all—the *northern cubit*. This unit of measure was in existence before 3000 BC, and was used in the Indus civilization of India, Mesopotamia, Europe, North Africa, and China. In Europe, it was associated with the Teutonic nations, and travelled wherever they migrated. As a *cubit, ell* or *elne*, it survived in everyday use in Europe as a measure for cloth, and its half, the foot, is the basis of British and American land measure.

Natural measure is based upon two related *feet*—the *natural foot* and the *northern foot*, sometimes called the *Saxon foot*. The northern foot is equal to half of a northern cubit or ell, measuring 13.2 Imperial inches or 33.53 cm. This measure has been found at Mohenjodaro, incised on a shell dating from around 2500 BC, divided into tenths and accurately cut. In Egypt, wooden cubit measures of the XIIth dynasty from Kahun c.1900 BC) bear the northern foot; and on finely-inscribed Egyptian *royal cubit* rods of the XVIIIth dynasty (1567–1320 BC), the northern foot is marked on or next to the eighteenth *digit* in Egyptian measure.

In northern Europe, the northern foot has been intimately connected with land measure, the delimitation of sacred enclosures, and ritual artifacts. Two thousand years ago, its use was so entrenched that in 12 BC, the Roman governor of Lower Germany, Nero Claudius Drusus, was forced to adopt the northern foot as the official measure for the provinces of northern Europe, rather than the shorter Roman foot. Officially, to the Romans the northern foot was 'two *digits* longer than the *pes*'.

The northern foot was primarily a measure of land, the basis of the rod, the rood, the acre, the furlong and the mile. As the Earth is deemed sacred in the Northern Tradition, so land measure must automatically be sacred measure. The various land measures are also integral multiples of the natural foot, which was used in Celtic countries. The natural foot and the northern foot are both sub-multiples of the rod (16 feet 6 inches Imperial), the natural foot being one twentieth and the northern foot one fifteenth. This gives a 3:4 relationship between the two feet, and allows direct conversion.

The subdivision of both the natural foot and the northern foot is into *palms* or *shafthands*, three making a natural foot, and four making a northern foot. Each shafthand is subdivided into three thumbs, each of which is again divided by three into *barleycorns*. The barleycorn is thus the smallest unit of measure, being 0.37 Imperial inches (9.3 mm). Each thumb is 1.1 Imperial inches (27.9 mm); and each shafthand is 3.3 Im-

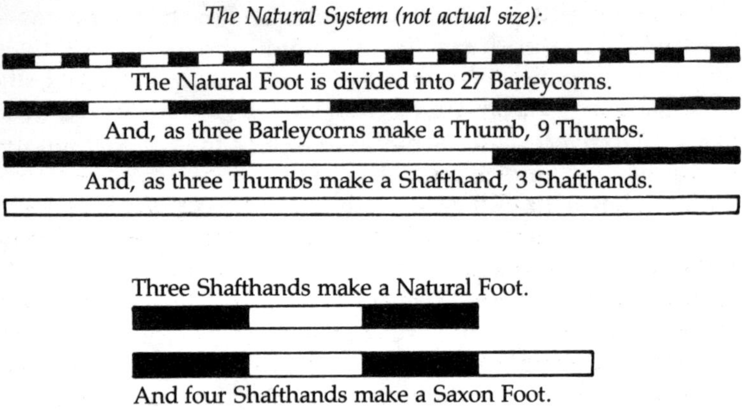

The Natural System (not actual size):

The Natural Foot is divided into 27 Barleycorns.

And, as three Barleycorns make a Thumb, 9 Thumbs.

And, as three Thumbs make a Shafthand, 3 Shafthands.

Three Shafthands make a Natural Foot.

And four Shafthands make a Saxon Foot.

Fig. 24 Natural measure.

perial inches (83.8 mm). The natural foot is thus 27 barleycorns in length, and the northern foot 36. These are multiples of the Northern Tradition sacred number nine. The various relationships can be summarized as follows:

One shafthand consists of 3 thumbs (9 barleycorns).

One natural foot consists of 3 shafthands (9 thumbs, 27 barleycorns).

One northern foot consists of 4 shafthands (12 thumbs, 36 barleycorns).

Above this level (the measurements used in craft and building) an eightfold structure predominates:

One ell consists of 8 shafthands (2 northern feet, 24 thumbs, 72 barleycorns).

One fathom consists of 3 ells (6 northern feet, 24 shafthands, 72 thumbs, 216 barleycorns).

One rod consists of $2\frac{1}{2}$ fathoms (15 northern feet, 20 natural feet, 60 shafthands, 180 thumbs, 540 barleycorns).

One furlong consists of 40 rods (600 northern feet, 800 natural feet).

One mile consists of 8 furlongs (4800 northern feet, 6400 natural feet, 800 fathoms).

Square measure is derived from the rod (15 northern feet), the *rood* of land being one rod by one furlong (15 × 600 northern feet; 20 × 800 natural feet = 9,000 square northern feet; 16,000 square natural feet). Four roods of land make one acre (60 × 600 northern feet; 80 by 800 natural feet = 36,000 square northern feet; 64,000 square natural feet). One acre is therefore an area of 10 by 100 fathoms (1,000 square fathoms).

Ten acres make one *ferdelh* or *Ferlingate* (one square furlong, 600 × 600 northern feet; 800 × 800 natural feet), and four *ferlingata* is equal to one *townyard* or *virgate*. Four *virgata* are equal to a *hide* of land (160 acres). Traditionally, towns were divided into four, the extent of which was ideally a *ferlingate* each. The extent of these areas, the geomantic division of a town into four *quarters*, are still recorded from many places, for example the English town of Huntingdon and the German town of Brilon. In many places, these sacred divisions were converted into parishes, each controlled by its own church.

Imperial measure, used today mixed up with metric measure, was a conscious attempt by King Edward I to unify the various measures of England and Wales. Until his time, the northern foot was used as the main measure in former Saxon areas, while the natural foot was preferred in Celtic parts. In addition, the Norman foot, the Greek common foot, modified Roman feet and other 'local, variants' were in use. In 1305, the *Statute for Measuring Land* ordained that a new foot should be the only measure allowed. This is the foot used now (304.8 mm). Its relationship to the northern foot is 10:11, making $16\frac{1}{2}$ Imperial feet of 198 inches rather than 15 northern feet of 180 thumbs equal a rod. It is from this compromise that the strange figure of 5,280 feet in the mile comes.

The numbers encountered in the smaller range of natural measure can be interpreted according to the runes. The number nine, which is the sacred number of the North *par excellence*, occurs in the arrangement 3-3-3 underlying the natural foot. The rune equivalent to nine is ᚺ *Hagal* or *Hœgl*, the hailstone, that icy egg or seed of primal cosmic pattern and life underlying the mystical framework of the world. Within this framework, the sacred geometrical structure of matter, natural measure acts as a reference point through which the Mysteries can be approached. Through it, craft, the application of materials, mind, tradition and insight, can bring human artifacts to fruition according to natural principles and so be in harmony with the world—a fundamental tenet of the Northern Tradition. In mystical tradition, the number nine exists in the Nine Worlds, the various states of being and consciousness strung out along the Cosmic Axis, viewed from Allfather Odin's high seat *Hliðskjálf*. The handle of Thor's hammer, *Mjöllnir*, was nine thumbs in length, having been made somewhat short by the dwarf smiths. In Anglo-Saxon law, the King's *Grith* (King's Peace) was defined as: 'Three miles and three furlongs, and three lineal acres and nine feet and nine shafthands and nine barleycorns'. Within this area, the magically-charged zone surrounding the initiated sacral monarch, criminals could claim sanctuary from punishment. Conversely, certain crimes committed within the royal *Grith* were punishable with greater severity than normal. This principle is still held to, theoretically, by modern Wiccan covens, whose *covenstead* is supposed to stretch for a *League* (three miles) from the covendom where meetings are held.

Natural measure is a rich store of numerical symbolism. The number 12, the number of thumbs in the northern foot, is equivalent to the rune ♦ *Jer* or *Jara*, representing the cyclical pattern of the universe, completion and the cycle of the solar year. Like *Hægl*, *Jer* is connected with totality, the encompassing of a whole; the foot encompasses the lesser measures.

The rod, fundamental unit in land measure, is 15 northern feet in length and in the Futhark, the fifteenth rune is ᛉ *Eolh* or *Elhaz*. The rune name is related to the old Gothic word *alhs*, meaning 'sanctuary', with the connotations of limitation, boundaries and protection. The rod is the canonical measure of ancient tradition for the *mystic plot*—sacred ground set aside for ceremonies—used by the secret semi-official *Vehmgericht* courts of Westphalia, Germany, until the eighteenth century. This is a cardinal-direction-orientated square with sides of one rod surrounding a foundation offering, usually ashes from a sacred fire, unburnt coal and a square tile. In Westphalia, the mystic plot of each Vehmic court was at a central point in the *Freigrafschaft* (free county) over which the court had jurisdiction. Every time the court was convened, the plot was laid out anew and measured with the *mete-wand*. Measure was an important function of justice, and the geolocation and structure of the place is a concrete example of the link between the sacred and measure. The *mete-wand* or measuring-rod was an important symbol of office, and can be seen in many ancient representations.

The outlaw Robin Hood, whose acts can be interpreted as a form of summary justice like the *Vehm*, was buried with a *met-yard* (mete-wand), perhaps the symbol of his jurisdiction. In 'Robin Hoode his Death', a fragment from the *Percy Folios*, as he is dying, Robin Hood instructs Little John to bear him to his grave:

> . . . And sett my bright sword at my head,
> Mine arrowes at my feete,
> And lay my yew bow by my side,
> My met-yard wi. . .

[the text breaks off at this point]

Fig. 25 The French martial arts techniques of *Canne* and *Bâton*, which are survivals of the ancient art of stick-fighting, once practised all over Europe. Engraving *c*.1910.

Apart from the bow, Robin Hood's greatest fighting prowess was with the peasant's favourite weapon, the *quarterstaff*. Originally, this was a stave one quarter of a rod in length, five natural feet, linking the combat of the martial arts with traditional sacred measure. It is possible that Robin Hood's *met-yard* was actually his quarterstaff, being used for laying out sacred plots when not in use as a weapon. The use of natural measure in the northern European martial arts survives in the French fighting techniques of *Canne* and *Bâton*. *Canne*, uses a shorter rod, whilst *Bâton* has the traditional quarterstaff. A longer *Canne*, used in traditional land-measure in the south of France, is eight natural feet in length.

In sacred writings the world over, the dimensions of holy places, physical and supernatural, are given in great detail. The *Bible*, for example, has many examples of the dimensions of artifacts such as Noah's Ark, various temples and the New Jerusalem, derived from earlier Egyptian and Assyrian models. These special dimensions play a great part in the Northern Tradition, too, sometimes being found in the underlying sacred geometry of churches which susperseded a Pagan *Træf* or *Wih*. Wherever they occur, these numbers and dimensions refer to the same basic system of natural measure. Thus, in the *Edda*, the number of doors of Valhalla is the same as the number of barleycorns in one rod—540. From each door of Valhalla ride 800 *Einherjar*, the chosen warriors of the Æsir, making the cosmic number 432, 000. This is the number of barleycorns in 20 furlongs—two and a half miles. It is also the number of years in the final cycle of Hindu cosmology, *Kali Yuga*, one of the many connections between the traditions of northern Europe and India. Perhaps most significantly, it is the radius of the sun in miles!

Practical applications of natural measure

The near-universal triumph of the metric system and its successor, the *système internationale*, over traditional measures has removed people from a direct experience of the world into an abstract area. The craftsperson, the cook, the dealer in materials at a direct level, however, needs means of measurement for use, and this means easy and natural division, two being the most obvious and widespread. Thus, cooks' measure, still used despite irrational attempts to force through 'metrication', is a practical and direct way of measur ing edible materials. The *teaspoon*, the *fluid dram*, is the basic unit. Two of these make a *dessertspoon*; two dessertspoonsful make a *tablespoon*; and four *tablespoonsful* make a *wineglassful*, which is two *fluid ounces*. This simple division into 2, 4, and 8 is accomplished with ease, avoiding any time-consuming weighing or other numerical calculations. Yet the dominant way today is the world of paperwork, number-crunching and everything which that mode of thought represents. At one time, the use of secular measures in sacred acts would have been unthinkable. Anyone who practises in the Northern Tradition has a rich resource of interrelated sacred measure with which to work.

Sacred equipment in the Northern Tradition should be made according to natural measure. It is convenient to make one's own *mete-wand* or measuring rod from wood strip, which can be purchased at any 'do-it-yourself' supplier. An ell is a convenient length, which should be marked off carefully in northern feet, shafthands, thumbs and barleycorns. For laying out large areas, such as the mystic plot, labyrinths and other sacred enclosures, a piece of stout cord can be marked in northern or natural feet with knots—the traditional way of the *Druids' cord*.

The Runic Circles of Day and Year

Geomantic convention divides the horizon around us into 24 equal sections, each of which has the power of that rune present in it. Each part of the horizon is directly related to the wheel of the day, with due south being noon and due north midnight, and so on. So each hour of the day is ruled by its own rune. The 24 runes can be arranged in a circle which corresponds to the eight *airts*, in which several of the major runes will be found to correspond significantly with a time of day and season of the year. This system allocates a rune to an hour of the day, with the *o'clock* hour of the middle of the hour. For example, the final rune, *Dag*, occupies the hour of noon, from 11.30 a.m. until 12.30 p.m. The first rune, *Feoh*, runs from 12.30 p.m. until 1.30 p.m., and so on around the clock/day/year/direction circle. In this way, each rune represents a time of day, time of year, and direction. During each hour of the day, when the sun is in the corresponding direction, the power of the corresponding rune can be

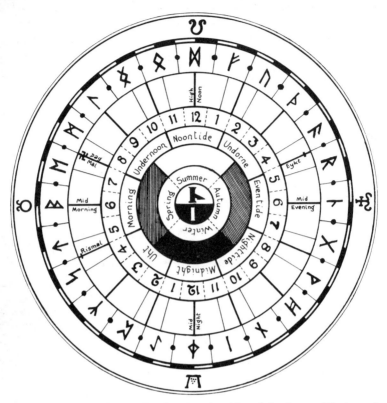

Fig. 26 The runic day-circle, showing the tides of the day and their runic correspondences.

visualized as streaming through with the rays of sunlight. In each 24-hour cycle, each rune is energized for one hour, its maximum power coming at the *o'clock* hour itself. As each rune has a specific meaning and quality, that *sele*, or hour of the day is infused with that property. Consequently, it is best to carry out acts at the time corresponding with the most favourable rune, when that power is at its maximum. It is from these directions that the *önd* or runic power comes, for, relative to our position, the sun is in that direction.

It must be remembered that the times are *by the sun*, that is, taking midday as *sun due south*. Using local time zones, which are set for the convenience of politics and commerce, is usually incorrect. In Britain, only sites on the Meridian of Greenwich are at solar time, and even then only during the winter, when Greenwich Mean Time is in force. One should deter-

mine the local time of midday by the time that a shadow cast
by the sun is due north on any one day. From this, local hours
can be worked out. At each hour, the sun is actually in that
direction from us, and so the power inherent in the rune is
added to by the solar power coming from the direction. It is as
if the sun is shining through a stained-glass window bearing
the rune and its attributes, bringing illumination. Even during the hours of darkness, the sun is still in its hour-direction,
even though below the horizon. In the landscape, any ley,
solar line or spirit path running to the horizon from a sacred
nowl (*omphalos*) will magically draw in the appropriate runic
quality of the direction, especially at the corresponding *sele*.

Because each rune relates to an hour of the day cycle, it also
relates to one twenty-fourth part of the year cycle, a period of
15 days, 5 hours 27 minutes 38 seconds, the *half-month* or *fortnight*. The old definition of the fortnight was actually 15 days,
bracketing 14 nights, and appears to be a survival of the
twenty-fourth part of the year. Each of the divisions is thus
365.24218 hours in length. Because they are $365\frac{1}{4}$ hours in
length, each hour of the half-month is a microcosm of the
whole year itself, and may be treated magically as such. Just
as each day has its own hourly runic *seles*, so then does each
year, though, unlike the hour, the changeover from one to
another needs careful calculation. When the runes of the day
and the runes of the year coincide, these are especially
powerful times for anything connected with the rune, during
which time, actions appropriate to that rune have additional
power or chance of success. Fig. 26 shows the correspondences. Because of these correspondences, there is a
little-known but powerful system of *birth runes*, which has a
significant bearing upon everyday life. One's birthdate has a
correspondence of a time of day (*hour rune*) and a half-month
or *fortnight rune*. So it one's birth time was 10 a.m. on 2
September, the runes would be ᛝ *Ing* and ᚱ *Rad* (*Rid*).
Because the runes have names, appropriate names for the
hour/fortnight can be determined. An appropriate name for
the runic correspondence given above would be Ingrid, for
example. When working out the hour/fortnight runes, one
must remember that the changeover from one half-month to
another takes place at sunset on the last calendar day of the
half-month. The time of sunset, and and hence the hour-rune
in which the changeover occurs, depends on the time of year
and the latitude in which one lives. Space does not allow me

to publish a full runic almanac here, but one is in preparation.

Clearly this system has many exciting applications. Visualizing the circle is a potent protective method, which should be used before undertaking activities such as sitting out and wood-taking. To carry out the rite of the rune ring, you should face north, the direction of prayer in the Northern Tradition, facing the axis of the heavens. The runes should be visualized as fiery red staves burning on a silver-blue band of protection at waist height around you. The band should be visualized first, beginning in the southern *airt* at *Feoh* (over the left shoulder), and proceeding *deiseil* around to the west, the north, the east, and then back to the south. Then, in the same way, the runes should be projected upon the band, again beginning with *Foeh* and ending with *Dag*. This band can then be visualized as merging with a protective sphere of light.

Having set up the runic ring, you can concentrate upon the rune appropriate for the work in hand, and draw in the power of that rune from that direction. Of course, the most appropriate time is the hour when the *seat of the sun* is in that runic 24th, and the solar power is literally behind the rune in the ring. Once this has been done, then the stage is set for further rituals and actions, in the knowledge that the best possible conditions have been set up for the working.

The winds

The direction of the wind is an important factor not only with regard to the weather, but also on a more esoteric, runic, level. Just as each direction has a quality related to its *sele*—the time and tide of the day and the year—so each direction and its wind have qualities which subtly affect people. When a circle of runes is visualized around one for protective purposes, then each rune is guardian of one twenty-fourth part of the horizon, and the corresponding directions. These correspond with the *eight winds* and *16 breezes* of the Southern European Tradition, which were the basis of landscape layout and town planning in ancient Greece, Etruria and in the Roman Empire. The eight major winds correspond with the eight major runes of the directions, and the eight festivals of the year, and the 16 subsidiary breezes with the other 16 runes. Each wind and its subsidiaray thus forms a triad within each *airt*. The direction of the wind can also be used in foretelling events, though it is an ill wind which blows nobody any good!

Circle and Labyrinth

The circle symbolizes eternal life, the cycle of the year, its seasons and the day, and stone circles are a physical image on the ground of the forces working at that spot. The position of their stones are related to the horizon and its phenomena, linking with possible underground watercourses, geological factors and customary-social traditions, the holistic balance of all elements which is needed for a full realization of the human and earthly potentials. From the greatest megalithic circles like Stonehenge to the smallest collection of stones little larger than pebbles, stone circles have the power to evoke other-worldly emotions and experiences. They are an intermediate link between totally natural sacred places of power, like rock pillars, and completely artificial structures such as temples. Wherever they exist, they stand as witness to the mysteries of the Northern Tradition.

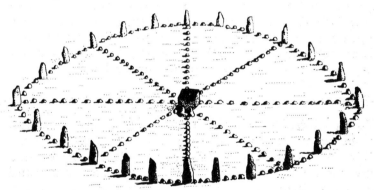

Fig. 27 Sjöborg, the eightfold megalithic meeting-circle at Sola, Norway.

Like most sacred places, stone circles have been multipurpose. An important stone circle, Sjöborg, which existed near Sola in Norway, was a *thing*, a council or meeting-place for the people of eight local districts. Being a microscosm of the local area and of the world, it was an eightfold wheel of stones with a hut at the centre. Around the circumference stood 24 standing stones, marking the 24 hours of the day, the 24 *fortnights* of the year and the 24-fold division of the circle upon which runic divination is based. Between these 24 megaliths were 72 smaller stones, regularly arranged around the circle, making a 96-fold division of the circle. Sola, whose name is redolent of the sun, is an archetypal wheel of life, symbol of completion, the image carried by several of the Pagan gods of the North. The parallel with Northern American native *medicine wheels* is obvious.

In recent years, there has been a resurgence in interest in one of the most potent of human mystical symbols—the *labyrinth*. Although the names *maze* and *labyrinth* are often confused, and seen to be the same thing, there is a distinction. The word *maze* is applied correctly to the puzzle maze, usually made from hedges, in which it is possible to get lost, having many alternative paths and dead ends. The labyrinth is not the same as the puzzle maze whose reason for existing is entertainment, where getting lost is part of the thrill of walking it. The sacred labyrinth is unicursal, i.e. it has only one path to the centre, covering the entire area of the labyrinth with no dead ends. The unicursal labyrinth is a symbol of wholeness, birth and transformation which has been used in many parts of the world for thousands of years. It is a universal symbol, known from most cultures of the world except China and sub-Saharan Africa.

As a symbol it is unique because it can be of any size from a motif on a coin to one large enough to walk through. It represents difficult entry, and as a pathway of the pilgrim, soul or spirit to transformation by a single, if circuitous, route. Only the unicursal labyrinth has protective, initiatory and geomantic uses. For example, in India, it is used as a *yantra* (charged sacred diagram) for focusing the mind during childbirth; to the Hopi of North America, it is an emblem called 'Mother Earth'. Small flat stones with the classical labyrinth design carved into them are used in Britain and Ireland as trance-inducing agents. Known as *brainstones*, *troystones*, *moonstones* or *serpent stones*, these labyrinth carvings can be used to induce a state of mental hypnosis or trance. This is done by staring at the pattern, and following the gyres of the labyrinth with a finger, in and out, in and out, until one is *amazed*. During the process, a rhythmic hum or chant based on a deity's or rune's name should be made until the desired state is attained. Labyrinth stones used by day are known as *serpent stones*, to be stared at in bright sunlight. *Moonstones*, carved at night by artificial light, should never see the light of day, but be used by the light of the full moon.

Either type of stone should be kept wrapped in cloth and kept in a safe place when not in use. In the magical protection of buildings, the labyrinth is used as a small protective symbol beside or over doorways. One notable medieval example is in Augustinergasse in Zürich, Switzerland, which has recently been restored by the civic authorities as a notable ancient relic. On a larger scale, the labyrinth has been built of loose stones, pebbles or boulders, cut into the turf, or laid out as a pavement of brick or mosaic stones.

In the Northern Tradition, there are three basic types of unicursal labyrinth. The most widespread is the classical labyrinth, with a single, relatively simple pathway to the centre characterized by intricate turns. Simpler than this, but less common, is the labyrinth which has one-way loops leading to the centre, and related to this is a type, known from Scandinavia and Germany, the 'in-and-back' labyrinth, where the path does not end at the centre but returns the runner to the entrance. Finally, the most complex form is the medieval

Fig. 28 Labyrinths. *Top left*: 7-ring classical labyrinth *Top right*: 11-ring classical labyrinth *Bottom left*: 'in and back' turf labyrinth, formerly at Kaufbeuren, Germany *Bottom right*: the medieval labyrinth design, the basic pattern for most English turf labyrinths. Pathway shown in black.

labyrinth, with a most elegant geometry.

In Scandinavia, there are several hundred large labyrinths, made of stones ranging in size from tennis balls to boulders the size of a human head. These are laid out so that they form the walls of a path which runs between them. These are the oldest known walkable (or danceable) labyrinths in existence, some of them dating from the Bronze Age. Some of them are found on remote islands, and others are associated with places used for traditional religious observances. In England and Germany, the traditional labyrinth form is cut from turf, usually with grassy pathways divided by small trenches. Over the years most of the ancient turf labyrinths have been destroyed, leaving only a handful still existing. The names of some of them, such as Shepherd's Race or Robin Hood's Race, record former customary games and dances. Except where they are done on ice or snow, labyrinth games and dances take place in the *airts* of late spring or early summer, roughly between the equinox and the summer solstice. In Finland and Sweden, there are traditional games where a girl stands in the middle of the labyrinth whilst young men try to get through to her to free her from captivity. Because of this custom, some Finnish labyrinths are called *jungfrudanser* 'virgin's dances'. The type of dance or race to the girl in the middle depended on the type of labyrinth. Those with a continuous 'in-and-back' path, i.e., with two paths to the centre, involved two boys starting close to one another and running in opposite directions. Those with one path to the centre involved running it without making any mistakes. In England, the great turf labyrinth which exists today on the common at Saffron Walden had a system of wagers associated with running it properly without stumbling. The maze was run by youths to reach a young woman at the centre.

The Northern Tradition contains a legend which is one of the keys to the mysteries of the labyrinth. The *Song of Grimborg* is a Swedish ballad which tells of the hero Grimborg breaking through fences of iron and steel to reach a beautiful princess. Once the king found out that Grimborg had entered, he ordered his men to kill the hero. Grimborg fought his way out, killing 12,000 of the king's men in the process. Returing to his mother's house, Grimborg was surrounded by another army, but, killing another 12,000, he fought his way out and rode alone to the king's palace, where he was reconciled with the king and allowed to marry his daughter.

A Swedish winter custom which re-enacted Grimborg's saga involved drawing labyrinths on ice or snow, with paths wide enough for skating on. At the centre stood a girl representing Grimborg's princess, and just before the centre or *castle* stood a guard blocking the way, who attempted to stop the youth playing the part of Grimborg from entering. During the game, the *Song of Grimborg* was sung. In a Swedish legend from Nordingrâ, the labyrinth was the home of a troll, who

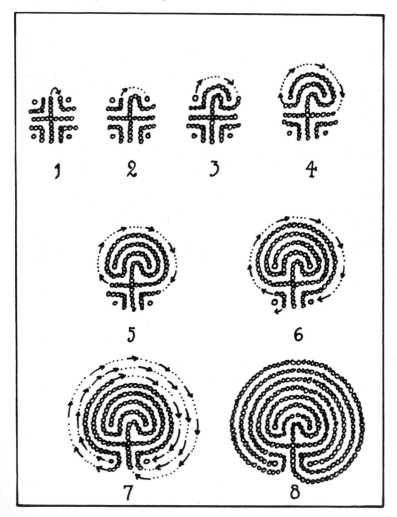

Fig. 29 Stepwise technique for constructing a stone labyrinth, starting with the 'cross, corners and dots' pattern (1), and joining up corresponding points until there are no 'loose ends' left.

had taken a girl and held her prisoner at the centre. The village people were assembled to rescue the girl from the troll's lair in the mountains. They walked back and forth seven times until they gained entry, and then watched until the troll fell asleep, when they rescued the girl.

Geometrically, the *fylfot* figure is based on the same nine-dot pattern as the classical labyrinth. So the *fylfot*, symbolic of the male generative, power, is immanent within the labyrinth, symbol of the female, enclosing, nurturing power. The labyrinth is a symbol of spirit coming into matter within the womb of the mother-goddess, which is the first entry into labyrinth. Birth, or coming into the world, is symbolized by leaving the labyrinth for the first time; then, at death, the spirit is ingathered once again to the goddess, to be released into the spirit world at the second egress from the labyrinth. The *Song of Grimborg* expresses this double entry and exit well, for the name *Grim*, one of the 49 by-names of Odin, means *the masked one*, a shaman.

The goddess of the labyrinth also symbolizes an element of shamanry—out-of-the-body and out-of-this-world experiences. For those who are chosen, this shamanic ascent is achievable through practice at and especially on such structures as labyrinths. Many believe that ancient labyrinths are physical representations of underground forces personified as the *Wouivre*, the Earth dragon of the Earth-Mother goddess, which act in subtle ways upon the body and mind of anyone who walks the labyrinth, subtly altering their brain-wave patterns and creating in them religious experience. The centre of a labyrinth is an ideal place for sitting out. The path to the centre forms a valuable preparation for this. Also, because of its orientation and geolocation, a labyrinth is in touch with the subtle magical energies which interact with the weather, and it was long customary for becalmed mariners to build labyrinths to use them to raise the wind.

Wherever a labyrinth of traditional design is made, the character of that site is altered; a formerly unimportant area becomes a focus of human interest, and energies are generated there. Wherever one is built, there is an immediate change in human perception of the place. The construction of a labyrinth can cause the immediate regeneration of an abandoned area, which takes on a new character because of the labyrinth. It is possible to create a new atmosphere at any place by constructing a labyrinth. Whenever a permanent

labyrinth is made, the work of construction focuses consciousness upon the area, and changes attitudes towards a
place that previously might have been considered negatively.
It brings people to a place where human activity may have
been absent, and as nobody can resist walking, running or
dancing round a labyrinth, it creates movement at a site. In
geomantic terms, a labyrinth collects or generates an interior
concentration of *önd*, and therefore is an artificially-created
place of power which will alter the balance of *önd* in the landscape around it.

The most simple way to build a labyrinth is to use the cross,
corners and dots pattern. Once this form has been made at
the centre, joining up opposite points with whatever material
has been chosen—sawdust, deal apples, wood blocks,
stones, bricks or an earth bank—will complete the labyrinth.
Scandinavian stone labyrinths are usually located with their
entrance towards the western quarter of the sky, though
others, such as the Saffron Walden turf labyrinth, face the
north. The main rule to remember when building a labyrinth
is that basic orientation should take the surroundings into account. No geomantic feature will work if it does not harmonize with its surroundings.

IV

Tools and Equipment

I guard myself with this rod.,. . . .
Against the painful stroke,
Against the grim dread,
And against all evil which may enter the land. . . .

Anglo-Saxon Charm

Every sacred tradition has its own collection of signs, symbols and sigils, correspondences and techniques unique to that system. Many of the techniques explained here come from my own part of the tradition, the East Anglian, of which several have never been published before. In the *calls*, for example, the final word, *Ka!* means 'Let it be', or 'So!', the East Anglian equivalent of 'Amen' or 'So mote it be' in prayers, *calls*, spells and incantations.

Magical Vestments and Paraphernalia

The traditional equipment of magicians, shamans, wise women, cunning men, locators and the rest has always included certain essential items which enable the practitioner to contact the other worlds. These are the hooded robe or cloak, with which to envelop the body and partially obscure the vision when entering shamanic trances; a ground-cloth, upon which to sit out; a bag in which to carry magical items; and a staff made from the wood appropriate for the specialized activity of the practitioner. All of these items are usually adorned with appropriate symbols of power, totemic beasts and consecrated amulets. Many ancient examples of these can be seen in museums: small figures of animals and birds, stars, discs and whorls of metal, seemingly without use, for the clothes to which they were sewn have long since perished.

These are truly the 'ritual objects' beloved of museum catalogues!

The essential equipment of the *Völva* (female practitioner), recorded in Norse sagas, is a dark blue cloak with a hood and set with stones along the hem; an inner hood or head-dress made from the skin of a white wildcat, fox or badger, extending around the neck; an animal skin large enough to sit on or be wrapped in; a small woven rug with appropriate designs, the *stol*; a kerchief, traditionally red with white spots; gloves made from wildcat skin, with the fur innermost; fur boots; a skin bag to contain objects of power; a *mete-wand*; a runestaff of *shaft height*; and, of course, a wooden platform for sitting out. Archaeological investigations of ancient burials in Scandinavia have found the remains of similar equipment, including leather pouches containing power objects such as amber beads and other power stones, snake bones, squirrels' tails, bird claws and sea shells.

Ceremonial robes used today are based on a very simple construction, taken from peasant clothing of former times, though of vastly superior modern manufactured material. A piece of material related to body size is used, with the width of the fabric equal to the future wearer's personal *fathom*, from hand to hand with outstretched arms. In length, the material should be twice the body length from the nape of the neck to the heels. The material is folded over, and four triangles cut from it to form a pair of sleeves and the flared sides of the robe. Another cut should be made for the head. When sewn up, it is appropriate to protect the openings in the material with a *tangled thread* pattern, such as an interlace or proprietary borders, so long as their design is appropriate to northern Europe. It is advisable to make a cowl-shaped hood of similar material, which can be attached if wished. Reflective material, such as jewels, semi-precious stones or mirrors, can be added around the hems.

In former times, the colour of one's clothes was prescribed by law. The Celtic rules stipulated specific colours and combinations and, in a rigid society, none could break the regulation. They were:

King/Queen	7 colours
Druids	6 colours
Lords/Ladies	5 colours

Governors of fortresses	4 colours
Young gentry	3 colours
Soldiers	2 colours
Commoners	1 colour

Today, in the magical tradition, people are free to wear any colours they consider appropriate, but earthy colours, such as greens, browns and yellows, are favoured. The magical colours associated with the East Anglian branch of the Northern Tradition, however, are red, yellow, and sometimes, black or dark blue. The traditional wizard's robe, of course, is dark blue, bedecked with stars and sigils of the planetary/godly powers.

Inside-out clothing

One of the traditional attributes of the shaman or wise person is the wearing of clothing inside out or back-to-front. The magical symbolism of this is the inversion of the normal ways of doing things, setting one aside from the run-of-the-mill. Inside-out clothes are also a confusing element, and as with all confusion, assists in the defeat of malevolent sprites and entities, enhancing the magician's *mattr* or *megin* (personal force for good fortune and success). The 'dog collar' of Church of England vicars is an example of this. Odd socks and other odd pairs also have a similar effect. The traditional *motley* costume of medievel court jesters, where many colours were set asymmetrically, had a magically-protective function.

The red cap

A red cap has always been the sign of a person wise in supernatural lore and praxis. To wear a red cap was formerly a sign of magical ability. There are several historically recorded English wise women who were called Old Mother Redcap, and many depictions of warlocks and wise women show them wearing the red cap. The person who wears the red cap carries a token of someone who is set aside from 'ordinary' society. Because of this, it was used as a symbol of heresy by the medieval church, and as a symbol of revolution by the French of 1789. Today, paratroopers, members of an élite, separate military corps, wear the red beret. Charles Perrault's fairy tale *Little Red Riding Hood*, written in 1697, used the motif, which Erich Fromm in *The Forgotten Language* considered a symbol of menstruation. According to Patrick Kennedy's collection of traditional Irish tales (*Fictions of the Irish Celts*, 1866), Irish witches used the *cappeen d'yarrag* or *birredh* in their flight. The formula for flight was:

> By yarrow and rue,
> And my red cap too,
> Hie over to England

with which the Irish witches would ride on a twig, flying across the sea. The herbs yarrow (*Achillea millefolium*) and rue (*Ruta graveolens*) were both used by herbalists in former times for controlling irregular menstrual cycles, and the red cap has obvious connotations in this connection. But the red cap should not just be seen as the badge of office of a women's herbalist or procurer of abortions. A sprig of yarrow held over the eyes was believed to make a person *ófreskr*, possessed of second sight. A red cap is also associated with the hallucinogenic fungus *Amanita muscaria*, the fly agaric, whose use by shamans and wise women of the North is well known. The design of the famous red kerchief with white spots, beloved of traditional dancers, is derived from the red cap of this fungus with its white flecks.

A red cap is also symbolic of supernatural beings. Traditional representations of leprechauns and other 'little people' often show then in a red cap—even plastic garden gnomes wear it! The *Fear Dearc* or *Red Man*, a spirit from the province of Munster in Eire, who visits farms to bring good luck, is a small man, about an ell tall, who wears a red sugar-loaf hat and a long red cloak. He comes to request to be let in to warm himself by the fire, and it is bad luck to refuse. Today, the red cap is set to return as a sign of practitioners of Northern Tradition magic.

Magic belts, girdles and collars

Belts and girdles are associated with power, both physical and magical. Thor's strength comes from his belt of power, *Meginjord*. To wear a belt around the body helps to channel energy, and for this reason a magic knotted cord is sometimes worn around the body. A girdle of untanned wolf-skin, wolf hair or wolf leather has been used in *hamrammr* (shape-shifting), where the practitioner transforms into a wolf! Belts of other animal skins are said to work similarly. Girdles and belts can contain pockets in which talismans, herbs and other magically powerful objects are placed. Whatever it is made of, the girdle should be of traditional dimensions, three fingers in width (two thumbs). When it is made into a belt, the buckle should have seven tags or tongues. Magic belts or girdles can be used around objects as well as people. The *balderick*, a girdle of horsehair placed around a bell, infuses it with *önd*, making it a powerful instrument of consecration. In East Anglian tradition, three polecat, stoat or weasel skins, joined together and worn around the neck, are a ceremonial symbol of hereditary magical power.

Several traditional remedies use a girdle or garter of animal skin. A formula from the Cambridgeshire Fens considers an eel-skin garter as a preventive and cure for rheumatism. Eel-skins should be prepared in springtime, being sun-dried until stiff, then greased and worked to pliability over a round piece of wood. The skins are then tied at both ends and stuffed with chopped leaves of thyme (*Thymus vulgaris*) and lavender (*Lavandula angustifolia*). The skins should then be placed in linen bags laid between layers of fresh marsh mint (*Mentha aquatica*) and buried all summer in the ground. At the beginning of autumn, the bags are dug up, the skins taken out, lavender and thyme removed, and the garters polished on a smooth stone. They are then ready for use. Known as a *york*, the garter should be worn just above the knee, women's knotted on the right, and men's knotted on the left. A snake-skin wrapped around the head has often been used as a cure for headache.

Headband

A white headband embroidered with a complete runic row in red is a useful magical protection and *megin* enhancer. You should embroider your own runes, putting the force of will appropriate to each stave as it is embroidered. A useful way of doing this is to do it over a 24-hour period, embroidering each rune at the correct runic hour, and facing the correct runic direction whilst doing the work. In this way, the embroiderer faces the sun as the runes are made, and a complete circle of time and space is programmed into the runic headband. It should then be dedicated to use at a geomantically powerful place. If possible, this should be done at one of the ancient centres of Northern Tradition observance. Mine was infused with *önd* at the Externsteine, the ancient continental Saxon sacred centre, a place of great numinous sancity.

Ceremonial Knives and Carvers

The knife is an essential tool for the performance of magical acts, for gathering herbs, for cutting staves and slivers and for the carving of runes and other sacred sigils. Traditionally, these functions have often been performed with the same knife, because the more it is used with conscious will, the more beneficial power known as *megin* will accumulate.

The blade of the knife should be made of iron or steel, a metal which has always been credited with magical properties, and which is serviceable for cutting. It is better to make your own knife rather than to buy one in a shop or market. It is certainly a bad idea to use a purchased magical knife, especially a second-hand one, for it is impossible to know what bad on-lays might be present. Ceremonial and functional weapons such as Nazi daggers or military surplus bayonets are certainly to be avoided. Literally, one does not know where such weapons have been!

If you want to make sure that it has never been used for anything else, a knife can be made from a piece of metal, shaped and ground to sharpness yourself. In this way, you know every action that the knife has ever been used for. It should have a handle made from wood, bone or horn, not plastic. Traditional woods include rowan, hazel and ash, though any serviceable hardwood which feels appropriate should not be rejected. Again, the purity of materials used should be ensured, and so it is best to cut and season the wood yourself. The ceremony for taking wood should be used when cutting it (see below).

However it is made, the knife should be a natural foot (nine thumbs) in length, the handle measuring four thumbs and the blade five. Such knives have different names. The name *athamé*, taken from the Wiccan tradition, is often given to a ritual knife, but equally the Saxon name of *seax* is viable. I always refer to a knife as a knife. The tool known as a *boleen* is sometimes used exclusively for gathering herbs. This is a small sickle, not more than a natural foot in length.

An engraving-tool or *carver* separate from the knife is often used for making runic inscriptions. Again, such tools have various names: *burin* from the Celtic–Wiccan tradition, and *ristir* from Old Norse. As with the knife, it is customary to engrave appropriate runes upon the handle to consecrate it to the special, non-secular use, and to enhance its power.

(a)   (b)

Fig. 30 Staves in English folk-custom: (a) attendant in the Haxey 'Hood' ceremony; (b) Norwich *Whiffler* from the former St George's Day dragon parade.

Sacred Staves, Sticks and Mete-wands

Whenever wood is used ceremonially, it should be cut from a living tree or shrub. Wood which has been cut already is not recommended, as whoever cut it will, knowingly or unknowingly, have put their own *álag* (on-lay) into the wood, which may well interfere with or negate the practitioner's intentions. Cutting wood ceremonially will infuse it with magical power, an on-lay which will interact with the powers present in the wood to enhance them. The practitioner should explore local woodland and hedgerows for an appropriate tree or shrub from which to cut the wood. Of course, permission should be sought first from the owner of the land before attempting to take wood. When the tree is located, one should approach it in a reverent manner. The best time to cut wood is at sunrise, high noon or sunset. The branch to be cut should face towards the *airt* corresponding with the use to which it will be put. For a sliver with a specific runic intention, it is best to use wood which faces the correct runic direction, that is one twentyfourth of the circle. First, the practitioner should perform a short ceremony of protection. Then, taking the knife, the practitioner addresses the tree's soul:

> Hail to thee, O [*tree's name*]!
> Old Lady, give me of this wood,
> And I will give thee some of mine,
> When I grow into a tree.
> Send thy power into this branch,
> That thy strength will flow through it
> For the good of all.
> Ka!

Then the branch is cut, with a single stroke if possible, starting the cut underneath and cutting upwards. The branch should not be allowed to fall to the ground. If it has been necessary to climb the tree to get the branch, then it should be passed to an assistant, not thrown down, for touching the ground before it is worked on is said to negate its power. When the branch has been taken, then the tree should be thanked for its gift. The soul of the tree should be addressed again:

> Old Lady [*tree's name*]!
> Accept my thanks

For thy power in this branch.
That its power there will remain,
Working for the good of all.
Ka!

A small offering should be given to the tree in thanks for the
wood. This may be a coin, a piece of red ribbon, a libation of
ale, or a candle lit in front of the tree. If a candle is burned,
then the practitioner should stay with it until it is finished—there is always a danger of fire in woodland. After the
ceremony, the wood should be taken to the place where it is
to be worked upon. Whatever the final use of the wood, it
should be consecrated to the intended use by means of the
runes, using the ceremony detailed in Chapter 3. There are
many different sorts of magical artifacts which are made from
wood, ranging from small talismanic slivers to long staves
and building materials:

Staves are often whole saplings, using the root end as the
knob on top. Staves such as this are an inversion of the way
that the tree grows, with its upper part inverted. Croomsticks
(see below) and other artificially-distorted magical staves can
be made by deliberately pinning the sapling in a certain way
as it grows, then harvesting it for use one, two, three or five

Fig. 31 Consulting the runestocks. (Engraving from O. Rudbeck's
Atlantica.)

years later. Croomsticks and staves created in this way are especially powerful. An alternative is to seek out a distorted sapling or bush which has grown that way naturally, having been affected by natural forces in such a way that is is perfect for the practitioner's uses.

Croomsticks — The croomstick is an East Anglian stave with a curved top rather like a shepherd's crook or the end of a conventional walking-stick. The croomstick, however, is longer than a walking-stick. It is used for various functions, including laying out magical enclosures, hooking down mistletoe and 'witches' brooms', and warding off psychic intrusion. The dimensions of the curved upper part are important. When held at arm's length, one sixteenth or one twenty-fourth part of the horizon should be viewed by looking at it through the space made inside the curve of the croomstick. The sixteenfold croomstick is used for the delimination of the eight *Airts* and their mid-points, whilst the twenty-fourfold is for the 24 runic directions.

Pilebogar — These are staves which have a small fork at the top end into which a red-painted egg or crystal is wedged to act as a psychic protector. A version of these has three branches, and is used to support a libation bowl or a *glódhker* (brazier) used in ceremonial ritual. Hazel, hawthorn or blackthorn are suitable woods for this.

Clog staves — The word *clog* means a piece of wood, transferred to mean a shoe composed entirely of wood or with a wooden sole. A clog almanac or runestave is thus an almanac, a record of the days and festivals of the year, made from a piece of wood. Northern European custom is to use a piece of wood which has been made into a square section, that is, with four faces. These faces then represent the four quarters of the heavens, and the four seasons. On the edges between the faces, notches or scratches—*scotches*—are made to signify the days of the calendar year. The Irish traditional script known as Ogham was also cut on staves in the same manner, each character straddling the corner (known as an *arris*).

Mete-wands — A mete-wand is a measuring rod or stick, an ell in length, graduated in the subdivisions of natural measure—shafthands, thumbs and barleycorns. It is used for making sure that ritual objects are the correct sacred dimensions. (It should not be confused with the *wand* or *Gandr* that is primarily a magically-charged talismanic stave.) The wand can measure between a shafthand and an ell in length. Preferably, however, the wand should be an ell in length, and not more than a thumb in diameter at the thick (lower) end. Only the largest staves are held with the lower (root) end of the tree uppermost; all other staves are held in the direction of growth, with the smaller end uppermost. This is the case for the wand.

The quarterstaff — This is best known from the legend of Robin Hood, the medieval outlaw practitioner of the martial arts. Among the traditional martial arts was combat with the quarterstaff. Technically, the quarterstaff is a hardwood stave one quarter of a rod in length. This is five natural feet (15 shafthands) in length. Being a secular rather than a sacred tool, however, the quarterstaff varied in length considerably. In 1550, a document spoke of the quarterstaff as being between six and eight feet in length, tipped with iron. The iron spike at the lower end was an important part of the weapon. Medieval travellers, forbidden by class to carry swords, were taught to use it in defensive techniques which were effective against wild animals as ferocious as wolves and bears. The modern French systems of *canne* and *bâton* are versions of the ancient art of stave-combat, using a short and long stave respectively.

Shaft-height measurements — In ancient times, the popular method for announcing an agreed time to stop work, or to perform a ceremony, used the height of the sun instead of its direction. Ancient northern European laws defined the *shaft-height* of the sun in the afternoon as the point when 'the lower edge of the sun appears to rest on the point of a spear set up nine feet from the observer'. The spear in question had to be the observer's own, set up so that he could reach out comfortably with a shafthand, with the thumb held out from the fist, up to the socket of the spearhead. In the tradition of natural measure, the length of the spear is related to the height of its owner, and so the shaft-height is always the same angle, regardless of who measures it. Effectively, the spear becomes an artificial horizon, around 10°.

Wands — A wand, also known as *gandr*, is often considered the magician's tool *par excellence*, and is of hazel or blackthorn. The word *gandr* also has the meaning of the *blast*, the directed energy or *önd* which is projected from the end of the wand

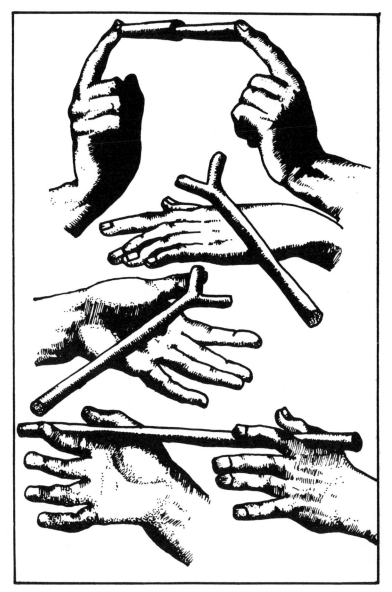

Fig. 32 Variations of stick-hold in traditional rhabdomantic divinations.

during magical acts. A standard wand should be an ell in length.

A wand with a deal apple (pine-cone) at the end can have either a real deal apple or a carved representation of one. Wands such as this are sacred to Freyr, and sometimes have a representation of a phallus carved at the end in place of a deal apple. The Cosmic Axis itself was sometimes known as the 'Earth's Hazel Wand', and consecrated staves of hazel should be used for supporting the ropes around a sacred place. This enclosure of hazel staves or wands is called a *vébond*. Staves for a *vébond* should be cut specially with appropriate ritual shortly before the enclosure is constructed.

Rhabdomantic rods — The art of *rhabdomancy* or *rhabdoscopy* is known better nowadays as *dowsing*, though technically they are not exactly the same. The word *dowsing* is used to describe attempts to divine the location or water, oil or minerals in the ground, and, in recent years, many kinds of esoteric 'energies'. Traditional rhabdomantic rods for water divining (or *water witching*) should be cut from a hazel tree with a single stroke at the time of a full moon, on a Wednesday and a runic hour corresponding with Odin's power. The traditional rhabdomantic rod for finding lost property, however, should be made of yew wood. The rhabdomantic rod, which should be about an ell in length, should be carried horizontally, each hand grasping one end, holding it with a pressure sufficient to bend it slightly. When the materials sought are beneath the rhabdomant's feet, then a torsion will be felt in the rod. An alternative to this is the forked hazel wand, one end of the 'Y' being held in each hand. When water is encountered, the rod bends downwards or upwards. Today, most dowsers have abandoned the magical side of rhabdomancy, or do not realize that there is one, and use pieces of wire or plastic in their quest.

Slivers and Albion knots — A *sliver* is a small piece of wood cut for the express purpose of making a runic inscription. An alternative name for it is a *tine*. The *Albion knot* is a stick about a shafthand in length with a knob-like projection at one end. It has been infused with magical power for the accomplishment of a specific task. Like the sliver, it should be destroyed ceremonially after use.

Sacred Flags

Today, flags and banners have an air of sanctity about them. In many countries, the national flag is protected by law, and any act of indignity towards it is punished by legal sanction. This is very apparent with *Old Glory*, the *Stars-and Stripes* flag of the United States of America, which is treated with great respect, backed up with legal sanctions against those who would 'insult' the flag in some way. In earlier times, flag magic was an important part of military pagentry. In Germany in the 1930s, every Nazi flag was 'consecrated' by being touched against Hitler's personal *Blood Flag*, which had been with him when he attempted to seize power in 1923, and which, the Nazis believed, had special qualities because of that. Nowadays, old military banners of British regiments are hung up in churches and cathedrals after their ceremonial days are past. And, of course, the ceremony of *Trooping the Colour* is one of the high points of British royal pageantry. In earlier times, a more overt magical function was ascribed to flags and banners. The Raven Banner was the consecrated luck-flag of Viking warriors, and each banner, when consecrated, was given a name. One of the most famous Raven Banners was *Landwaster*, the standard of Harald Hardrada. This had been sewn by the daughters of the great Viking Ragnar Lodbrog, and was carried from Norway to Constantinople in the campaigns of the Norse warriors known as the Varangians. Finally, at the Battle of Stamford Bridge in 1066, the banner's luck ran out, when Hardrada was defeated by the Saxons. In the same year, William of Normandy won the Battle of Hastings under two sacred flags, his own banner, Gonfanon, and another specially consecrated by the Pope.

Some Raven Banners, it was said, were not made by the hand of woman, but obtained by paranormal means. One, *Ravenlandeye*, hung in St Mary's church in York for many years. According to William Ramsay, writing in the *Crowland Chronicle* in the twelfth century, Siward the Stout, *Jarl* of Northumbria under the Danish King Cnut, acquired a supernatural flag. Whilst riding along the rocky Northumbrian coast, Siward was stopped by an old, cloaked and hooded man. The old man took a Raven Banner, called *Ravenlandeye*, from his cloak, and gave it to the *Jarl*. Of course, the old man was in the typical guise of Odin, and the raven is Odin's tutelary bird. Siward, in an age when the old religion had been absorbed by the newer, donated the banner to the Church as a protector of the City of York. Today, unless you are lucky enough to inherit a fairy flag or to be given one by an old man on a beach, if a luck-flag is needed, it must be made. Luck-flags can be made from any suitable material, preferably in the colour which corresponds to the activity being undertaken. There are several appropriate designs for these flags, which should bear a sigil proper to its function. They are illustrated and explained in Chapter 5.

The Sacred Hammer

The Hammer of Thor, *Mjöllnir*, is a symbol of protection and consecration. It represents the power of thunder and lightning, the divine manifestation of *önd*. In the Northern Tradition, the sign of the hammer, the *hammermark*, is made as a benediction. The ceremony known as *Hammarrsettning*, projecting the image of the hammer to the four quarters, above and below, is performed today as a magical protection. When the hammer is in its sacred form, it is shown with the handle uppermost, and when worn as an amulet, it hangs from the chain by a ring. As an amulet, silver is the preferred metal for a Thor's Hammer, but, of course, a full-size version should be made of iron or steel.

The *crowned hammer* was the emblem of the Guild of Hammermen, a Scottish and Scandinavian traditional union of craftsmen. The Hammermen included carpenters, cabinetmakers, masons and other craftsmen whose main tool was the hammer. The crown over the hammer denotes the divine regal power of Thor, protecting those whose craft it is to use the sacred emblem. The fylfot or swastika is a dynamic form of the hammer, representing its circular motion when in use, transmitting energy from the wielder to the job in hand. For this reason, the swastika was generally considered a very lucky charm until the Second World War. The Swastika Laundry in Dublin, founded in 1912, continues this lucky charm use today. However, in the Northern Tradition, the misuse of the swastika from 1919 to 1945 by a criminal organization does not remove its true meaning, any more than it has done so to Hindus and Buddhists. It remains an image of the power of the Hammer of Thor.

Despite attempts by the Church to suppress it in favour of the cross, the hammer's sacred use was never abolished. Images of saints bearing the hammer or axe are common, and in Lappland, altars of Thor, complete with hammers, were erected at sacred places until the nineteenth century. In Britain in former times, it was a funeral custom to bury a hammer with the corpse. This tradition has been associated with the Gypsies, such as the much-reported funeral of Caroline Penfold in 1926, but it was much more widespread than that. In Montgomeryshire it was customary for *Gorgios* (non-Gypsies) to be buried with a hammer in one hand and a coin in the other. Some folklore states that the hammer was for the deceased to knock for admittance to heaven, or that it was a precaution against premature burial, but it is clear from the paramount position afforded the hammer as a sacred symbol that it was placed in the coffin primarily as a symbol of sanctification or magical protection, as was salt. Often, in addition to the hammer and coin, a candle and a piece of bread was buried with the corpse. In former times, a sacred hammer was sometimes used in euthanasia, to put a dying person out of their misery. The last known instances from Europe are Sardinian. In the Roman Catholic Church, a silver hammer is used symbolically when a pope dies, three taps upon the forehead signifying that he is indeed dead.

The name of Thor's hammer, *Mjöllnir*, is recalled in the word *mallet*, and the old hammer-ball game of *pell-mell*. The traditional formula for nailing up a horseshoe as the magical protection of a doorway includes the lines:

> Thrice I smite with holy crock,
> With this *mell* I thrice do knock,
> One for God,
> One for Wod,
> And one for Luck.

God in this charm is clearly Thor, the god of the hammer. As a sacred tool, the hammer drives in nails, which themselves are sacred protectors. The high-seat pillars of temples of Thor had sacred nails driven into them, and there was a form of divination known as *onychomancy*, the interpretation of patterns glimpsed in the sunlight reflected from nails on a sacred post. Holy trees, posts and doorframes throughout Europe can be found which have had thousands of nails driven into them over the years by passing tradespeople. The tree-trunk known as the *Stock im Eisen* in Vienna, now preserved in a glass-fronted case on the corner of a nineteenth century building, was once a standing tree into which nails would be driven. Over the years it accumulated so many nails that there were scarcely any patches of wood visible, and at its death it was preserved. Many ancient inns in Britain have many nails hammered into the main post or doorframe, for example the Skirrid Inn, the oldest inn in Wales, and the Cross Keys at Saffron Walden, Essex, said to have been built on a living tree. Today, in many European countries, alongside old ones, new nails can be seen hammered into trees at crossroads. Anyone can find examples in their own locality. Hammering in these nails is a direct continuation of tradition.

The Norse *Erbyggja Saga* tells of how Thórólf Mostrarskegg transported his wooden temple of Thor to another location. When it was dismantled for trans-shipment, the soil on which it stood was excavated with it (one reason why archaeologists today may not find much when they excavate an old temple site). From his ship, he threw overboard the main high-seat pillars of the temple (*öndvegissúlur*—pillars of sacred *önd*), so that where they came ashore would be the currect geolocation of the reconstructed temple. Finally they came ashore at a place which he named Thórsnes, where

'He had a temple constructed, and it was a mighty building. There was a doorway in the side-wall, nearer to one end, and inside stood the main pillars in which nails were set, called *divine nails* (*reginnaglar*). Inside was a great sanctuary. Further in was a room of the same form as the chancels in present-day churches'.

From the reflected sunlight on these *reginnaglar*, the runemasters would glimpse evanescent, shimmering runes, by means of which the divine will would be communicated. Hammering in the nail is a microcosmic version of the geomantic act, where the energies of the earth are fixed at the *nowl* or *navel of the world* by the lance, sword or stave of the hero. Similarly, the act of hammering is believed to fix certain energies or qualities in the object being hammered. This is a modern interpretation of the ancient custom of hammering in nails or striking stones to sanctify them or other objects. In the days before electromagnets, blacksmiths made iron magnetic by hammering it in a north-south direction. Similarly, the dowser J. Havelock Fidler, in his book *Earth Energy*

(1988), claims to be able to charge stones by hammering them, and to create various sorts of 'charge' which causes a reaction in a dowser's pendulum.

The Wheel

At the summer solstice, it is customary to roll a wheel, often fiery, down a hill. A correspondent to *Current Notes* for March 1854 noted that at Norwich 'it was the custom to turn or roll a wheel about, in signification of the sun's annual course, for the sun, then occupying the highest place in the Zodiac, was about descending'. As a symbol of the year, the wheel is used as a protection on buildings, either painted on or as an actual cartwheel fixed to the wall. Wheels are fixed to the walls inside the Suffolk churches of Long Stratton and Yaxley, where they are known as *sexton's wheels*. These have six holes in the rim, through which thread was passed and the wheel rotated as a means to determine upon which day a penance should be made. In the calendar, there are six days sacred to the Madonna, and the penitent had to catch a piece of thread as the wheel spun. The hole that the caught thread was passed through was examined to see which of the festivals on the year-cycle it represented. The spinning wheel, rotating around the former pole-star, *Tir* or the Nail, is one of the symbols of Frigg in her aspect as Queen of the Heavens, ruler of time. This attribute is present in the old Norse name for the Arctic Circle, *Hjolgaddsringr* (Wheel-nail-circle). The church wheel was a transference of the rites of the goddess to the festivals of the Madonna.

Magic Sounds: Protective, Invocatory and Divinatory

Bells, rattles, whistles, clappers, handclaps, drums and fireworks all have a subtle effect upon the environment. Bells and drums are the most readily made and make the most potent noise of music-makers. Bells are a means of signifying and amplifying the presence of desirable sacred powers, whilst suppressing unwanted intrusions. The resonance of a bell depends on its material, dimension and, to some extent, its shape, so the sound is a physical manifestation of these qualities. It is possible to make a bell by bending sheet metal

Fig. 33 The bell-reliquary of St Cuilleann, an ornamented shrine for a
   sacred object of magical power.

to shape and then riveting it, as bells were made in the old
days, and Swiss cow bells are today. Like all sacred objects,
bells are given names which express their innate magical
qualities.

The sanctity of bells was recognized by the monks of the
Celtic Church who enclosed notable bells inside ornate relin-
quaries. The bell of St Cuilleann, a ninth century Irish priest,
shown in Fig. 33 is a classic example. This one was deposited
for many years in a hollow tree at Kilcuilawn in the parish of
Glenkeen, County Tipperary, and was used in the eigh-

teenth century as a sacred object upon which oaths were sworn. Sacred bells and other holy objects were entrusted to hereditary relic-keepers, and handed down in families. Another notable Irish bell, the Bell of St Conall, was kept by the O'Breslen family who lived on the island of Inishkeel off the coast of Donegal.

The drum is the most important instrument in many rituals, and its use in shamanism is legendary. The beat of a drum can accelerate or slow the heartbeat; it can modify the brain-wave patterns and alter emotions. Because of this, sacred drums have been made with great ritual care, from the correct materials, and at the times most conductive to creating objects of magical power. The wood and skin from which the drum is to be made must be taken in the correct ceremonial manner, which endows the materials with the correct qualities. The wood should be cut at full moon, and the skin laid on at midday, the point of the sun's zenith. The wooden part of the drum is thus sacred to the lunar power, whilst the skin is endowed with solar qualities. In shamanic traditions, including Northern Tradition magic, the drum is seen as a receptacle of spirit, either a soul infused into it by ritual, or its own special portion of the universal *önd*.

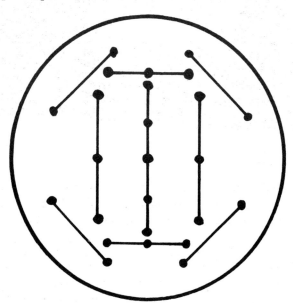

Fig. 34 Layout of lines and points on Kate 'the Gull' Turner's shamanic drum.

The Lappish shaman's drum and the Celtic *Bodhran* are of common origin: they are flat and circular, with a handle so that they can be held in one hand whilst dancing and drumming. The drum, which is painted with emblems of divinity and worldly existence, is held in the left hand and struck with a small club or drumstick held in the right. The drum's main use is in shamanic ritual and ceremony, but in divination, the drum also plays its part. Divinatory drums are identical in structure, but have different designs painted on their skins. The 'talking tambourine' of Kate 'the Gull' Turner, a famous early twentieth century West Country wise woman with powers over the sea, is still preserved. This is a shaman's drum with a divinatory pattern painted on it. This pattern is composed of nine lines, upon which 25 shells were placed at specific points (see Fig. 34). The 'tambourine' was then struck, and vibrations set up, causing the shells to dance across the surface into new positions. From these positions, Turner was able to make predictions. If all of the shells migrated to a point inside the four oblique lines, then a positive outcome is indicated. It is even better if they come within the cardinal rectangle. If most migrate outside, then the outcome will be unfavourable. Within these criteria, of course, there are more subtle nuances. Along the Baltic coast and in Slavonic countries, an identical pattern is used. There, the seeds of the highly toxic thorn-apple (*Datura stramonium*) replace the shells or beans of British practice. Between nine and 21 of the black, pitted, kidney-shaped seeds are used, being placed on the lines at the beginning. Thorn-apple seeds are extremely dangerous, containing hallucinogens which may have been used in shamanic practices of the past. However, they should *never* be used in this way, as even the few used in drum divination constitute a fatal dose.

Binding Magic, Strings and Knots

Protective bottles

Ever since their invention, bottles have been used as receptacles for unwanted entities which could not be allowed out in the world. There are two types of bottle: those which entrap and contain a troublesome spirit, and those which have been prepared as a magical protection against psychic attack. The former tradition is known by every child from the tales of

The Arabian Nights, where a *djinn* or *genie* is let out of a bottle and finally re-imprisoned there. The second kind are known in the eastern counties of England as *witch bottles,* and many from earlier centuries are found each year when old houses are rebuilt or demolished. These are not considered to contain a sprite, but are more of a spiritual barrier, containing materials which will nullify malevolent forces and reflect back any psychic attacks upon their sender.

There are several formulae for preparing witch bottles, of which there are two kinds. The larger bottles contain sharp metal objects, such as pins and nails or, less traditionally, razor blades and screws, even broken glass. Along with the sharp objects, it was customary to urinate in the bottle before sealing it and burying it under the doorstep of a house or in the ground outside. The sixteenth and seventeenth century *greybeard* or *Bellarmine* jars found in eastern England, the Low Countries and Germany are made of stoneware, but in modern times, people have been known to use instant coffee jars and the like! Unlike the stoneware, glass jars do not have the protective element of salt, used in the glaze of the pottery vessels. Often used as an alternative to urine is red wine and the herb rosemary (*Rosmarinus officinalis*). Herbally, red wine and rosemary will act as a pain reliever, though very strong doses are poisonous. This is appropriate for a prophylactic against attack. Whatever the filling, the bottle should be corked and sealed with red or black wax.

Thread magic and spirit traps

Spirit traps are made with red thread. 'Rowan tree and red thread gar the witches' speed' celebrates its use. The spirit trap illustrated here is a type used in Britain to deal with psychic disruption attributed to harmful sprites, entities or energies. It is prepared by cutting blackthorn staves of appropriate length and attaching a copper wire loop to them. Around the copper circle, red thread is twined to make a radial pattern, except at the point where the *Dag* rune is. This is made from metal, preferably silver, although I have seen aluminium used. The *Dag* is consecrated in the midday hour, whilst the final sprite trap is assembled at sunrise on the day when it is to be set up.

Once made, the spirit trap is set up by the practitioner using concentration on the function of the trap, and a short ceremony calling on the powers of the trap to entangle,

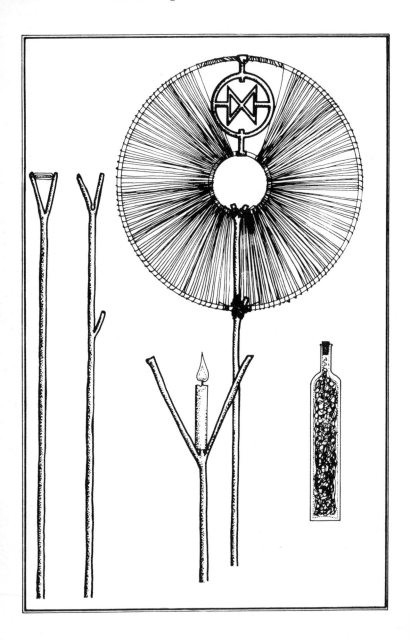

Fig. 35 Spirit traps. *Left to right*: *Pilebogar* with and without crystal (a blown egg or pebble may be used in place of the crystal); thread spirit trap with candle in front; Cambridgeshire witch bottle.

ensnare and entrap these harmful sprites. It is then erected on the pathway or spirit track (perhaps a ley line) which the sprites will take to cause their disruption, for example, between a cemetery and a house, or at the entrance to an abandoned sacred place or any other place where *álfreka* (desecration) has occurred.

At night, a candle, held in the cleft end of a short stave, should be lit in front of the trap. After an appropriate time, the spirit trap is examined, and tested to see whether it has trapped the offending spirit. If the test is positive, then the trap is taken away, and the thread is cut from it and placed in a previously-consecrated spirit bottle, preferably of the Cambridgeshire type (see below). This is then sealed with a cork and red wax, and buried in an appropriate place.

Another version of this magic is the preparation of the so-called *Cambridgeshire witch bottle*. The prepare one, one needs a small bottle, less than six Imperial inches (15cm) long, preferably of blue glass, and a quantity of thread. If possible, the thread should be red, but any other colour, except black, may be used as long as red is predominant. The thread should be cut into small pieces, no longer than a *shafthand* (3.3 Imperial inches) in length, and then each is placed in the bottle separately, saying:

> Thread, tie up this sprite,
> Free us from its spite,
> Tangle up the bane,
> Let not a jiece* remain.
> Ka!

* A small piece

With the final 'Ka!', you must put full concentration into the meaning of the words and act, to give it its full magical force. Once the bottle is full to capacity with tangled threads, it is corked and sealed with red wax. It is then placed in a window, over a door, or, if possible, in a niche in the wall which has been appropriately psychically cleansed, saying this formula:

> In this place
> I put this power,
> To guard my home
> On from this hour.
> Ka!

The niche must then be sealed up and preferably plastered over, so that the presence of the bottle is known only to the person who has put it there. If the bottle is to be buried under a threshhold, then the call

> You will go
> Down Below!
> Ka!

should follow the first formula, as the bottle is located in its resting-place.

Further binding and fetching

Red is *par excellence* the colour of magical protection, as with the red cap. Sacred bushes decked with rags (*rag bushes*) which mark places of power in the landscape, or the *yries* ('Pagan trackway'), are best dressed with red rags, which are considered the luckiest. Gypsy tradition is that at funerals, each mourner should wear 'a scrap of crimson', a red rosette or ribbon, and that the hearse should be decked with red plumes. Red ribbons or woollen threads should be tied to the thorn or rose trees growing on someone's grave, and Gypsy tradition is to bind up the tombstone with plaited ropes of red wool. All of these are precautions against spirits. It is the thread which entraps a spirit, but it is also the thread which may be used to fetch a lost soul trapped in a spirit trap back into its rightful place. The classical labyrinth tale of Ariadne's *clew* (ball of string) in the legend of Theseus and the Minotaur is an example of this.

Glory-twigs are a form of wood magic which involves taking twigs of the appropriate trees for the magic to be performed, and binding them together with thread. If someone looking for stolen property comes across willow twigs with natural in-growth into a knot, then this can be tied up with the call: 'I tie up the thief's luck. Ka!' To undo such a natural knot is to court disaster. In the preparation of twigs to protect against the hostile sprites of the night, red thread is used as a binding. A twig each of ash, oak and thorn are cut at the waxing moon, and are bound together at each end by red thread to make a small faggot which is then placed above the door or window which is felt to be under threat. The faggot may also be carried as a personal protection. It is effective only for one cycle of the moon, and must then be replaced by a new faggot, the old one being buried.

The *thread of many colours* is a sustainer of boundaries and barriers. It is a skein of threads of the seven colours of the rainbow—red, orange, yellow, green, blue, indigo and violet. It is symbolic of *Bifröst*, the *Rainbow Bridge*, which links the lower worlds with the abode of the gods.

The knotted cord

In many religious traditions of the world, a knotted or beaded cord is used as an aid to memory in devotional exercises. These all have their own names but are known commonly by the name of *rosary* from their Christian example. In the Hindu religion, there are the rosaries of Vishnu, with 108 beads, and that of Siva, with 32 or 64 beads. The rosary of the Sikh religion has 108 knots of wool. The standard buddhist rosaries of Burma, China and Tibet each have 108, but the Korean version has 110 (108 plus two larger ones, one marked with a swastika). The Jewish rosary has either 32 or 99 beads. The Muslim rosary has 99 beads and one terminal, whilst the rosary of the Roman Catholic order of friars Dominican has 150, connected to a pendant cross by a string with one large and three small beads. The Coptic Church has a rosary of 61 beads, whilst that of the Eastern Orthodox Church is again different. The Greek Orthodox *Komvoschinion* of Mount Athos has 100 knots, divided by three beads into four equal parts, whilst the Russian Orthodox *vervitsa* has 103 knots or beads. The Wiccan rosary, the *witches' ladder*, has 40 knots or beads.

From this, it is apparent that drastic variations exist between religious traditions, and even within them. Nevertheless, the rosary as a devotional object has an almost universal occurrence. In Anglo-Saxon, the word *bead* meant both a bead and a prayer. The standard cord of the Northern Tradition has nine knots, each of which represents one of the nine worlds. A piece of red cord one ell in length is used, and nine knots tied equidistantly in it, with the formula (tying each knot as each number is said):

By knot of one, it is begun; by knot of two, the power comes through; by knot of three, so must it be; by knot of four, the power will store; by knot of five, the power's alive; by knot of six, the power to fix; by knot of seven, the power to leaven; by knot of eight, ties up the fate; by knot of nine, what's done is mine. Ka!

There are several other variant formulae for tying the nine-knot cord. I have also seen a Northern Tradition rosary with 81 knots, which multiplies the ninefold ninefold.

Strings of objects

Like the knotted cord or the rosary, strings of objects hung in a room have a protective function. In the kitchen, a string of onions hanging up may appear to be merely a functional way of storing them. But the magically protective function of onions is the primary reason for hanging them in that way. Their smell and their many protective layers of skin are both off-putting. They are said to ward off everything from snakes to ill-wishers!

Strings of snail-shells, too, have a magical function, being considered a charm for promoting fertility, prosperity and well-being. The spiral is the basic universal pattern of growth, and a string of spirals repeats the motif both of the spiral and of the knotted cord. In the garden, too, lines of snail-shells are a traditional charm for growth. This practice is enshrined in the nursery rhyme, *Mary, Mary, Quite Contrary*, which tells of 'cockleshells all in a row'.

Step patterns and binding knots

The custom of magically protecting a dwelling with *step patterns* has been reinstated in the last few years after a period of disuse. This reinstatement is partly due to the identical tradition being brought to this country by Hindu immigrants. One unbroken tradition continues at Knutsford in Cheshire, where sand patterns are made in the street during the May celebrations. The patterns include circles, spirals (like the string of snail-shells), interlaced (*tangled thread*) patterns, curved swastikas, *Ing* runes and patterns of dots.

Binding knots are closely related to step patterns, being a means of magically preventing entry or exit of sprites and entities, and psychologically reinforcing the users. The basic pattern involves the sacred grid, but with the corners turned in on themselves to make continuous figures. The sigil known as the *shield-knot* is the simplest binding knot. It is useful as a protection for a doorway, window or a place known to be subject to problems. The most common of the binding knots is the sigil for Samhain, and a group of similar figures from medieval graffiti in churches is illustrated here.

Fig. 36 Step patterns (*top three lines*) and binding knots.

Unlike the sacred grid, which is open to the influences of the external world, binding knots are an enclosure, a full stop to harmful influences. These binding figures are also an entrance to the non-material world. The Norse saga titled *The Tale of Thrond of Gate* describes an instance of wizardcraft in which Thrond calls up the wraiths of two murdered men by making 'a four-cornered lattice work'. This figure is known from surviving historic examples, some earlier and some later than the saga period. A version of this magical diagram exists on an ancient Egyptian vase in the Fitzwilliam Museum in Cambridge and as medieval graffiti in the churches at Little Waltham, Essex, and Barrington and Chippenham in Cambridgeshire.

Sprite flails and besoms

There is a parallel here with the construction of both sprite

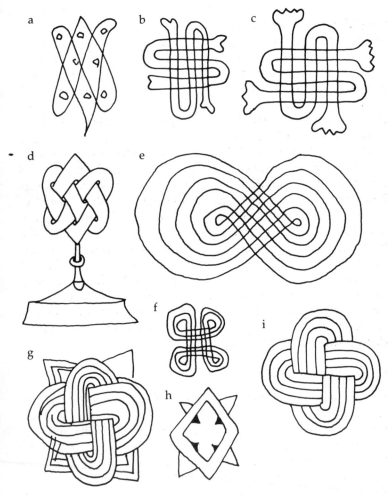

Fig. 37 Binding knots and magic grids. Medieval church *graffiti* from (a) Landwade, Cambridgeshire; (b) and (c) Stoke-by-Clare, Suffolk; (d) Hoxne, Suffolk; (e) and (i) Little Waltham, Essex; (f) Kingston, Cambridgeshire; (g) and (h) Lydgate, Suffolk.

flails and besoms. Both involve a form of 'warlock' magic, binding up the power within the object, which is to be used for the control or suppression of spirits and powers.

The sprite flail is made from nine bramble branches about an ell in length (26.4 Imperial inches, 67.06cm), well covered with thorns, and tied near the base traditionally by willow bark, though latterly string or even wire has been used. Willow bark, collected at *barsel*, the spring collecting time, is recommended. The sprite flail is used in clearing pathways which have not been walked on for a long time, and generally opening access through areas which may be felt to have some sort of on-lay upon them. It is used held in the left hand (outward side), and used in a ninefold sweeping action away from the person, to drive away the unwanted entities.

The traditional *besom* or *witch's broomstick* is made from three woods. The actual broomstick itself is made from ash, to which an array of birch twigs are tied with osier. The birch twigs should be cut at Michaelmas, and, when on the besom, should not be cut. The stick itself can be adorned with red and green ribbons, or painted with a *deiseil* spiral of the colours blue, red, green and yellow (clockwise with the colour sequence from the end of the stick towards the twiggy end). The East Anglian broom-tiers of the past often made the business-end of brooms from ling (heather) but, unlike the birch besoms, the heather was trimmed at the end. The ling was bound to the broomstick by long pliant bonds of split bramble. It is considered unlucky to make a besom during the month of May or the Twelve Days of Yule, and using a besom made of birch twigs or green broom is disastrously unlucky during the month of May.

Sweeping luck

When sweeping a house, it is customary to sweep the dust inwards for luck. Sweeping outwards will sweep out good fortune. Magical sweeping is similar, except that luck is being swept rather than dust. The traditional sweepers for luck are the wings of a goose. The right wing of a goose should be taken in the right hand and swept towards the body, to bring the good luck in, whilst the left wing should be held in the left hand and swept away from the body to sweep away bad luck. The whole motion is therefore *deiseil*. The *Donnerbeson* (thunder broom) is a German version of the goose wing, being a small handled wide brush using goose feathers instead of the bristles on a secular hand brush. This is sacred to the god Thor. An alternative to goose wings is the witches' broom, a twiggy outgrowth on trees often induced by certain types of parasited fungus. These are like small, dense, bushes, and should be cut with the wood-taking ceremony. Sprigs of vervain (*Verbena officinalis*), picked at the moment when Loki's Brand (Sirius) is rising, make a herbal broom with which to sweep sacred places, such as *hofs* and *hörgrs*. Vervain is also efficaceous for magically sweeping ordinary homes.

Protection sachets or pouches

In recent years, the ancient custom of making protective pouches containing herbs, powerful plant parts of other magic objects, has become widespread once more. It is now possible to buy pouches for various purposes, for protection, health, wealth or any of the other human preoccupations. However, as with other ready-made 'magical' objects, it is advisable to make them oneself, for only then are the ingredients and processes truly known.

A standard pouch widely used today is for protection. It involves collecting together equal parts of nine magically powerful ingredients: ash, basil, clover, elderberries, mandrake (or bryony root), rosemary, rue, tarragon and a clove of garlic. A paper with the nine-square pattern containing bind-runes appropriate for the preservative powers sought is made. The pouch itself is made from a square of blue or white cloth nine thumbs square. A ceremonial area is prepared, and a piece of each active ingredient is placed into the square, with the formula:

> Ash, Basil, Clover, Rue,
> Eldern, Tarragon, Rosemary too!
> Mandrake and Garlic,
> Yerbes old and new,
> For preservation,
> I call on you!
> Ka!

The nine-square parchment is put on top of the herbs, and the pouch is tied up with red thread. Thirteen knots, one for each moon of the lunar cycle, are used to tie up the pouch. As the knots are tied, the practitioner says: 'I bind thee to preserve [*name*]. May the virtues in this pouch preserve and guard the cause which I intend for all who surround it. Ka!'

If you are making a pouch for yourself, then this forumla is used:

By the power of three times three,
This pouch is bound to protect me.
Ka!

Incenses

Most religions and magical paths use some form of incense, and the Northern Tradition is no exception. Many different sorts of incense are available commercially from occult and ecclesiastical suppliers, but many of these are composed of materials which are not always appropriate for Northern Tradition ceremonies. Frankincense, which is a purifier and protector; jasmine, for intuition, sandalwood, for heightened consciousness; and myrrh for healing and purification, are commonly used magical incenses. There are, however, a number of traditional incenses which use plants indigenous to northern Europe, or introduced many centuries ago and cultivated here ever since. These can be made at home from readily available herbs. Some incenses are composed of the dried leaves, seeds or resin of single plants, whilst others are more complex concoctions, sacred to specific deities or times. They enhance the mood of a ceremony, and magically call down appropriate qualities into it. Incenses should be burnt on a block of charcoal, or in a specially made censer, preferably of pottery in a traditional style. Naturally, incenses are to be burned in relatively small quantities away from the immediate vicinity of people, and are not intended to be smoked or inhaled directly. If this is done, harmful effects are certain. In addition to the traditional names the plants' scientific names are given because some of them have close plant relations with the same name which are potentially harmful.

The commonest single-plant incenses are:

Honeysuckle (*Lonicera periclymenum*): a plant used in house-protection, brings a protective psychic atmosphere for a runic working.

Mugwort (*Artemisia vulgaris*): for clairvoyance and dreams, visions.

Rosemary (*Rosmarinus officinalis*): a protector and purifier, healing and bringing a sense of well-being.

The following are traditional incenses, but their use is not recommended as they may be toxic when inhaled:

Mistletoe (*Viscum album*): was a Druidic incense.

Yew (*Taxus baccata*) resin: a shamanistic incense, communing with the elements of winter and darkness.

More complex incenses include:

EOSTRE (SPRING) INCENSE
1 part sweet marjoram (*Origanum majorana*)
1 part thyme (*Thymus vulgaris*)

MANI (LUNAR) INCENSE
5 parts apple blossom
5 parts lavender
1 part white rose oil
(This should be made on a Monday at a runic hour appropriate to Mani. It is mixed into spherical pills and allowed to dry completely before use.)

FREYR INCENSE
Equal parts of:
Garden mint (*Mentha* × spp.)
Spearmint (*Mentha spicata*)
Sage (*Salvia officinalis*)
Bay laurel (*Laurus nobilis*)
Sorrel (*Oxalis acetosella*)
Vervain (*Verbena officinalis*)

ODIN INCENSE
4 parts gum mastic
3 parts lavender (*Lavandula angustifolia*)
3 parts valerian (*Valeriana officinalis*)
2 parts hyssop (*Hyssopus officinalis*)
4 parts wormwood (*Artemisia absinthum*)
(These should be mixed together on a Wednesday in a runic hour appropriate to Odin.)

PROTECTIVE INCENSE
An incense for protection, which mixes traditional herbal materials with more cosmopolitan elements and consists of:
1 part basil (*Ocimium basilicum*)
2 parts frankincense
2 parts myrrh
2 parts pine (*Pinus* spp.) resin (or deal apple, ground up)
1 part sage (*Salvia officinalis*)

V

Protective Techniques and Objects

Courage, Truth and Honour; Fidelity, Discipline and Hospitality;
Industriousness, Self-Reliance and Perseverance.
The Nine Noble Virtues

Talismans and Amulets

The basic function of protective magic is to ward off harm of
all kinds as far as is possible. Of course, any magical steps
taken must be in addition to normal precautions that any sen-
sible person takes. It is no use covering a car with protective
sigils and then driving it carelessly, for example. Protective
talismans, amulets, sigils and sacred objects have various appropriate functions, and have been used by human beings
since the end of the last Ice Age if not before. They can range
in size from that of a small coin to a flagpole or even a whole
building, and are designed and constructed according to
mystic principles.

A talisman is an object which has been charged with *önd* by
means of a ceremonial consecration. It is dedicated to a
specific purpose by the agency of the inscription upon it and
the magical formulæ performed during the consecration.
Having a function and purpose known to the owner or
wearer, the talisman exerts a psychological or autosuggestive
effect on her or him, evoking innate but untapped powers
within the wearer. An amulet is a charm, which may or may
not have been consecrated, but which, through its form, exerts a protective or *Megin*-enhancing capability. Generally,
amulets are protective in function, either against specific
classes of harm, such as illness, attack or bad luck, or against
evil spirits and entities such as *black weasels* and *meinvættir*.

The materials of which talismans can be made have been

discussed in Chapter 2. It is essential that appropriate materials be used to enhance the talisman's qualities rather than creating an inner conflict. When deciding on the use of a talisman, the material chosen for it must be appropriate. If Mani (the moon) rules the area dealt with by the talisman, then silver is the proper metal to use, not copper or aluminium. When making the talisman, the metal, wood or stone must be matched with a corresponding sigil. Sigils are written, drawn, carved, painted or printed alphabetic or pictographic characters, which encapsulate within them the quality of a specific idea or power. Sigils are the means by which the talisman is charged, drawing into it the force which it is intended to represent. These are frequently inscribed upon talismans and amulets during their construction, but they may also be used by themselves as a mark on a tool, a vehicle or a building to protect them and enhance their power in some way. Talismans made by one person for another are less powerful and effective than those made for oneself.

Talismans can take many forms, but those worn on the person tend to be rings, bracelets, necklets, pendants and lockets. Rings, bracelets and necklets should bear appropriate runes and/or sigils on the outside as a protection and on the inside as secret knowledge and power. A pendant can be an image of a deity, a medallion bearing an image or sigil, or a physical representation, such as a solar disc or Hammer of Thor. A *Bulla* or traditional sacred locket is a circular container which is worn on a string or chain around the neck, or kept in a pouch when it is not possible to wear it. It is convex on each side, and comes apart so that it will take a consecrated object or lucky charm. It generally contains a piece of stone, bone or other sacred object which the wearer considers is of importance to him or her. Either the object inside, or the *bulla* itself, should be inscribed with appropriate runes or sigils.

Runic inscriptions on talismans

The construction of one's own talismans requires a considerable understanding of the symbolic and runic magic of the North. No one should try to make a talisman without a good working knowledge of the principles and philosophy underlying them. With a magical system as potent as the runes, a mistake can be disastrous. However, so long as basic principles are well understood and applied carefully, the outcome should be successful. For example, when you want to select an appropriate rune for protection, you should consider just what it is you want to do. What is the nature of the thing or person being protected? Do you want to ward off bad luck, or attract good luck? Do you wish the nature of the warding to be one of invisibility, so that nobody notices it, and walks past? Or one of defence, where people notice it and shy away, as if from a fierce dog? These and similar considerations should be meditated upon.

Writers on ancient skills and wisdom often assume that everyone in the past who practised magic was a skilled adept. Like today, when in every profession there are skilled practitioners and incompetent people, so in former times, not every 'wise person' was highly skilled, and some were com-

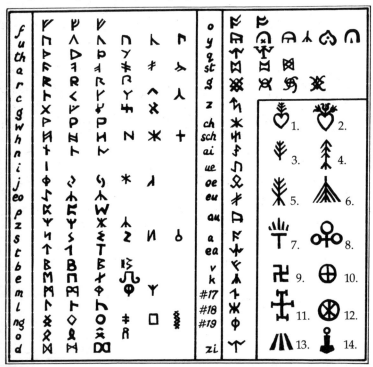

Fig. 38 Alternative versions of the runes, from Germany, Scandinavia and England. (1) and (2) *Mother Earth* sigils; (3) Tree of Life; (4) Tree of upward growth, with three roots; (5) Yggdrassil, with its three roots; (6) Autumnal tree; (7) Thunderbroom; (8) Three-leafed clover; (9) Fylfot (swastika); (10) Sunwheel; (11) Runic cross; (12) *Hagal* in circle; (13) Awen; (14) Thor's Hammer.

plete bunglers. This is especially true of the time when such knowledge was suppressed deliberately, and practitioners were few and far between, with little formal training. Even in the days before wholesale persecution, the old Norse account of the runemaster Egill tells of an unskilled person with a little knowledge who tried unsuccessfully to cure a woman suffering with a fever. Called to the bedside, Egill found a whalebone sliver on which 10 incorrect runes were scored. Removing it, he applied the correct formula for the cure, with the dismissive statement: 'A man should not score runes unless he can read them properly, because many a man has fallen down on an unclear runestave. I saw ten staves cut on a scraped whale-bone, which prolonged an over-long sickness.'

The runes are a magically potent means of protection and assistance. Each rune is in resonance with the aspect of *önd* which it represents, and when two or more are joined together by the agency of the human will, then that combined power will be present. Runic words of power come from several sources. Of course the names of deities carry their own special potency, Odin, Frigg, Freyr, Freyja, Balder, Hlín, Bragi etc., each invoke their appropriate power in the wearer of a ring or talisman. *Ansur*, the gods in general, or *Asyniur*, the goddesses, make powerful invocations. The names of practitioners of the Northern Tradition are also words of power:

Erilaz, runemaster

Gothi, minister, priest

Vitki, magus, wizard, runemaster

Qualities, too, make fine inscriptions. The main traditional ones are:

Alag, on-lay

Asatru, faith in the gods

Auja, good luck

Framsynn, far-sighted

Gybu auja, give (bring) good luck

Gina, charged with sacred potency

Hailagaz, full of sacred potency

Hamingja, mutable magic energy

Lathu, a summons, invocation

Mattr, personal beneficial force

Megin, personal magic power for good fortune

Ofreskr, second-sighted

Odhroerir, the mead of inspiration

Önd, the vital breath or universal soul

Ørlög, fate, destiny

Rammaukinn, possessed by superhuman strength

Salu, sun-kissed, health

Ungandiz, unaffected by magical attack

Wihaz, sanctified

Wihyan, to sanctify

Wodiz, inspired frenzy.

Human and divine artifacts of power also produce traditional runic protection:

Alu, ale, the primal water of the gods, ecstacy and divine guardianship

Medu, mead, inspiration, transformation

Gandr, wand, and the power emanating from a wand

Gar, the ash-shafted spear of Odin

Mjöllnir, Thor's hammer for divine protection against the forces of disorder

Ve, the power of the sacred enclosure

The power of natural things:

Ac, oak tree, the potency of Thor's sacred tree

Æsc, ash tree, stability

Aurgelmir, the Primal Being

Bar, bear, the power of a show of strength as the best means of defence

Ehwe, horse, transmission

Hjolgaddsringr, the Wheel-nail-ring, the Artic Circle

Hrafn, raven, intelligence and knowledge

Iorth, the Earth

Laukaz, leek, the power of irresistable growth

Lina, flax, fertility, the sacred plant of the goddess Frigg

Stan, stone, the power of blocking

Svin, wild boar, formidable opposition

Ulf, wolf, active protection

Yggdrassil, the World Ash tree, eternal stability, reliability

Ymir, the Primal Being

Often these words of power are made up into word formulae, using the combined power of runes, as a means of invoking the power represented by the runes into oneself. They may be written as *bind-runes*, where two or more staves are combined together. Often bind-runes create further runic shapes, so their use should be monitored carefully to avoid unwanted runic input. The runes themselves are shown in Fig. 38.

A new talisman to deal with a specific problem can be produced by creating bind-runes. A bind-rune is a sigil composed of a series of runes superimposed upon one another in the manner of a personal monogram. Unlike most monograms, however, by their nature bind-runes create new runic forms within themselves, giving the sigil additional power. The skill in making bind-runes is to create a form which contains *only* the runes needed for the desired effect. Usually, bind-runes are made up from a series of runes spelling a sacred name or a word of power, but they can also incorporate sigils such as the Tree of Life and other northern pictograms.

Sigils and symbols as talismans

In the Northern Tradition, there is also a series of sacred symbols which are appropriate for use as protective talismans. The most important ones are as follows.

The valknut is composed of three interlinked equilateral triangles. The nine lines symbolize the nine worlds of the Norse tradition, the power of three times three. Specifically, it is a symbol of Odin, and is sometimes used with an eye at the centre. As a protector, it invokes the power of eternal unity. Its name means *the knot of the fallen* (or *chosen*) *ones*.

The triskele or *trefot* is a version of the *valknut*, being composed of the six lines at its centre. It is composed of three *Lagu* runes, signifying magical inspiration. As a heraldic device, three armoured legs, it is the sign of the Isle of Man.

The triple circle is composed of three interlinking circles. Like the *valknut*, it signifies the interlinking of the three forces or

Fig. 39 The valknut (*top*), triskele and triple circle.

states which rule the universe: space, matter and energy; body, mind and spirit, etc.

The three-leafed clover is an allied version of the triple circle.

The Awen is a Druidic sigil, composed of three radiating lines, sometimes within an equilateral triangle. This symbolizes the divine, generative power and its triadic manifestation. It is closely allied to the *Eolh* rune.

Eolh — This rune is a sigil of the protective power of the elk, a formidable beast, but also, in its *Awen* aspect, it is a symbol of healing and the Pagan equivalent of the Red Cross and Red Crescent.

Fig. 40 *Top left*: the 'farmer's fylfot.' *Top right*: eight-mark. *Bottom left*: fylfot from medieval English church bell. *Bottom right*: Fionn's Wheel, Ogham protective shield.

The Gammadion, otherwise known by its Sanscrit name *swastika*, or its Old English name, fylfot, symbolizes solar power, the dynamic energy of Thor's Hammer, magical force directed by the will. Like the *Triskele*, it has two forms, left and right-handed, which are considered male (outgoing) and female (ingathering) respectively.

The 'Farmers Fylfot' is a version of the *swastika*, being composed of a swirling, four-armed, continuous line enclosing five dots of a nine-dot pattern. This is the male sigil whose construction is based on the classical labyrinth's basic pattern. It symbolizes the male, godly force immanent within the goddess's female form.

The sun-wheel is a circle divided into four by an equal-armed cross. It is a pictographic version of the rune *Rad*, and signifies the solar power, manifested as santification, enclosed and controlled sacred power. It is sometimes called the Celtic cross, for the Celtic Church, many of whose priests were former Druids, assimilated it and extended its arms.

The spiral is a symbol of the forces and patterns which underly all growth. Talismanically, it brings the wearer into harmony with the universal *önd*.

The fire wheel is composed of multiple spirals radiating from a central point, multiplying the power of the spiral eightfold.

The Gar rune, the runic form of a square set on edge, intersected by an equal armed-cross, is a symbol of stability, the spear of Odin.

The runic cross is a sigil which looks like three letter 'H's superimposed on a vertical central line. This is a symbol of the three divisions of the Cosmic Axis, with the central, *Middle Earth*, one larger than the other two. Being an invocation of the earthly powers, the runic cross is a protection against the demonic empire in all of its forms—ghosts, demons, evil spirits, etc.

The grid of nine is a square divided into nine smaller, equal squares. Inside each of these squares, which symbolize the seven astrological planets and the lunar nodes, appropriate sigils or runes can be inscribed.

Fig. 41 *Ing* grid, consecration cross and *scutcheon*, (from Beauchamp Chapel, Warwick, *c.*1460.)

The grid of eighty-one is a ninefold version of the grid of nine.

The Ing rune takes several versions. It can be the simple 'diamond' shape; the full *Ing* with extensions, or expanded versions of this, such as the *Ing grid* and *God's Nail*.

The Ing grid is a development of the rune *Ing*, which signifies universal expansion and protection. The grid is formed of two squares superimposed over the *Ing* rune, and subdivided into 50 squares in all. This sigil invokes the power of dynamic balance between two interchangeable states, resisting attack by both direct and devious means.

God's Nail is the *Ing* rune, in the centre of which is an eight-petalled flower representing the sun standing due north at midnight at midsummer north of the Artic Circle, a time when the power of the Pole Star (the Nail) and the sun are in alignment.

Hagal is a six-pointed rune, sometimes shown in folk-art as a six-pointed star, but not the same as the two interpenetrating equilateral triangles known as the Star of David. It is the formative structure of matter, the three axes of the three dimensions, x, y and z, the power of magical protection working through the underlying laws of physics.

The Lucky Star is a version of *Hagal*, being drawn with a pair of compasses inside a circle. It is the basis of triangular geometry, the *ad triangulum* of medieval masonry, and is a powerful house-protector, once very popular in the timber-framed architecture of Germany, still prevalent in Westphalia and in North America in Pennsylvania Dutch buildings as the *hex* sign.

The Heavenly Star is an eight-branched figure which signifies the eight *Airts* of the horizon, the eight legs of Sleipnir, steed of Odin, and the eight winds. It is a symbol of balance and right orderliness.

The Eight-Mark is a version of the Heavenly Star, being a circle at the centre of eight radiating lines, each of which end in a circle. This symbol can be found on early medieval grave slabs and standing stone crosses in the north of England. It is an appropriate sigil to mark a nowl-stone (*omphalos*) or any central mark-point in the landscape.

The Ægishjalmur is an even more elaborate version of the heavenly star, but is much more powerful, symbolizing the force of irresistibility, being the power of a whole collection of runes projected outwards from the centre, which they protect.

The classical labyrinth, either in its seven-ring or 11-ring variants, is a symbol of the generative principle, outgiving and ingathering, wholeness and return. It is a powerful binding sigil against harmful psychic forces.

Fig. 42 *Top left*: Ægishjalmur, symbol of irresistibility. *Top right*: Heavenly Star. *Bottom left*: Ægishjalmur crest of Sir John De Warenne, 1329. *Bottom right*: medieval eight-mark cross from Gilling West, Durham.

Mjöllnir, the Hammer of Thor, takes several forms, ranging from an inverted letter 'T' to a full representation of the hammer, complete with its ring. It is a sign of consecration and the exercise of the conscious will in doing so.

The thunderbroom is another version of the Hammer of Thor, in the form of a broom. It represents the goose-feather brush used to brush away bad luck and evil on-lays. As a worn talisman, it cleanses away all harm.

The double axe, sometimes known by its southern European name of *labrys*, is a physical manifestation of the rune *Hagal*. It invokes the power of the Norse god Forseti (the Celtic Esus).

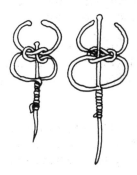

Fig. 43 Wire Caduceus charms from holy spring at Finthen, Mainz, Germany, 1st century CD.

The caduceus is the sigil of the southern European deity Hermes/Mercury, identified in the North as an aspect of Odin. This, wound from wire, was a popular offering to sacred springs in Germany, and can be made readily as a protector of water sources.

The heart is a symbol of the mother-goddess, representing the pubic area. It is still the prime symbol of love, and a love talisman of great power.

The triple mountain takes several forms. It is often seen in the form of three inverted 'U's, with the largest in the centre. In central European heraldry, the triple mountain sometimes bears embedded swords or trees. It signifies the triadic nature of things, with the central process—the *Now*—as the major factor. So as a protector, this sigil invokes triumphant resistance, overcoming adversity.

The Tree of Life is a single stem bearing six straight side-branches. It is a powerfully protective sigil, symbolizing the generative power of nature in its resistance against destruction. It is closely allied to the thunderbroom.

The World Ash Tree — This is depicted as a Tree of Life growing from a vessel which symbolizes the holy well of wisdom.

As a talisman, it promotes spiritual and intellectual growth.

The serpent — Either as a snake biting its own tail, or as a looping figure, the serpent symbolizes magical containment and the power of the unconscious.

The sun — Images of the solar disc, with or without a face and 16 radiating rays, invoke the blessing of our solar system's power source, smooth progress according to right orderliness.

The lunar crescent — Depending on the direction it is facing, the lunar crescent can signify the waxing or the waning power of Mani, bringing ordered, sequential change according to natural law.

The horn is allied to the lunar crescent, but also signifies the draught of inspiration, bringer of plenty through the application of skills.

The raven is the sacred bird of Odin, signifying rapid thought and the application of memory. Its magical use is in outwitting opponents and gaining advantage through the application of superior skill and knowledge.

Fig. 44 Dragons and *God's Nail* as door protection on a medieval house at Hitchin, Hertfordshire.

The cock is a symbol of alert watchfulness, and brings these qualities to its talismanic form. As *cock's-head hinges*, it provides protection for a door or a piece of furniture. In former times, it was a popular form of hinge in traditional cabinet-making.

The horse is one of the sacred animals of the Elder Faith. It is a talisman of transformation, defence and communion with the gods. Images of horses are amongst the largest talismans in existence, being carved upon hillsides, mainly in southern England, as geomantic protectors of the landscape.

The dragon is connected with the Earth, representing the serpentine energies within it. Carved on buildings, the dragon protects the roof and doors from malevolent powers of the air.

The stag is shown with a sunwheel between its antlers. This form is known as far back as Romano-Celtic times. It invokes the power of the wild wood and the sun as protection against all evil.

Images

Images of deities and semi-divine beings exist in every religion. Over time, with changing opinions and fashions, images have sometimes been favoured, sometimes destroyed in fits of iconoclasm. Iconoclasts misunderstand the function of images, believing them and not that which they represent to be the objects of worship. In northern Europe, this problem was compounded with the arrival of beliefs which had little room for alternatives. Because of this, only a relatively small number of Northern Tradition images survive from former times. Most of the large images of the gods, kept in *hofs* and *Hørgrs*, were destroyed when the shrines were overthrown, but often the smaller, portable, images were concealed from the destroyers. A few large wooden images survive, such as that of the *Hooded Man* found near Geneva and now in the Landesmuseum in Zürich. This has been dated by tree-ring chronology to C.80 BC. Other images of the gods still exist in profusion inside churches as carvings in stone and wood. Although worship was forbidden at sites other than churches, adherents of the Elder Faith bent the rules by incorporating sacred images *in* them! One at Great Canfield, Essex, is particularly notable, with its image of Woden complete with attendant ravens and swastikas.

Small images

A small image of a deity which can be carried about as a talisman is known as a *hlutr*. This can take the form of a medallion showing the deity, rather like the popular talismans showing the ex-saint Christopher, or can be a small image in-the-round. Examples of these can be seen in most of the major museum collections in northern Europe.

Alrauns

An offshoot of mandrake lore is the practice of carving certain herbal roots into human form as talismans. In the Middle Ages, it was customary to plant grains of barley in the carved roots in the places where hair or a beard should be. The object was then buried in sand for three weeks, and dug up, by which time the grains had sprouted. The shoots were then shaped into the head of hair or beard of the mannekin. Such a talisman is known as an *erdmannekin* or *alraun*, a word cognate with *rune*, redolent of magic secrets.

These are supposed to represent members of a magical tribe or order, alluded to by Tacitus as the *Aurinia*, or the 'loose-haired, bare-legged witches who would slay a man, drink his blood from a skull and divine the future from his mangled remains' of Aventinus. The tribe of magicians known as the *Alyruninæ*, said to have interbred with wood-spirits, were believed in medieval times to be the ancestors of the Huns. In eighteenth-century Germany, certain witches were known as *Alrune*, who claimed their name was that of the goddess of the crossroads. The *alraun* itself was made by a wise woman or white witch known as an *alrune maiden*.

Carved *alrauns* had to be treated with the greatest care and reverence. They were wrapped in a white cloth, or folded in silk. They were kept in a box, and bathed every Friday, the day sacred to the goddesses Frigg and Freyja, of whom the goddess of the crossroads is an aspect. If these rites were omitted for some reason, then the *Alraun* was said to shriek its disapproval.

Ownership of an *alraun*, however, was always considered to have its dangerous side. Unless it could be sold for more

Fig. 45 Alrauns with runic inscriptions.

than it cost to buy, it would remain in the owner's hands, and would henceforth bring bad luck upon the owner. Places where people tried to get rid of their *Alraun* acquired an on-lay which was potent for many years afterwards. For many years, a house in Frankfurt, Germany, stood empty, because it had been the home of a baker-woman who had tried in vain, to abandon her *Alraun*, and who had died horribly as a result, leaving a psychic on-lay which made it impossible for anyone else to live there. In Lower Württemberg, a haunted spot was formerly pointed out to passers-by as a place where a merchant from Ulm had tried to dispose of his *alraun* in vain, leaving an on-lay at the place and suffering personal misfortune as a result. Stories tell of how people wishing to rid themself of an *alraun* would throw it into a river, only to find it waiting for them at home when they returned. The *alraun* was the family's protector, and so had to be tended carefully and respected, for, if neglected, misfortune would befall everyone. In old German law of inheritance, an *alraun* passed to the deceased's youngest son, on condition that he buried a piece of bread and a gold coin in the coffin with his father.

Alrauns have many uses. In the past, they were both helpers during childbirth, and the bringers of rejuvenation. In the Alps, *alrauns* provided a protection against the effects of bad weather, and, when laid on the bed, could prevent the sleeper suffering from nightmares. In the Tyrol, they were used for the divination of hidden treasure. The spirit present in them was sometimes trapped within a glass bottle, where it could be kept out of harm's way. One such object was kept until the early part of the nineteenth century in the cloister of a Capuchin monastery in Vienna.

Alrauns are a specialized sort of talisman, constructed according to esoteric principles and consecrated. When handled properly, they worked according to their makers' intention. But, when handled by those without the proper knowledge, they proved at best a nuisance and at worst positively dangerous. In some sense, this applies to any talisman, but if you make your own, then you will have control over 'what goes in' and consequently 'what comes out'.

Preparation of Protective Talismans

Making talismans is a straightforward procedure. Talismans of a constructive and protective nature should be made during the waxing moon, and, if possible, at a runic hour which corresponds most closely to their desired effect. First, consecrate the area where the work is to be carried out. This need only be the erection of a temporary psychic barrier, as described below, using salt, water, fire and incense. Then the materials of the talisman are worked upon. These should have been prepared beforehand, and the inscriptions or design already worked out. If the talisman is to be made of wood, stone or metal, then the runes and sigils are engraved using a *ristir*. This engraving tool will have been made ceremonially some time earlier. As the runes are carved, you should call their names, and visualize their quality entering the work from the corresponding part of the runic circle which surrounds you. When this is done, the sign of the hammer should be made over the talisman, with an appropriate runic call. Now, the talisman is enclosed in darkness, perhaps wrapped in black cloth or placed in a box. Then, a call such as the following can be made, whilst the cloth or container is rotated nine times, *diesal*:

In the name of Odin, Balder, Frey and Thor.
And by the might of earth, wind, water, ice and fire,
Ward off all harmful evil sprites,
The ill-natured demons,
The fiends who injure our bodies,
Who sap our strength,
Who blight our lives,
Who attempt to destroy us.
Ward off the ill-fortune of bad spirits,
The awesome giants,
The fearful trolls,
The mischievous yarthkins,
Envious humans,
Bad omens, injurious portents,
Unwanted on-lays and laid air,
And the ministrations of malignant entities.
May we be freed from all kinds of injury,
And instead be favoured with those real gifts
Which we seek.
In accordance with eternal Law.
Ka.

Then you should bring back the talisman into the light of day. This is its symbolic birth, when it is hailed as new-born. Then the talisman is named. Naming consecrated objects has a venerable tradition. Historic examples of named swords include Excalibur, Mistletoe, Head, Tyrfing and Skrep. Sacred Raven Banners were Ravenlandeye and Land-Waster. Many other tools and talismans also had their own names. This principle is recognized even by the most secularized; everything from rock musicians' guitars to ships, aircraft and locomotives are named. British Rail even have a diesel called *Odin*!

To name the talisman, first you should pass it over a candle or a fire-brazier (*glódhker*) three times, calling upon the powers of light and life to bring its qualities to their full strength. Then, to name it, scatter water over the talisman with a formula like:

I sprinkle water over thee
And name thee [*name*],
By the might of water, wind, earth, fire and ice.
Ka!

The final consecration involves infusing the talisman magically with the power to carry out its task. You should create a call especially for each talisman you make. It should declaim the special function and use of the talisman, for example:

> [*Name*], bearer of my will,
> I charge you to do as commanded,
> For the purpose of [*say what it will do and where it will do it*]
> May the talisman work my will
> In accordance with eternal law
> Ka!

Then three interlinked circles—the triple circle—are visualized on and around the talisman. If this is to be placed in a building, three circles can be chalked on it, or carved where they are not visible. This sigil can be found, concealed, on the roof-beams and brickwork of many old buildings, evidence of our forebears' magic. Finally the enclosure should be psychically closed down, and the ceremony ended with something like:

> Now is the work concluded,
> In which [*name of talisman*]
> Was brought out of the unformed world
> Into the world of manifestation.
> In the name of the gods,
> Ka!

Now, the talisman is ready for use, fully empowered.

Purification and Consecration

Any object or place which has been consecrated properly possesses a spiritual essence, a concentrated, formed part of the universal *önd*. In the consecration of a place, or in its protection against harmful forces, several parts of the enclosure require protection. The principle behind this is one of removing or neutralizing any forces present by means of an exorcism, then filling the void created by the power of an invocation or blessing. A most basic consecration is the utterance of sacred names of power which in themselves have the quality of altering a place. A common Northern Tradition opening is: 'In the names of Odin, Balder, Frey and Thor...' followed by an appropriate statement. Where a new character is created magically at a place, this is known as *álag*, an on-lay, which has a character stemming from the will of the magician who has laid it down there. Sacred objects placed at strategic points around the perimeter of the area act as sustainers of this power, being located at places where additional protection is needed. The interaction between the place, the ritual and the object consecrated in the ritual maintains the new sanctity. In order to sustain this, however, ceremonies must be performed periodically in the newly-consecrated place, or the power will drain away gradually. This is why the service of Holy Communion is held at least annually even in almost disused churches.

A sacred area is cleansed of unwanted influences and on-lays by an initial purification, using water which has been consecrated. The water, taken from a local holy well, should be about one pint in volume. Consecration of the holy water is accomplished by charging it by means of the directed will. Placing the forefinger of the right hand into the water, you should visualize a flow of *önd* as a stream of vibrant, blue-white light, coming from the body into the water. Here is a suggested formula to say during this process:

In the names of Odin, Balder, Frey and Thor,
Into this water
I direct my might,
That it will be pure and clean,
In the service of the gods.
Ka!

Then, when you feel that the water is charged, enough crystalline sea salt to cover a circle one thumb in diameter is poured in. Then it is stirred nine times *deisal* with the forefinger, with the call:

Here is salt,
Salt is life,
To clean this place,
Free from strife.

The water is sprinkled using the fingers, or with a sprig of hyssop, *diesal* around the area to be cleansed. As the sprinkling takes place, a song which enhances the cleansing can be sung. When all of the water is used up, incense should be burned at the centre of the area, and a protective shield visualized around it, excluding unwanted powers, but welcoming and encouraging those which *are* wanted there. Once the cleansing has been performed, an invocation should be made. This calls into the place an on-lay of the power which is needed. If the place is to be a place of worship, then the *genius loci* should be recognized there. Any object placed with conscious care and ceremony will retain a charge received at that time. So as well as the actual ceremony, the actual time of a consecration is important. To get the best results, a ceremonial cleansing and consecration should be done at a runic hour corresponding with the work that is to be done there.

In all nature religions, the sun is a vital element. *Önd* is seen to flow from the sun through the earthly plane, and for this reason, ceremonial sites, including traditionally-designed churches, are orientated. Meyryg of Glamorgan, a medieval Welsh Bard, stated that the *Gorsedd* or Bardic assembly should be held 'in the face of the sun and in the eye of the light: it being unlawful to hold such meetings under cover, at night, or under any circumstances otherwise than while the sun shall be visible in the sky'. Inside a sacred building, the sun's position should be apparent, and we find windows, doors, light-funnels and squints strategically placed to enable the sunlight to penetrate at the correct hour.

Whenever a ceremony is to be held out of doors, the area where it is to take place should be chosen carefully so that the optimal flow of *önd* is available there. The area should be laid out properly and cleansed both physically and psychically before any ceremony is conducted. When an area is being prepared for a ceremony, orientation, either by the sun or with a compass, should be the first consideration after the place itself is chosen. Ceremonies associated with the gods should be conducted facing northwards, and those concerned with the Earth in a southerly direction. Ceremonies to promote fertility and growth are east-facing, and those of death, in the western and north-western *airts*. Once north and south are determined, then the meridional line should be marked on the ground with wooden pegs and string. Blackthorn or hawthorn are recommended for layout pegs, used with a red cord. Then the knotted cord should be measured ceremonially with the *mete-wand*, to verify that the knotting accurately measures northern feet, ells, or whatever the ancient and accepted measure the cord is intended to use. Two flags or banners should then be set up, marking the line at right angles in front of the operative, meridional axis. These form two of the four corners of the mystic plot, which (if there is enough space), should measure one rod (15 northern feet, 5.0292 m). The square should be laid out from this, and the other two corners marked with appropriate hazel staves. Then, formulaic calls are made, cleansing and setting aside space and time for the ceremony to have the desired effect. These are followed by four libations, made *deisal* at the centre of each side of the square, facing the cardinal directions.

Protection of land and buildings

There are ceremonial means of protecting land and buildings. These use a version of consecration magic which sets up a barrier round the place, with local reinforcement at entrance-points and similar weak areas through which harmful forces may enter.

The *Four Holes* ceremony is a rite for the consecration of a plot of land so that it is fertile and unaffected by harmful influences. It is an especially appropriate land-remedy for gardens and farmland, based upon the oldest recorded English traditions. On the 'eve' ('at night, before dawn') of the day of consecration, four sods or divots of earth are taken from the four sides of the land. Sometimes they are from the four corners of a field, but, wherever they are taken from, their positions and identity are noted. Then the sods are treated with milk, honey, yeast, vegetable oil, and appropriate parts of trees and herbs, with the formula:

Grow and multiply and replenish the Earth
In the name of Frey and Freyja.
Ka!

The sods are then taken to a consecrated place, where an observance is made over them; then, before sunset, they are brought back to where they started. Aspen slivers with runes for growth and plenteousness are inserted in the holes from which the divots were taken, and the sods replaced, beginning at the south side and going *deisal* around the plot. At each hole, the formula above is recited nine times as it is done. When all four are replaced, the practitioner is on the east side of the plot. He or she bows nine times towards the east, the direction of the growing light, springtime, and the 'goddess' rune *Beorc*, and says:

Eastward I stand,
I pray to great Frey and Freyja,
The might of Vanaheim and the lofty Halls of Asgard,
That I call this charm
By their power;
Raise crops for worldly use,
Make beautiful these meadows.
Ka!

Then three sunwise turns are made, intoning the runes *Beorc* and *Lagu*. Seed is then taken, and placed with the implements which are to be used to sow it. Consecrated water, fennel seeds and soap are put along with the seed, and grain incense should be burned. The following formula follows:

Erce, Erce, Erce, mother of Earth,
May Allfather, the mighty, grant thee
Fields growing and flourishing,
Fruitful and reviving,
Store of gleaming harvests,
And broad barley-crops,
And white wheat crops,
And all the crops of the Earth.
May this land be kept safe from all foes,
And may it be guarded against all evils,
May no woman be eloquent enough,
Nor any man powerful enough,
To pervert these words thus pronounced.
Ka!

Then, the surface of the field is broken for the sowing, with the call:

Hail to thee, Earth, mother of all people!
Be fruitful, filled with food for our use! Ka!

Then, last year's corn dolly should be ploughed into a cornfield, or last year's vegetable token buried in a vegetable patch.
Finally, when sowing has finished:

Field full of food for mankind,
Brightly blooming, be thou blessed,
In the holy names of Frey and Freyja
And this Earth on which we live.
May we be granted growing gifts,
So that every kind of plant may prove of use. Ka!

Sacred space

The *Four Holes Ceremony* is the consecration of a place to promote its natural qualities. Sacred enclosures, however, are called upon to accomplish more than this, to become channelling-points for the communion between human beings and the divine. Sacred enclosures can take various shapes. The best-known is the *magic circle*, whose consecrated boundary excludes psychic influences. This can be truly circular in a geometrical sense, or, like many ancient stone circles, be laid out according to subtle and complex geometries. But in addition to the magic circle, there are several other traditional shapes for enclosing sacred space. In

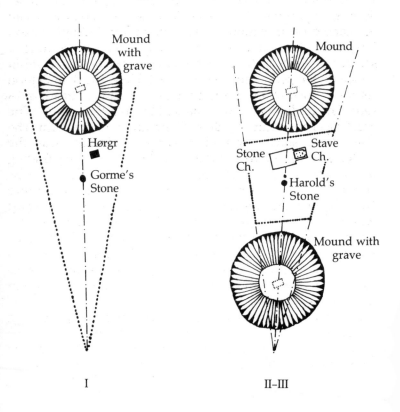

Fig. 46 The vé at Jelling, Denmark, (I) in Pagan times (II–III) after a church was built on the site of the Hørgr.

the Northern Tradition, the *mystic plot* is square, whether it be the small square for *útiseta* or the larger, rod-sized gridded plot. This should be orientated to the four quarters, i.e. with each side facing a cardinal direction. Also, there is the *Vé*, which, as its name suggests, is shaped like the letter V. This should be orientated with its open end to the north, with the vertex at the south.

Whatever its shape, sacred space is a piece of ground which has been set off from the everyday world, enlosed by some means, cleansed of unwanted psychic and physical energies, and then infused with sacred power by means of ritual. Ideally, the site should be chosen so that the powers or energies present there enhance the intended use of the sacred place. The techniques of geolocation and general geomantic practices are required for this. Once delimited, sacred ground can be marked off in various ways. The *frithsplot* (Anglo-Saxon *frithgeard*, Norse *friðsplott*), is a holy enclosure around a sacred tree, well or stone, marked by a hedge or fence, within which divine peace must be observed. Here, the delimitation serves to enclose and protect the sacred power already present. The traditional *vé* was marked by standing stones. The great royal enclosure at Jelling, Denmark, is of this form. The *stafgardr*, a stave-surrounded sacred enclosure, was the preferred form on the Baltic island of Gotland. Surrounding temporary sittings of juridicial courts was the *vébond*, a rope supported on poles of hazel. In *Egils Saga*, a tenth century Norwegian court is recorded: 'In the place where the court was held was a level field, and hazel poles were fixed in a circle in it, and ropes were placed around them on the outside: these were called *vébond*. Inside sat the judges. . .' Obviously, any present-day sacred enclosures can take any of these forms, but certainly the most common will be the *stafgardr* and the *vébond*.

For a temporary mystic plot, grid lines marked by string, or on a floor, in chalk, are appropriate. The edges of the mystic plot can be protected by returning the lines like those in Thrond's story, 'locking in' the power and 'locking out' unwanted influences. Also, this can be done by placing talismans placed at corresponding points. When the lines of the plot are left 'open', that is without terminal protection, the grid is linked in to whatever is present in the locality, drawing it inwards. This is the form of the grid used in *Útiseta*.

The Bardic Tree Circle

In the Bardic system of ogham writing, each character corresponds with a tree, incorporating all of that tree's powers
and uses in the stave in a manner similar to that of the runes.
Thirteen of the oghams correspond with periods of the year,
and the whole circle makes a powerful magical protection.
This system was long forgotten until it was re-constructed in
the 1950s by the poet Robert Graves from the work of the
seventeenth century Irish bard Roderick O'Flaherty. The correspondences are as follows:

Ogham character	Tree	Time period
Beth	Birch	24 Dec – 20 Jan
Luis	Rowan	21 Jan – 17 Feb
Nion	Ash	18 Feb – 17 Mar
Fearn	Alder	18 Mar – 14 Apr
Saille	Willow	15 Apr – 12 May
Uath	Hawthorn	13 May – 9 Jun
Duir	Oak	10 Jun – 7 Jul
Tinne	Holly	8 Jul – 4 Aug
Coll	Hazel	5 Aug – 1 Sep
Muin	Vine	2 Sep – 29 Sep
Gort	Ivy	30 Sep – 27 Oct
Ngetal	Reed	28 Oct – 24 Nov
Ruis	Elder	25 Nov – 22 Dec

In addition, there is the 'blank day', 23 December, known
as the 'secret of the unhewn stone', which is said by those
who use it to correspond with the blank rune. This makes a
very uneven 14 fold division of the circle, which can be laid
out on the ground as a sacred enclosure for cermonies and
rituals. Each of the divisions can be signified by the corresponding wood, or can be laid out permanently by planting
the corresponding 'tree' in its appropriate place. The fourteenth sector, towards the divine direction of north, is the un-
shielded *vé*. The 14 Stations of the Cross of Christian tradition, enacted at the lunar festival of Eostre, are derived from
this lunar-based cycle.

The great strength of this tree-cycle is that it can be laid out
easily in physical form. A circle of the ogham tree direction-
correspondences was set up at the Tree Fair, held at

Rougham, Suffolk, in 1979, where a *Beth-Luis-Nion* ceremony, devised mainly by Gill Gillilan, was enacted. The wheel of change during the year was symbolized by people dressed in ceremonial costumes signifying each of the 13 trees in order. Since then, several tree-circles have been planted, including one near Glastonbury and one in France. The tree-circle—a miniature sacred grove—is an appropriate magical enclosure when one wishes to use the powers of the trees in a ceremonial fashion.

Sacred Pillars and Wooden Temples

Wooden pillars supporting the roof of a hallowed building are sacred in their own right, corresponding to the trees of a sacred grove. The *öndvegissulúr*, or high-seat pillars, were the most sacred part of the halls or temples (*hofs*) of Norse Pagan times. These are the posts which stood on either side of the high seat, which were carved with the *Ing* rune, *God's Nail*, and peppered with consecrated iron nails hammered in during sacred rituals. When Norse settlers emigrated to the then uninhabited island of Iceland, a number of them took with them their high-seat pillars. When their ships drew near to Iceland, the high seat pillars were thrown overboard so that where they came ashore, so would the settlers. Among these were Thorólf Mostrarskegg (who had an image of Thor carved on one pillar), Thord Skeggi, Ingolf, Hrollaug and Lodmund. Thorólf Mostrarskegg and Thorhadd the Old both transported entire wooden temples from Norway to Iceland, including the hallowed soil on which they stood.

Only wood from trees marked out in some special way is suitable for high-seat pillars. Hallstein, son of Thorólf Mostrarskegg, called upon Thor to send him high-seat pillars. Shortly afterwards, a tree was washed ashore from the sea on his land. It was 63 ells in length (a magic dimension: 7×9) and two fathoms thick, sufficient wood to make new high-seat pillars for every farm in the neighbourhood. It is a universal tradition with sacred wooden architecture that after a period of time, the sacred virtue of the wood is lost, and the temple must be reconstructed. This is still carried out in the Shinto religion of Japan, which has many direct parallels with the Northern Tradition of Europe. There, a spiritually outworn wooden temple is replaced by a new one next to it within the sacred temenos. The new Shinto temple is identical in design and dimensions with the old one, which is demolished once the new one is complete and consecrated. The Icelandic record of Hallstein Thorólfsson indicates that the same tradition once existed in northern Europe.

Non-Sacred Buildings

Modern problems

The principles of geomantic location and magical protection do not apply only to sacred buildings but to any place in which humans or animals dwell. All over the world, traditional societies have systems of geomancy which relate to the siting and design of dwellings. Only since the Industrial Revolution, a very short time in the history of human beings upon this planet, has geomancy been ignored. The supposed technological objectivity of modern architectural design is a deliberate rejection of anything natural. This principle, which goes under the misleading name of 'functionalism', has been refined to a means of lowering costs and the raising of profit margins without regard to any subtle effects which might be created by ignoring traditional methods. *Building sickness*, the condition where office workers suffer from various chronic illnesses directly caused by their workplace, has only recently been recognized by scientists. Only after long, exhaustive studies had eliminated every other possible cause was it admitted, reluctantly, that the buildings themselves are to blame for the malaise of their users. Any traditional building practitioner would have pointed out a dozen ways in which the building fell foul of subtle harmful influences. At present, only Hong Kong, where *Feng-Shui*, Chinese geomancy, is consulted even for the most prestigious modern buildings, is attempting to avoid these problems by traditional methods. Even most so-called 'post-modern' buildings, with their neoclassical and neo-*Art Deco* ornament, recall an earlier, less austere, age of 'functionalism', that of American skyscrapers of the early part of this century.

The 'functionalist' view of former methods rejects them as superstitious, as though superstitions had no function. This view is wrong. Those areas of behaviour now called superstition certainly possessed a social function for those who observed them. In addition, many superstitions were a response to a problem, often in ways that 'functionalists' would recognize if the problems were defined in other ways. For example, if bed orientation arose as a means of dealing with the effect of the Earth's magnetic field upon individuals, then this practice would have a functional validity. Even though those performing the orientation now might have no idea of the reason, or give spurious explanations, the actual function would still be effective. It is a form of gross arrogance to dismiss any traditional practice just because it does not fit in with a specialized and necessarily partial view of the world. One has only to look at the rediscovery of antibiotics by science after their herbal and fungal predecessors had been discarded as 'old wives' medicine' to recognize the folly of imagining that 'we know it all already'.

Traditional Building Protection

In traditional buildings, it is difficult to distinguish 'functional' from 'magical' elements, for they originate in a time before that artificial distinction was made. Although it has lapsed in most parts of Europe, the traditional house building of India still recalls the techniques used in European traditions. Every possible factor is taken into account, from soil quality, direction of slope, prevailing winds and materials to be used, to more esoteric qualities such as astrology and auspices. So-called vernacular architecture in northern Europe, too, was constructed according to an analysis such as this. In addition, the ornament of buildings is related directly to talismanic magic of the Northern Tradition. A walk through an old town which has not suffered total 'redevelopment' will reveal numerous examples. As in former times, talismanic objects should be installed with a ceremony which evokes their power.

The ceremony of foundation-stone laying, or unveiling plaques in public buildings, is the last public survival of the magical protection of buildings. There, the presence of a member of the Royal Family, or some other notable person imparts some of their personal *megin* to the place. Ceremonies for installing external house protection such as images or painted sigils are similar to that for the Cambridgeshire witch bottle, detailed in Chapter 4. When the object is being carved or painted, the worker should will into it the function for which it is being made. This will involve calls of appropriate runes, etc. When it is ready, it should be in-

stalled at a correct runic hour with a ceremony which effectively switches on the power at that moment. The libation of
champagne at ship-launchings is a perfect example of this.

Building protection is accomplished by several traditional
techniques, which either deflect harmful energies or draw in
beneficial ones.

Animal skulls are potent protectors of the threshold and the
hearth. In former times, it was customary to bury the skull of
a wolf, dog, ox or horse in the foundations of a new building.
Every year, a few are unearthed when old buildings are
demolished or renovated. The custom of burying bottles may
be derived in part from an earlier use of skulls.

Horseshoes combine the magical power of iron with the crescent symbol of the lunar goddess Mani. As a protection, they
should be nailed up on or over doors with the points upper-

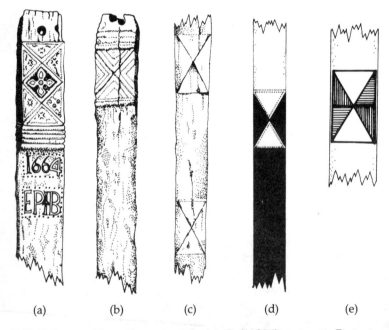

(a)   (b)   (c)   (d)   (e)

Fig. 47 Posts with runic protection: (a) *God's Nail speer-post*, Postgate
Farm, Glaisdale, Yorkshire; (b) *Dag speer-post*, Church View, Gillamoor,
Yorkshire; (c) *Dags*, house door-post at Lerbeck, near Minden, Germany; (d) traditional painted dag in blue and white; (e) door-post of
house at Witersheim an der Weser, Germany—vertical hatching, green;
horizontal hatching, blue; plain, white.

most, 'so that the luck doesn't run out'.

Lady's trees are small dried seaweed plants hung above the hearth, or put in a vase on the mantelpiece. These protect the house and its inhabitants against fire and malevolent sprites.

Nails are a symbol of the power of Thor in his capacity as stabilizer of orderliness. Nails hammered into main beams or supporting posts of a building are considered to bring good luck and protection from fire and intrusion.

Runic protection includes the use of a number of runes, of which the most important are *Ing, Dag, Gyfu, Gar* and *Odal* (*Ethel*). These can be made in contrasting brickwork, or be carved or painted on the outside of a building in appropriate positions. *Ing, Gyfu* and *Odal* are appropriate as wall-protection, whilst *Dag* and *Odal* are appropriate for door and window-frames. Speer-posts and other structural posts of timber buildings, the equivalents of high-seat pillars, are marked with the *Ing* rune as *God's Nail*, or *Gyfu, Gar* and *Ing* can be made into lattices to protect windows and other openings. The 'leaded lights' beloved of cottage-dwellers are an *Ing*-rune protection. .

Sacred images are uncommon today, but in former times they were powerful building talismans. Carvings on exposed wooden parts, pargeting in plasterwork, or painted figures of giants, saints, heroes and deities were common once, calling on the power of those beings to defend the house and its inhabitants against all evil.

Mirrors reflect various sorts of energy. They reflect not only light, but also more subtle energies dealt with by dowsers, geomants and magicians. The Abbé Mermet, one of the most eminent dowsers of the 1920s and 1930s, noticed that the 'rays' he attributed to the dowsing reaction were able to be reflected by a mirror. In more recent years, J. Havelock Fidler has used a mirror in his experiments with 'energy lines', and in *Feng-Shui*, the octagonal *Pak Kwa* mirror is an important part of the geomant's armoury against *sha qi*—harmful energies. Women's dress from the Indian subcontinent often retains many small metallic mirrors sewn into the fabric, and the highly-polished metal talismans on the shaman's costume serves the same function of reflecting harmful forces. Sometimes the mirrors are replaced by silver or gold coins, as in traditional Romany women's costume. On a larger scale, all over England today, large blue, green or occasionally yellow, glass balls, silvered inside with mercury, can be seen hanging up in house windows. These are known as 'witch balls'. They are sought-after 'antiques', but it is their property of deflecting harmful projections that makes them so 'collectable'. The 'witch ball' is a larger version of the glass Christmas tree ornament, which serves the same function.

Every building-protector works on several levels. If it is a sacred object recognized as holy by passers-by, such as the image of a Hindu deity in India, or an effigy of a saint in a country where Roman Catholic devotion is strong, then it will elicit certain thoughts and feelings in the person who sees it. A devout person will acknowledge its sanctity in some way, such as with a short prayer or an offering, which will recharge that object with spritual power. If, as some people suggest, consecration creates a physical field inside and around an object, then this field will be reinforced by ceremonial observances. It is clear that some objects, placed deliberately, or occuring naturally at certain locations, produce certain effects even when they are not consecrated. The protection of a building can be seen as the creation of beneficial fields which obliterate other, harmful fields, bringing harmony where there is discord, health where once was illness, and fertility in place of barrenness.

Protective Plants

Finally, the medicinal and magical virtues of herbs and trees are also apparent in their use as protection. Many of these have been dealt with in Chapter 2, but there are a few important ones which should not be omitted.

Groundsel is a plant which has associations with magic. In East Anglia, a large patch of the weed is said to be the assembly-place of witches, and a small plot a place where a witch has urinated. The plant can be worn as a charm against the Evil Eye and malevolent magic.

Hawthorn invokes the power of the rune *Thorn*, and is a powerful protector when twigs are placed in the rafters of a house.

Hemp — Although formerly hemp-growing was widespread, for rope-making and medicinal uses, it is now illegal, and re-named *cannabis*. In the days before its possession became a criminal offence, hemp seed was used in charms of protection and binding.

Honeysuckle is another protective plant used on May Day to cover entrances and windows.

Mugwort has a curious root structure which contains black nodules which have protective and medicinal properties. It makes a useful incense, too.

Oak is the sacred tree of Thor, and the fruit, the acorn, invokes the protective power of the god. Acorns turned on the lathe from oak wood are a magical protection for the end of window-blind cords and as traditional stair bannister finials.

Rowan is a protective tree, like the oak, connected with Thor. Grown outside a house, by the path approaching the front door, it wards off malevolent magic and psychic attack.

St John's wort hung in bunches over doors and windows on Midsummer's Day protects and cleanses the home from harmful forces.

Yarrow strewn across a doorstep is said to prevent the entry of malevolent people, and a cushion stuffed with yarrow suppresses the magical powers of anyone sitting upon it.

Local Tradition

When you are considering the most appropriate magical protection for yourself or your home, then you should look around at local tradition. Once you start looking, it is surprising what exists. Even a small village may have witch balls or symbolic 'light-catchers' in windows, runic brickwork, roof protectors, carved dragons, appropriate trees growing outside houses and cryptic sigils in plaster-work. Local museums also contain collections of magic objects which are listed under *folklore*, *bygones* or 'superstition'. Once you start looking, you will soon get a feel for the local tradition, and will be able to become a worthy inheritor of the practice.

VI

Ceremonies and Rituals

Hail to thee, Mother Earth,
Mortals maintaining,
Be growing and fertile,
By the goodness of the gods,
Filled with fodder
Our folk to feed.

Anglo-Saxon prayer

Traditional times have their own ceremonies and rituals which express and explain the nature of those times in a symbolic way. In Britain, there are a few times of year which are noted as public holidays or events in which the majority of people participate. These are Christmas, New Year, Easter, Hallowe'en and Guy Fawkes' Night. The first three are public holidays, when work stops and customary activities take place. Christmas (Midwinter) and Easter (Spring Festival) are dual Christian–Pagan festivals. New Year is a Pagan tradition. The other two are closely related, Guy Fawkes' Night being part of the week of Samhain, Hallowe'en. These autumn festivals are not official holidays, yet they are celebrated in the traditional ways. In addition to these celebrations are the remaining six of the Eight Festivals: Imbolc, vernal equinox, Beltane, midsummer, Lammas and autumnal equinox. As well as these, traditional days of deities and saints must be added. It is clear that today only a fraction of customary festivals are celebrated or even commemorated, a telling indictment of how far removed most people are from the natural cycle of the year. However, despite this lack of national recognition, the festivals and their ceremonies continue to be observed, and by a growing number of people. This chapter deals with some of the ap-

propriate ceremonies, rituals, decorations and food for the
festivals. Participating properly in these festivals is more than
being a consumer of spectacle or entertainment. It is to commune with the powers and qualities existing on Earth and in
the non-material realm at that time. We can tap this current in
our lives through the medium of the sacred festivals and their
traditional observances, re-enacting the sacred drama of the
year as millions have done before us over the millennia.

Most ceremonies have the same basic pattern. The details
depend on the time of year and the purpose of the ritual. The
first part of a ceremony involves assembly, where the participants come together, either at the place of the ceremony,
or at another place, from whence they make a procession to
the sacred site. The site will have been magically 'set up'
before the participants arrive. Then an act of homage to the
deity or deities is made in word or song. An enactment of the
ceremonial motif is made, followed by a declaration. Finally,
there is a closing ceremony of dismissal. The wording of all of
the basic ceremonies decribed here is by way of suggestion
and example. Only the sacred scriptures of the North such as
Hávámal, and the holy runes have a prescribed form which
cannot be altered. Whether their origin is ancient or modern,
these ceremonies tap the cosmic pulse of the time. Readers
may choose to use them, adapt them, take others from alternative sources, or to devise ceremonies of their own. Many
people believe that, except in the case of certain fixed magical
formulae, it is more natural to speak 'from the heart' in a
ceremony than to read it from a printed text. If you choose a
written text, it is best not to read it off, but to learn it by heart.
By so doing, one may gain a greater understanding of the rite.
Whatever the form and words may be, however, one thing
should rule any ceremony: it must be composed of elements
which correspond to the qualities and traditions of the time of
year. The recipes given here are all traditional, and of considerable antiquity, as are the artifacts and customs covered.

Common to all ceremonies of the Elder Faith are song and
dance. They are the means of reaching a state of ecstasy, getting out of oneself into other states of consciousness. Sacred
dances for the festivals of the year should be an enactment of
the motifs of the season. Above all, sacred dance is imitative.
In hunter-gatherer societies, hunting dance enacts the
movements and tactics of the chase. Dances for fertility im-
itate the actions of reproduction and growth, and dance at

Fig. 48 Sacred dance: (a) medieval *graffito* from Sutton, Bedfordshire; (b) traditional Lappish shaman.

rites of passage symbolize the changes taking place. One almost universal labyrinth dance imitates the mating dance of the crane. Imitative dance often includes imitative costume. Mumming, wearing animal skins, masks and antlers, is usually a New Year's custom. It was prohibited by several medieval Church edicts. Dancing back-to-back is another custom which has almost lapsed. Medieval illustrations show that it was once common, but at a later date, like Mumming, its connections with the Elder Faith made churchmen denounce it, and it was suppressed. Those most extreme churchmen, the self-styled 'Puritans', thought that *all* dancing and physical activities other than work was evil. In Britain at

Fig. 49 Medieval mummers in animal masks, a continuation of indigenous British Pagan tradition.

least, they caused a serious disruption of folk customs of all kinds. Because of this the Abbots Bromley horn dancers are one of the few folk-dance groups that have continued the animal-dance tradition unbroken. They carry reindeer antlers dating from the time when it was an indigenous animal. This, and other customs, is a powerful reminder that the Northern Tradition practised today is in direct continuity with more ancient times.

Yule

The period of Yule really begins a fortnight before the winter solstice with the festival of St Nicholas's Day, associated with a bowdlerized shaman-figure, Santa Claus, who has aspects of Odin in his attributes. This is the true meaning of 'Old Nick'. A few days later is St Lucy's Day, the winter festival of the goddess of light. In Sweden, the youngest daughter of the family becomes the 'Lucia Queen'. On St Lucy's Day, she gets up early—at first cock crow between 1 and 4 a.m., during the *tide* of *Uht*. She dreses in a white costume with a red sash, and wears a crown composed of whortleberry twigs and lighted candles. Singing a special St Lucy's Day song, she wakens the other members of her family with food, and also takes food to the animals. Then she presides at a specially good breakfast in a brilliantly illuminated room. St Lucy's Day is the Northern Tradition *Festival of Lights,* and should be remembered if only by burning a single candle in the morning.

The 6th and 13th December are precursors of the main festival of Yuletide, which begins around the solstice and includes the New Year of the present calendar. The festival of Yule/Christmas has a plethora of traditions associated with it, which still flourish today. Their symbolism is one of light in darkness, warmth in coldness, life coming out of death, greenery amid barrenness, plenty amid dearth and hope in time of despair. The symbol of the new light of the Undefeated Sun underlies the ceremonies. Yule is the fourth *station* of the mystic year, signifying enlightenment, the rebirth of light in the darkest hour. St Thomas's Day, 21 December, is the solstice, the real festival of the Undefeated Sun. In Belgium, this is the traditional day for the feast of Cakes and Ale. Ceremonies around this time are interlinked and cross-reference with one another. On St Thomas's Eve,

Fig. 50 Ulli (Ullr), god of midwinter, skiing and archery, from an 18th century Swedish engraving.

Christmas Eve, New Year's Eve and Twelfth Night, houses and farm buildings should be visited with holy water and incense.

The greatest symbol of light in the darkness is the fire which should burn throughout the Twelve Days of Yule, symbolizing the eternal light shining through the 12 months of the year. The Yule log should be lit at sunset on 24 December from the remains of the previous year's log, kept for the purpose. It should be done with the formula: 'I charge the log that it shall burn brightly and well on the wide hearth of this hospitable mansion, shedding a glow of warmth and friendliness.'

Sometimes, the Yule log is decked with greenery, cones and berries before being burnt. The greenery, deal apples, etc., can be stuck on with paraffin wax which aids combustion. In Devon and Somerset, the place of the Yule log is taken by the *ashen faggot*, a bundle of logs cut from an ash tree. This is bound with nine withies. As each band bursts in the flames, so a quart of cider is passed around as a toast. In dwellings where a Yule log or ashen faggot is not feasible, then a candle or other light should be kept burning during the 12-night period to signify the light of the Undefeated Sun.

Because Yule is a festival of light in the darkness, candles have long played an important part. Today, many people make a *Yule candle*. A large, thick, candle which will burn for at least 24 hours is needed. It is lit at sunset on the eve of the solstice, when it should be extinguished, for it has continued the light through the lowest part of the sun's power, the shortest day. Juniper incense can be burned at midwinter and through the Yule holiday period. It has the magical function of cleansing the home of unwanted left-over emotions and other on-lays.

The Yule tree or Christmas tree is the best known symbolic decoration of Yuletide. Customarily it is a spruce, which symbolizes the continuance of green life through the barrenness of winter. Holly or mistletoe should be brought into the house by a man on Christmas Eve, that is, after sunset on 24 December. Another Yule tradition is the kissing bough, a globe of evergreens, often seen today in a flattened form as a holly wreath. In its traditional form, this globe is made of osiers, bound with evergreens, traditionally box or rosemary, with red apples hanging from coloured ribbons in the middle. Beneath the bough, a sprig of mistletoe is suspended. Whilst it is being made, it should be hung from the ceiling by a hook, but *not* the hook from which it will hang once completed. Customarily, holly denotes the male principle, and ivy the feminine, and preparation should be done accordingly. Another Yule structure is the light tree, an apple or several apples supported on sticks, from which hang nuts, and to which are attached sprigs of holly, evergreen leaves and candles. This is stood in the centre of the table at the Yule feast.

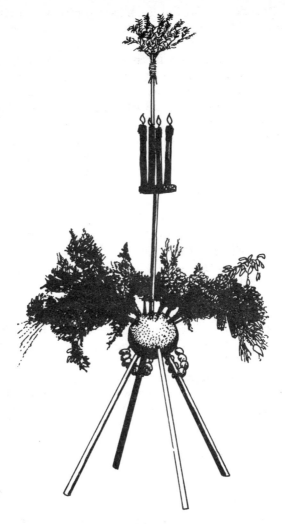

Fig. 51 Yuletide light apple, supported on four sticks, bearing evergreen foliage, nuts and candles.

The traditional Yule or Christmas puddings should be made on Stir-up Sunday, the last Sunday before the Christianized Advent period, the run-up to Yuletide. The mix should be enough for 13 puddings, one for each of the Twelve Days of Yule. The thirteenth should be given away. The pudding itself should contain 13 ingredients, and be stirred *deisal* with a wooden spoon nine times by each member of the family, in decreasing order of seniority, so that the smallest child is last. During the stirring, nine silver coins or charms should be dropped into the mix, invoking the lunar power of growth. The pudding symbolizes the Earth, its harvest of grain and fruits, fermented liquor and precious metals, and the sprig of holly with which it is topped, the Cosmic Tree, Yggdrassil.

Dumb cakes are the traditional food made during daylight on 24 December. These should be made in total silence by young women who wish to know their future husbands, to the recipe of an eggshellful of salt, another of wheatmeal and a third of barley. When the cake is in the oven, she should walk to the door and open it. If all is well, then the future husband should walk in at midnight and turn the cake.

Making *sowens*, cakes baked on Christmas Eve before sunrise (early on 25 December) is a Scottish custom. Sowens are made by boiling the floury matter from the husks of oats, and then making it into cakes. The liquid remaining should be kept and drunk at Hogmanay. A sowen is given to each member of the family, who has to keep it safe and unbroken until the main feast in the evening (after dark on 25 December, and therefore the eve of the 26). If the sowen breaks, then this bodes ill luck, but if it remains intact until eaten, then health and happiness will be the owner's lot in the next year. Traditional cakes known as *Gods kitchels* are made in Suffolk for the Twelve Days of Yule, to the following recipe:

1 lb puff pastry
$\frac{1}{2}$ lb currants
2 oz butter
3 oz candied peel
2 oz ground almonds
$\frac{1}{2}$ tsp cinnamon
$\frac{1}{2}$ tsp ground nutmeg

The puff pastry is divided into two portions and rolled out into squares. The filling is spread inside one square, and the edges of the other one are moistened with water and the two pieces are brought together to enclose the mixture. The top is then marked out into squares measuring two inches along each side, making the whole kitchel into the sacred grid. The kitchel is then baked in a hot oven for 25–30 minutes, and finally sprinkled with caster sugar and cut up along the marking-out lines into squares.

Another food customary for the festival of Yule is pea soup, of which the following recipe is a Norwegian version:

5 pints (one pottle and one pint) of water
2 cupfuls of dried, split peas
2 cupfuls of diced bacon or ham
1 diced onion, medium
2 cupfuls of sliced carrots
2 cupfuls of chopped celery
1 tsp pot marjoram
4 tsp ginger
$\frac{1}{4}$ tsp small-leaved thyme
$\frac{1}{2}$ tsp pepper
2 tsp sea salt
1 bay leaf

Fig. 52 Traditional West Frisian Yule biscuits are made with a carved wooden stamp bearing images of deities of the Elder Faith. This one, dating from the 18th century, has Frigg, wearing a lunar crescent head-dress, and holding her distaff and spindle.

Place all of the ingredients together in a large pot and bring to the boil. Cover and simmer for 3 hours (one eighth of the day cycle), with occasional stirring until the peas break up. The cooking of the soup should be done in the tide of *Undernoon*, from 7.30 a.m. until 10.30 a.m., the time of the rising light.

Wassailing

Wassailing is a Yuletide celebration of wholeness, being a toast or series of toasts drunk from a communal wassail bowl turned from maple wood. The word *wassail* is from the Anglo-Saxon, *wes hal*, meaning *be whole*. It is the Yuletide toast, when one says 'Wassail' to be answered by 'Drinkhail'.

The wassail bowl contains the celebratory drink, whose recipe, recorded in the time of King Charles I, is as follows.

'Boil three pints of ale; beat six eggs, the whites and yolks together; set both to the fire in a pewter pot; add roasted apples, honey, beaten nutmegs, cloves and ginger; and, being well brewed, drink it hot.'

Even when the recipe is not so rich, leaving out the eggs which may not be to some people's taste, the common recipe contains hot ale, the pulp of roasted apples, spices and sugar. Some less traditional recipes have cider as the base of the drink, which some believe to be a more appropriate ceremonial toast to the apple tree. In some places, it is customary to carry the wassail bowl, bedecked with ribbons, garlands, and a golden apple, from house to house. Wassailing has its own songs. The *Worcestershire St Thomas's Day Song* is typical:

> Wassail, wassail, all over the town,
> Our toast is white, our ale is brown,
> Our bowl is made of a maplin tree;
> We be good fellows all—I drink to Thee!

Another wassailing song praises and encourages the tree from which the fruit comes:

> Here's to the old apple tree,
> Whence thou mayest bud, and whence though mayest blow!
> And whence thou mayest bear apples enow!
> Hats full! Caps full!
> Bushel, bushel sacks full!
> Any my pockets full! Wassail!

New year

New Year's Eve (after sunset on 31 December), is the time to eat triangular *kitchel cakes*, made with the same recipe as the kitchels above, eaten with spiced elderberry wine. The apple-gift, an apple on a tripod of ash twigs, decked with hazel nuts and yew vegetation, signifying sweetness, fertility and immortality, should be the centrepiece of any table used in Yule and New Year ceremonies. In Scotland, the solar nature of this festival, transferred from the solstice, is still recognized. It is celebrated under the special name of Hogmanay, a time sacred to the solar hero-giant Hogamagog or Gogmagog. After midnight, when the New Year has been 'seen in', the front door should be opened to receive the New Year, and the first act through the door should be to take something in, for as the East Anglian adage warns:

Take out, then take in, bad luck will begin:
Take in, then take out, good luck will come about.

Some people burn the old year's calendar at sunrise on New Year's Day. It should be wound nine times with red wool or thread, and cast into the flames, accompanied by the formula:

Burn, burn, burn,
Old day book, burn!
Old year's troubles
Never return.
Ka!

The house should be cleaned, and dirt, household rubbish, old newspapers, ashes etc. cleared away. Then silver, bread and a piece of coal or charcoal should be brought in. These signify wealth, plenty and warmth for the forthcoming year. New Year's Day is a time for looking forward, and many divinatory arts, such as card and rune reading or bibliomancy, should be done before midday. The first new moon of the year should be greeted with nine bows, and by turning over of money in the pockets.

Imbolc

Imbolc is another festival of lights, as indicated by its Christian name of Candlemas (*Lichtmesse* in German, meaning Light-Mass). This is commemorated with the *Crown of Light* a circle of 13 candles (the number of full moons in the solar year). An Imbolc ceremony should be one of welcoming the returning light after the darkness of midwinter-time. Ceremonies include the lighting of the Crown of Light, with the call:

Hail to thee, Lady of Light,
Welcome to thee, threefold Goddess of Life!
Mother of the Sun, we welcome thee.
Patroness of Fire, we invite thee to enter.

The Spring Equinox

This is a time of cleansing and renewal, the fifth *station* of the

Fig. 53 Before the advent of high-rise buildings, the weathercocks on the church steeples were the first objects to catch the rising sun each morning. Rotating in the wind, they indicate the qualities of the air present at that time. Installation of weathercocks was usually carried out in springtime. This one is a medieval example from Obliers, Rhineland, Germany.

mystic year, a time of reconciliation, when the seed, apparently dead, comes to life once again. The tradition of spring cleaning the house, its opening up after the closed months of winter, is also one of spiritual cleansing. An incense of pot marjoram and thyme can be burnt prior to the spring clean. These herbs also make a good addition to a symbolic bath which can be taken on the equinox.

Eggs are a rich source of traditional springtime lore, for the egg is a symbol of the potential of life. Symbolically, the yellow egg's yolk represents the solar deity, its white the white goddess in whom the god is immanent. The egg is associated with springtime and its festivals for a good physiological reason. Egg production in the hen is stimulated only when the retina of its eye receives more than 12 hours of light at a stretch. Under natural conditions, this occurs in the light half of the year between the equinoxes. Laying begins, then, around the vernal equinox, when there are 12 hours of daylight for the first time since the previous autumn. The festival of Easter, of the vernal goddess Eoestre or Ostara, is the time when hens begin to lay, and the Easter egg is the customary reminder of this, when the first eggs of the year were made into sacred offerings, being painted symbolically and then kept in shrines. Painted Easter eggs celebrate the transition from the dark half of the year, with its cold, dampness, depression, death and decay and the light half of the year, with its warmth, dryness, elation, life and growth. Traditional Easter egg painting in Northern Europe still reproduces the ancient sacred motifs of the Northern Tradition today. Eggs are encircled with lines which bind in the energy, and symbolize the eternal circle of life. The *tangled thread* pattern, binding in the energies, is a common motif, as are grids, which again serve a magical function. The eightfold heavenly star and sunwheels commemorate the seasonal cycle. Triangles are emblematical of the triadic nature of things. Trees of Life and other generative sigils are appropriate for egg-decoration.

An egg, painted or not, hung on a string in the window is a means of psychic protection of a household. According to the sixteenth century writer Reginald Scot, 'to hang an egg laid on Ascension Day in the roof of a house, preserveth the same from all hurts'. The hanging egg is probably the origin of the silvered *witch-ball*, which combines the egg-symbolism with the protective power of the mirror. Also, eggs were buried sometimes in the foundations and walls of buildings, to prevent psychic attack, and were carried around a fire to prevent it spreading.

May Day

May Day is the sixth *station* of the mystic year, signifying mystical union, the plant in full growth in perfect harmony with its environment. This is the time of honouring the household sprites. The May branch, bush and May-pole are the best known symbols of this important festival. In their simplest form, May-poles are felled trees moved to a traditional site and set up there. In Germany, where the custom continues in a much more widespread and stronger form than in Britain, the May-pole is frequently a real tree—felled on May Eve (*Walpurgisnacht*)—upon which some or all branches are allowed to remain. A tree I saw in Horn, Westphalia, in May 1986, was an intact birch decked with ribbons. Current traditions in Germany range from freshly-cut trees to painted May-poles. In parts of Bavaria, poles are made from conifers which retain a small amount of foliage at the top. In that land, the poles are usually painted with a spiral in blue and white, the Bavarian national colours. Garlands such as those illustrated here are common, representing the planes on the Cosmic Axis. Sometimes May-poles had a broomstick attached to the top in place of the uncut foliage. May trees are sometimes set up on steps, reproducing the Cosmic Axis–World Mountain correspondence.

England today has still not recovered from the blow against Maytide festivities at the hands of seventeenth century fanatics. At that time, most of the dual faith celebrations (where Pagan and Christian elements are combined in an event which has its own character, such as Christmas and Martinmas), were suppressed. In April 1644, the government ordered the eradication of all permanent May-poles. But after the overthrow of the Commonwealth, and the restoration of the Monarchy, many were never re-erected. However, the custom of having permanent May-poles has survived into modern times in several English villages: Barwick in Elmet, Yorkshire, (100 feet tall, painted like a barber's pole, in red-and-white spirals); Welford-on-Avon, Warwickshire, (also red-and-white); Temple Sowerby, Westmoreland; Ickwell, Bedfordshire (70 feet tall); and Paganhill, near Stroud,

Gloucestershire. The abolition of permanent poles was easier to achieve than the abolition of tree-related custom. Local obervance in private homes or on private, isolated, land is almost impossible to police. In Herefordshire, country people would fell a birch on May Day, deck it with streamers and set it against the stable door to bring good luck for that year.

A Beltane sunrise ceremony

This is a short ritual which marks the end of May Eve (Walpurgis Night, sacred to Walburga, an aspect of the lunar goddess) by hailing the rising sun of Beltane morn. It can be done alone, or with a group of people. A comparable ceremony, using the appropriate correspondences for the time of year, can be made at the midsummer solstice. Shortly before the sun rises, the following prayer can be made:

> May Balder give us his brilliance,
> May the light of Sól bless us,
> May Tyr, the bright warrior,
> With the might of his shining sword,
> Ward and watch over us.
> May Odin, endow us with the wisdom
> To comprehend the mysteries of being.
> May Freyja bring to us her verdant growth
> And bounteous gifts to come.
> Hlín, thrice gentle and fair goddess,
> Your face shining in comely beauty and compassion,
> Draw near to us, and give us comfort.
> Ka!

Immediately before the rising of the sun, a red candle is lit and placed in a bowl or cauldron into which is poured consecrated water from a holy well. As the sun's rays are seen to break over the horizon, the following is said:

> In the face of the sun
> And in the eye of the light:
> The eye of Sól,
> The eye of the Queen of Day,
> The eye of the Lord of Light,
> The eye of the White God,
> Pouring thy brilliant light upon us
> Hail to thee, O glorious sun,
> Full of the power of life-giving.
> Ka!

Bells, rattles, drums, horns and other musical sounds are made before the call:

> Hail, mighty Sól, source of life,
> Hail, mighty Balder, Lord of Light.

From the consecrated water, the participants take a small amount with thumb and forefinger of the right hand, and make the sign of the *Lagu* rune, the rune of flow and growth, ruling rune of the time of year, on their foreheads. Then, each person in turn passes her or his hand through the candle flame (quickly!), and makes a secret resolution of something that he or she will try hard to accomplish before the summer half of the year is through. The rite ends with the call:

> Brilliance of Sól,
> Hallowed balefire
> Spreading light and warmth,
> And driving out the darkness,
> Expelling winter's cold,
> And bringing us the welcome summer
> Hail and farewell, Ka!

The candle is then extinguished, and the water poured out of the bowl as a libation to Mother Earth. The rest of the May festivities can now take place!

The May Day hobby-horse

The *hobby-horse* is a curious artifact which is generally seen hobnobbing with Morris Dancers and other ceremonial perforers at traditional festivals. In its basic form, it is a stave with an attached horse head, which a dancer rides in the same way that the witch's besom is ridden. The horse is usually covered with cloth or canvas and may have a carved head with a snapping jaw mechanism. Hobby-horses are a continuation of an extremely ancient sacred tradition, the earliest known representation of which is of a man in a horse-head mask, dating from the Stone Age and found in Pinhole Cave, Derbyshire. Representations of medieval hobby-horses exist as *graffiti* in some English churches, including Girton, Cambridgeshire (see Fig. 54), Shillington, Bedfordshire, and Wallington, Hertfordshire. As the German name for them, *Steckenpferd* (stick-horse) infers, the framework of the hobby-

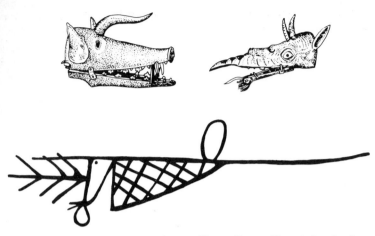

Fig. 54 The hobby-horse and its allies. *Above*: 'Snap' heads from Salzburg, Austria. *Below*: hobby-horse frame—sixteenth century *graffito* in the parish church at Girton, Cambridgeshire.

horse, over which a material covering is put, is a long stave attached to a wickerwork body, with a loop by which the operator holds it. On the heads of two of the earliest representations are the Northern Tradition Tree of Life.

The hobby-horse began as much more than just a piece of entertainment for May Day revellers. It is a supernatural beast, upon which the shaman rides up or down the Cosmic Axis. Yggdrassil, the axis-tree which May-poles symbolize, has a name meaning *the horse of Ygg*, Ygg being a by-name of Odin. The Buryat shamans of Baikal, central Asia, whose practices parallel the ancient usages of northern Europe, use horse-staves of wood or iron about an ell in length, with a horse's head and hooves at the ends. These staves symbolize the horse on which the shaman rides to the Upper and Lower Worlds. In its power of trance-induction, the horse-stave is connected with the ritual drum, whose skin is made from horsehide. Ritual drums accompany British hobby-horses, too.

Various forms of the hobby-horse are in use today, the most famous being that paraded through the Cornish town of Padstow on May Day. May is welcomed at dusk on the previous calendar day—May Eve or *Walpurgisnacht*—with the *Night Song*. In the morning, the *Old Hoss* is carried out from the Red Lion Inn, and parades through town all day. The visible part of the horse is black and boat-shaped, and the horse part has a ferocious mask with snapping jaws. Snapping is a characteristic of the hobby-horse, the *Hooden Horse* of Kent, paraded on Christmas Eve, and *Snap the Dragon*, formerly paraded through Norwich. At Norwich, the attendant *Whifflers* of the dragon carried ribbon-bedecked staves (see Fig. 30). At Padstow, the perambulation is attended by the *Teaser*, a man dressed in female attire, who directs the horse with a padded club. Now and again, the creature sinks to the ground as if dead, only to leap up again into life at a certain line in the *Day Song* which is performed continuously throughout the day. The horse chases after women and envelopes them under its skirts.

At Padstow, the horse festival was associated with a Maypole, which was abolished in the 1870s, but then reinstated more recently. The pole itself was a spar taken from the boatyard, set up at the top of Cross Street in the centre of a cross inlaid in stone. The pole is thus the symbol of the Cosmic Axis, set at the navel or *nowl* of the town. Part of the earlier festivities involved carrying the horse through the streets to Traitor's Pool, sacred waters a quarter of a mile out of town. Here, the horse pretended to drink. At Minehead, Somerset, another hobby-horse, the *Sailors' Horse*, was taken to a crossroads early on May Morning, where it would bow to the rising sun. There is a legend associated with Padstow that St George visited the town, where his horse 'made a mark' with one of its hooves and brought forth a spring—St George's Well. The Padstow *Day Song* has an explicit reference to St George, the dragonslayer:

Awake, St George, our English knight, O!
For summer is a-come, and winter is a-go.

In most places, where it survives, the parading of the hobby-horse is on May Day. There is a record of May Day hobby-horse and minstrels for the year 1557 in the churchwardens' accounts of St Mary's church, Reading, and it was customary in many other places where it may yet be reinstated.

Oak Apple Day

The *dressing* of oaks and other trees on Oak Apple Day—29th May—ostensibly in commemoration of the escape of King

Fig. 55 Notable monuments of the landscape have to be maintained, and in former times it was customary to make the scouring of white horses into a festive event. The *Pastime*, as the Uffington scouring was called, was one of the largest and most renowned. This engraving from T. Hughes's *The Scouring of the White Horse*, London, 1889, shows the Uffington horse being cleaned up.

Charles II from the forces of Parliament by hiding up an oak tree, was formerly a widespread custom in rural England. Oak leaves should be worn on this day, and made into garlands to deck houses. Dressing the black poplar growing at the crossroads at Aston-on-Clun, Salop, takes place every Oak Apple Day, and the custom continues sporadically in other localities. In parts of Scotland, Ireland and Wales, festooning sacred trees for votive purposes, or hanging of swatches of cloth on *rag bushes* and *fairy trees*, is customary. Oak Apple Day is a good time to do this.

The Wild Hunt

The *Wild Hunt* is a spectral phenomenon where Woden (Odin) leads a band of the homeless dead across the sky to the terror of anyone who witnesses it. This is seen as a pack of dogs with attendant hutsmen in full cry. The hunters ride black horses, and are attended by black hounds with staring hideous eyes. The Wild Hunt does not ride from the middle of May until the end of June, a 42-day period corresponding with the 42 by-names of Odin. Some believe that this period has special qualities for growth, but that divination does not work so well then.

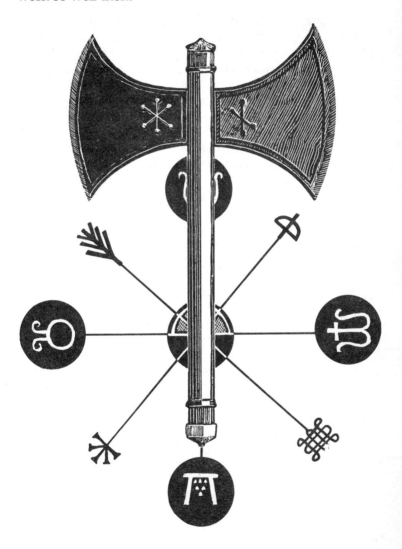

Fig. 56 Midsummer and midwinter are the two solsticial points of the year, the two making the *Axis of the Year*. This can be symbolized by the *labrys* or double-axe, here seen superimposed over a symbolic diagram of the annual cycle.

Midsummer Solstice

Midsummer, when the solar power is at its maxim, is a good time for rune magic and also for harvesting herbs. Markstones, boulders and rocky places of power should be remembered at midsummer and acknowledged with offerings of flowers and lights. The yellow flowers of St John's wort, a plant whose name literally means 'the herb of Midsummer's Day', make a useful guardian decoration at midsummer. At midsummer, there are other uses for flowers. A customary charm for *framsynn* dreams involves picking nine flowers and placing them under your pillow. An alternative to nine flowers is mistletoe.

One of the most publicly visible ceremonies of the Northern Tradition is the solsticial observance at Stonehenge by the Druid Order. Although in recent years this observance has been disrupted by problems, it is a tradition which has been held in some form or other since time immemorial. The Druidic ceremonies of midsummer take place at daybreak and high noon. The daybreak rite celebrates the arrival of the longest day. The sun is welcomed as a symbol of the banishment of darkness in a new Golden Age. According to the Druids, the first flash of the sun at midsummer symbolizes the descent of the *Awen*, the sigil of the Divine Name, of which the three rays of light are an outward sign. The ceremony involves greeting the sun and affirming goodness, truth, justice, peace and wisdom.

Arise, O Sun!
Let the darkness of night
Fade before the beams of thy glorious radiance!

At high noon, the Druidic ceremony involves crowning one of the assembly, representing the honour due to possessors of talent. The crowned one passes his crown on to his companions, sharing his honour, just as the brilliant light of the sun falls upon all at midsummer. This sharing of honour is manifest at midsummer as the seventh *station* of the mystic year, which signifies sanctification. This is the time when the flower opens and is fertilized, creating the potential seed within the glory of the bloom.

Lammas

Lammas is a time of ingathering, of summation of the harvest. It is a time of completion, the final (eighth) *station* of the year, when the seed, still present in the mother plant, reaches maturity. Sacred to Lugh, Celtic deity of illumination, it signifies regeneration at the place of original creation, *station eight* of the year cycle. An ancient Irish charge, known as the *Lammas Assembly*, gives the things appropriate to Lughnassadh:

> Heaven, Earth, Sun, Moon and Sea,
> Fruits of Earth and Sea-stuff,
> Mouths, ears, eyes, possessions,
> Feet, hands, warriors' tongues.

The Mystery of John Barleycorn is intimately tied in with the celebrations at Lammas. The old folk song *John Barleycorn Must die* is the explicit description of the mystery of death and rebirth which underlies the ethos of Northern Tradition shamanism and magic. As with all of the old songs, *John Barleycorn* exists in several variant versions, of which Robert Burns' ballad is classic:

> There were three kings into the east,
> Three kings both great and high,
> An' they hae sworn solemn oath
> John Barleycorn should die.
>
> They took a plough and plough'd him down,
> Put clods upon his head,
> And they hae sworn a solemn oath
> John Barleycorn was dead.
>
> But the cheerfu' spring came kindly on,
> And show'rs began to fall;
> John Barleycorn got up again,
> And sore surprised them all.
>
> The sultry suns of summer came,
> And he grew thick and strong,
> His head weel arm'd wi' pointed spears,
> That no-one should him wrong.
>
> The sober autumn enter'd mild,
> When he grew wan and pale;
> His bending joints and drooping head
> Show'd he began to fail.

His colour sicken'd more and more,
He faded into age;
And then his enemies began
To show their deadly rage.

They've ta'en a weapon long and sharp,
And cut him by the knee;
Then tied him fast upon a cart,
Like a rogue for forgerie.

They laid him down upon his back,
And cudgel'd him full sore;
They hung him up before the storm,
And turned him o'er and o'er.

They filled up a darksome pit
With water to the brim;
They heaved in John Barleycorn,
There let him sink or swim.

They laid him out upon the floor,
To work him farther woe,
And still as signs of life appear'd
They tossed him to and fro.

They wasted, o'er a scorching flame,
The marrow of his bones;
But a miller us'd him worst of all,
For he crushed him between two stones.

And they had ta'en his very heart's blood,
And drunk it round and round;
And still the more and more they drank,
Their joy did more abound.

John Barleycorn was a hero bold,
Of noble enterprise,
For if you do but taste his blood,
'Twill make your courage rise.

'Twill make a man forget his woe;
'Twill heighten all his joy;
'Twill make a widow's heart to sing,
Tho the tear were in her eye.

Then let us toast John Barleycorn,
Each man a glass in hand;
And may his great posterity
Ne'er fail in old Scotland!

John Barleycorn is the physical reality and spirit of the grain, through whose death and resurrection we are sustained. John Barleycorn's life is the cycle of the *stations of the mystic year* (see Chapter 1). He is pronounced dead and is buried, but in the spring undergoes a resurrection, grows through the spring and summer to manhood, symbolized by his beard. But at summer's end, he, too, begins to age and droop, when he is again cut down and undergoes the shamanic dismemberment and ordeal by the two elements of water and fire. But through his second death, John Barleycorn is transmuted into the sacred drink—ale. Also, through the process of being crushed in the mill, the grain is transmuted by water and fire into the staff of life—bread. A Lammas rite is not complete without some rendition of John Barleycorn—in song, recitation or as sacred drama.

Fig. 57 The spirit of Nature can manifest in many ways, as John Barleycorn, or here, as Robin Goodfellow, the northern equivalent of the Great God Pan, bringing joy and merriment to those who are receptive. (After a seventeenth-century engraving.)

Sacramental drink

Cakes or bread and ale are the sacrament of country tradition. The runic word for ale—*ALU*—is composed of the three runes, *As*, *Lagu* and *Ur*. The first rune has the meaning of the *gods* or *divine power*; the second, *water* and *flow*, and the third, *primal strength*. So its kenning is the primally strong water of the gods, an appropriately poetic description. The eating of bread and drinking of ale is the mystery of the transmutation of the energy in the grain into a form where it is reborn in our physical bodies. The grain, personified as John Barleycorn, is truly our sustainer. The runic word for the loaf of bread—*HLAF*—similarly has symbolic meaning, *Hægl*, *Lagu*, *As* and *Feoh*, with the kenning of the transformation of the flow bringing the wealth of the gods. As ale and bread are sacred manifestations of John Barleycorn, so is his ground-up body, flour. In many of the world's magical traditions, flour or grain meal is used as a ceremonial weakener of boundaries, seen as an offering to a divinity or *genius* to permit an entry to be made. Step-patterns made of flour are an appropriate magical protection for Lammas.

One of the most enjoyable traditional sacred drinks is mead. Like ale, mead is a sacred drink with a runic kenning—*MEDU*, *Man*, *Eh*, *Dag* and *Ur* (man, horse, day, primal strength)—signifying transformational magic. Traditional mead is made from honey, though some drinks sold commerically as mead may be white wine to which honey has been added. Real mead can be made at home, though it is a long process. Natural processes cannot be hurried! The basic ingredient is honey, but not any honey will do. Most commercially available honeys are so thoroughly processed that all of the wax and pollen has been removed, making it virtually useless for mead making. Honey on the comb is a vital ingredient. It you don't keep your own bees (few of us do), then honey on the comb can be bought directly from a beekeeper, or through a health-food shop. Just as good wine comes from the finest grapes, so good mead comes from the best honey. Basic wine-making equipment is used to produce mead. The ingredients are as follows:

1 gallon water
3 lb clover honey
3 tsp yeast nutrients

$\frac{1}{4}$ tsp tannin
$\frac{1}{4}$ oz tartaric acid
$\frac{1}{2}$ oz malic acid
Wine yeast starter*

The honey is dissolved in half a gallon of warm water, to which the acids, tannin and nutrient is added. It is then made up to 1 gallon with the rest of the cold water, and put in a wine-making demijohn. Two crushed Campden tablets are then added. The demijohn is corked and allowed to stand for 24 hours, after which the yeast is added, and an airlock put on the demijohn. Put the demijohn in a warm, indisturbed, place, and leave until fermentation stops, in 3–4 weeks. A week after fermentation has ceased, siphon off the mead into a clean, sterilized demijohn, add a crushed Campden tablet and cork. Leave it alone for three months, after which time a deposit will have formed. The mead should be racked again, siphoned every three months, with a Campden tablet added after every second racking. This should go on until there is no more deposit and the mead is totally clear. Then it can be bottled, and left to mature for one to three years.

Corn dollies and straw figures

Traditionally, the *corn dolly*, *kern baby* or *corn token* originates in the period after Lammas and before the autumnal equinox, at the first *station* of the year. This is a time of cosmic renewal, the start of the new life in the midst of the dissolution of the old. The dolly is a figure fashioned from the straw of the last wheat or barley cut during the harvest. In days before mechanization, the last stand would be cut by the labourers throwing their scythes at it. When it was cut down, it was bound up as the *Ben* and carried back to the farm. Finally, the straw was plaited into a traditional form and the dolly was kept in a place of honour until ploughing for the new crop commenced. Then, at the January festival of Plough Monday (*Charming the Plough*), or whenever the ground was suitable for ploughing, after the Four Holes ceremony, the old year's dolly was laid in the first furrow and ploughed under. The

* Yeast starter is made by boiling half a cup of pure orange juice with half a cup of water, adding two teaspoonfuls of sugar. The mixture is then poured into a bottle, and yeast is added. After about three hours, when the yeast has begun to ferment, it can be added to the mead.

Fig. 58 The cock is sometimes used to surmount harvest-time proces-
    sional garlands made from barley ears as celebration of the mysteries of
    John Barleycorn.

spirit of last year's corn, which had fled into the final stand,
was now returned to the earth for the task ahead of growing a
fresh crop.

As their name infers, corn dollies are often humanoid in
form, and it was traditional to dress them for the ceremonies
celebrating a successfully gathered-in harvest. But, in addition to humanoid dollies, there are many local variations,
spirals, loops and elongated forms, all of which have their
own lore and traditional usages. A straw goat is a 'dolly',
made at Lammas and sacred to Thor, which is part of the
winter solsticial festivities. It is popular in Scandinavia and
North America, promising plentiful food through the winter-
time until the spring.

The First Station of the Year

This is the part of the mysteries that is not defined by a specific festival. With most natural things, it is easier to define the precise moment of their end rather than the precise time of their beginning. When things are big enough or important enough to be noticed, or to attain formal recognition, they are then some time from their actual inception, which is usually indeterminate. In a real sense, there is no separate beginning for anything, for life and the multiverse is eternal and continuous, being defined only by cycles within it. The first *station* should be a time of rest and enjoyment, the traditional time of summer holidays, a space of rest between work. There is no specific ceremonial form which ought to be done at this time, but we can bear in mind the knowledge that the completion of one cycle is the beginning of another.

Samhain

Samhain is the third *station* of the mystic year, signifying awakening, letting-go, when the seed falls to earth from the mother plant. It is a time of freedom and excitement, but, of course, with freedom also comes danger, for in falling, the seed may be destroyed. Samhain is the *crack of time*, the boundary-point between the worlds, a time belonging neither to the old nor quite yet to the new. Any ending is also a beginning of a new phase, and at this time, memories and thoughts of the past mingle with hopes and fears for the future. (This applies also to New Year's Eve, of course.) In its guise of Hallowe'en, Samhain has a plethora of customs and ceremonies, almost all of them connected with commemoration of the dead, or of foreseeing the future.

Traditionally, part of any Samhain ceremony should involve throwing away all worn-out and superseded ideas and feelings. It is a spiritual cleansing of those aspects of our life which we have grown out of or no longer need. They may have served us well in the past, but now they are a burden which must be shed. Participants in a ceremony can write (on a small piece of paper or parchment) those things in their lives which they wish to leave behind or transcend. These are ritually burned in the cauldron, brazier or bonfire as the culmination of the ceremony, with the words (or equivalent):

By the power of wind and water, earth, fire and ice,
In times past,
These things have served me well,
But now that I no longer need them,
I hereby relinquish and release them all,
[*cast paper into the flames*]
And affirm only positive things,
Now and in the coming times.
May it go as I say.
Ka!

Samhain is a time of divination, and looking into the future, so part of the night's proceedings would involve the customary divinatory games of the time. These are well known, from the familiar 'trick or treat' games to apple bobbing in a water tub, and *Apple and Candle*. A small stick of rowan wood is suspended from the ceiling by a red thread. A candle is attached to one end, and an apple to the other, balancing one another. The candle is lit, and the assemblage is set in motion. Everyone present then has a turn at trying to bite the apple whilst avoiding the flame. Rune-casting and playing ceremonial board games like *Tablut* and *Gala* can also be undertaken at Samhain.

A triangular cake with a furrowed surface, known as the *bannock*, is a Scottish Samhain tradition. It is made ceremonially by specially chosen women, known as Queen Bride and Her Maidens. As it is being made, it should be rolled, *deisal*, by each person in turn. The recipe used in God's kitchels makes a satisfactory bannock.

The value of ceremony

Ceremonies can be performed at each and every significant time and event in our lives. They need not be elaborate, but should reflect the time and people present. In many encounters and events, the introduction of ceremony based upon traditional forms, can create a better atmosphere and enable people to come more into harmony with each other, and with the natural order, of which we, as much as the gods, are part.

Conclusion

Everything that exists moves in cycles, and, after centuries of

Fig. 59 Daily ceremonies can be part of everyday life, as they are in traditional, rural societies. Here, in an illustration after a German calendar of 1560, a shepherd hails the setting moon as the sun rises.

Fig. 60 The great wooden temple at Uppsala, Sweden, was destroyed early in the twelfth century. Yet although the shrines were extirpated, the spirit of the Northern Tradition has continued unbroken until the present. (Engraving from O. Rudbeck's *Atlantica*.)

surviving underground, the time has come again for the Northern Tradition. Now it can reclaim its rightful position as a valid and appropriate spiritual pathway for northern Europe and those of northern European descent. Its reinstatement comes at a time when increasing numbers of people are realizing that a predominantly materialistic way of living is leading to the destruction of the natural world and the break-up of societies. The self-evident truth that we should live in harmony with Nature has been ignored by 'modern thought' which is based upon the use of technology, without the realization of its harmful effects. Traditional ways of doing things have broken down gradually and have become marginalized from the mainstream way of doing things.

The Northern Tradition teaches that despite hundreds of years of physical abuse, Nature is not spiritually dead, but that spirituality is inherent in Nature. Nature is alive and hallowed by the immanent presence of the gods. People and gods are within Nature, and must work in partnership with the natural cycles or face the consequences. Through the techniques of the Northern Tradition, we can reclaim a harmonious relationship with the natural order. In times of great stress and change, of increasing ecological catastrophe and social disintegration, there is a romantic pressure for returning to the past, 'when things were simpler'. This can manifest as religious or political extremism, where simplification inevitably leads to intolerance and conflict. It also leads to the rejection of the many beneficial aspects of modern life.

But this is fantasy. We cannot return to the past, or even recreate the conditions of the past. Nor should we want to, for at the final count, it is no more than escapism, which is a retreat from life. Instead of trying to escape, we must have a positive attitude towards life. 'the creative Pagan acceptance of life' as Eugene O'Neill put it. The Elder Faith allows the reinstatement of the old spirit in a new form, and provides us with the means to implement it in our everyday lives. Through this creativity, we can apply the eternal spiritual essence to the new forms of today, Ka!

Appendix 1
Glossary of Terms

Many of the listed terms are from the tradition of East Anglia, a part of England where knowledge of the old ways has continued into the present day. The Icelandic or Old Norse equivalents, which are often used in the modern Northern Tradition, are also given, along with Celtic words which describe states of being on the Cosmic Axis.

Abred — This material world. The middle world (Norse *Midgard*).

Ætt — One of the eight directions.

Æsir — The gods and goddesses of the later Norse pantheon.

Airt — *See Ætt*.

Álag — *See On-lay*.

Álf-blót — Offering to the elves or *genius loci* of a place.

Álfreka — To defile a place so that the elves are driven away. To desecrate.

Alraun — Human image fashioned from a root of bryony or ash.

Annwn — the Celtic Lower World, also known as the *Loveless Place*, the *Land Invisible*, and the *Abyss*.

Ásatrú — Name given to the religion worshipping the *Æsir*.

Awen — The Druidic threefold symbol of the Godhead.

Back-end of the year — Autumn.

Balderick — Girdle made of horse hair, placed around a bell for magical purposes.

Beltane — The May festival, starting at sunset on 30 April.

Ben — The effigy of the grain-spirit placed in front of the last load of the harvest.

Besom — Broom with birch twigs, the *witch's broomstick*.

Black weasels — Evil, shape-shifting spirits.

Blast — Magical power projected from a stave.
Bregda sér — *See Shape-shifting*.
Brigantia — Candlemas, starting at sunset on 31 Janaury.
Bull's noon — Midnight.
Burin — Tool for carving runes, etc..

Call — Magical incantation.
Ceugant — The transcendent realm of the ineffable source.
Clim — Chimney spirit.
Corposant — The electric discharge also known as Saint Elmo's fire.
Croomstick — Staff with hooked end used physically or magically.
Cunning man — A man with knowledge of the use of spells, traditional medicine and magic.

Deal — The sacred pine tree.
Deal Apple — The pine cone when used in sacred rituals.
Dobbie stone — A cup-stone used for offerings and in wind-magic.

Ealh — A fully-enclosed, wooden Pagan temple.

Far-sighted — Blessed with the gift of seeing into the future.
Fate — Sometimes rendered as the Old Norse *ørlög* or the Anglo-Saxon *wyrd*, in this sense, close to the meaning of the Indian term *karma*. Also a name given to one of the three Norns.
Ferridge — A gingerbread biscuit or cake, bearing appropriate symbolic designs.
Fetch — A spiritual entity connected with every person, containing the summation of past actions affecting the present. A magician's guardian sprite or guardian angel.
Fetch, To — To be taken away by supernatural entities.
Fjölkyngi — Skilled in the magical arts, literally 'much knowledge'.
Framsynn — *See Far-sighted*.
Frith — Sanctuary.
Frithsplot — Sacred ground.
Fylgja — *See Fetch*.

Galdr — *See Call*.
Gandr — Wand, also the power emanating from one; *see Blast*.

Glódhker — Brazier or fire-bowl used in rites of consecration.

Gwynvyd — The spiritual Upperworld, *the White Land*.

Haliarunos — Wise women of the Gothic tribes.

Hamfarir — Travelling around in an assumed shape or form different from one's natural form.

Hamhleypa — A 'shape-leaper', rapid shape-shifting.

Hamingja — Mutable magic energy, through which shape-shifting or other skills are accomplished, personalized as a guardian angel or spirit.

Hammarrsettning — Sacred rite of protection using the power of *Mjöllnir*.

Hamrammr — The power of shape-shifting.

Hlutr — A small image of a deity carried about as a talisman.

Hof — Banqueting-hall used for sacred meals, such as the Yule feast.

Hörgr — Pagan place of worship, an altar covered by a tent or canopy, also known as *træf*.

Hytersprite — Benevolent Earth-spirit (*see Yarthkin*).

Ka! — There! 'So be it', 'So mote it be!'.

Kenning — Poetic analogy.

Lammas — The first harvest, starting at sunset on 31 July.

Landvættir — Guardian earth-spirits, *genius loci*.

Mattr — *See Megin*.

Megin — A personal force, distinct from physical power or strength, the possession of which assures success and good fortune.

Meinvættir — Evil spirits who do one personal injury.

Mell — Sacred hammer.

Messe-dag stave — Wooden almanac showing days only (*see Primestave*).

Mete-wand — A measuring-stick.

Mitchpool — Whirlpool.

Mjöllnir — The Hammer of Thor, the 'Crusher' or 'Miller'.

Nemeton — Sanctuary, often a sacred grove of trees.

Nimidas — The 'ceremonies of the woodland'.

Norns — The three *Fates* of the Northern Tradition.

Nowl — The navel of the body, or the sacred *omphalos* of a place.

Ófreskr — Second-sighted, one with vision of events in the spirit world.

Omphalos — Literally, *naval of the world*, a central place of power where magic can be performed, or where oracles can be given.

Önd — Vital breath or Universal Soul, equivalent to the *prana* of India and the *ki* of the oriental martial arts.

Öndvegissulur — Main pillars of a wooden temple. The most sacred part of the building as the name containing *önd* and *vé* indicates.

On-lay — A spell or incantation pronounced on a place.

Ørlög — *See Fate.*

Primestave — Wooden almanac with day, month, lunar and solar notation.

Rammaukinn — One possessed with superhuman strength through the practice of the northern martial arts.

Reginnaglar — Divine nails, driven into the main posts of a building as a sacred act.

Rimstock — Danish wooden almanac.

Ristir — Carving-tool, used for runes etc.

Samhain — Holymas/All Saints' Day. Beginning of the old Celtic year, commencing at sunset on 31 October.

Seax — Ceremonial knife.

Sele — Time of day, year or season.

Shape-shifting — To change one's shape, or the way others perceive one's appearance, by magic.

Shotsele — Evening time.

Sliver — Flat slice of wood cut to bear runes as a talisman or for divinatory purposes.

Spirit — Lightning.

Sprite — A spirit.

Stafgardr — Stave-surrounded sacred enclosure.

Stance — Any special posture assumed for certain magical procedures.

Svínfylking — Norse boar-cult warriors who fought in wedge-formation with two champions, the *rani* (snout) to the fore.

Temenos — Sacred enclosure around a temple, etc.

Tinley fire — Sacred fire kindled on 2 November.

Træf — *See Hörgr.*

Vé — Triangular sacred enclosure.
Vébond — Rope and posts enclosing sacred ground.
Völva — A wise woman.

Waff — A human being's spectral double, sometimes also called a *wraith* or *doppelgänger.*
Ward, The — The spiritual protection of a settlement at night by supernatural powers.
Warlock — A man with the power of binding spirits ('locking' them) using runes or calls (Old Norse *vardlokkur*).
Wih — An unsheltered, out-of-doors image of a deity.
Will — The Will-o-the-wisp, luminescent manifestation of *önd.*

Yarthkin — Harmful Earth-spirit (*see Hytersprite*).
Yries — Spirit-paths or 'Pagan trackways', marked by rags, shoes or other offerings.
Yule — The festival of midwinter, amalgamated with Christmas.

Appendix 2
The Northern Deities

This appendix lists the names of the major deities, godlings and sprites of northern Europe, with their basic attributes. Some, like Abandinus and Belisama, are purely local deities, whilst others are aspects of the infinite. Many are specialized aspects of others, having slightly different emphases on their qualities. Most of these are living names of power, used today by practitioners of the various aspects of the Northern Tradition. The names of goddesses and gods should be respected as should all holy names.

Key:

B	=	Baltic
C	=	British and Continental Celtic
E	=	English
F	=	Frisian
G	=	Greek
I	=	Irish Celtic
L	=	Lithuanian
N	=	Norse
P	=	Prussian
R-C	=	Romano-Celtic
R-W	=	Romano-Wiccan
S	=	Saxon (German and Anglo-Saxon)
W	=	Wiccan

Ægir (N) Sea god.
Abandinus (R-C) Tutelary god of Godmanchester, Huntingdonshire.
Afliæ (R-S) Goddesses of power.
Alasiagæ (C) Female Water sprites associated with the war gods.

Albiorix (C) 'The King of the World'.

Alföðr (N) The Allfather, 'the oldest of the gods'.

Ambactanos (C) *See Amœthon.*

Ambisagrus (C) 'The Persistent', identified with Jupiter/Thor (*q.v.*).

Amæthon (C) God of farming, identified with Ambactanos.

Andraste (C) Goddess of victory.

Angrboda (N) Goddess-consort of Loki (*q.v.*), mother of the Fenris-Wolf, the Midgardsorm and Hela (*q.v.*).

Annarr (N) By-name of Odin (*q.v.*).

Antrimpas (P) God of sea and lakes.

Aradia (W) Goddess of Wiccans.

Aramo (C) 'The Gentle', identified with Jupiter/Thor.

Arawn (C) Lord of the Underworld.

Arduinna (C) Goddess seated on a wild boar (*cf.* Freyja).

Artio (C) Bear-goddess, patroness of the city of Bern, Switzerland.

Arvagastiæ (R-S) Goddesses of healing.

Aurgelmir (N) The primal being, *see Ymir* (*q.v.*).

Balder (N) Solar god of the growing light.

Bagputys (L) Sea god, attribute: ship with golden anchor.

Bardoyats (P) Ship god.

Belatucadros (C) 'The Lover of War', Gallic war god.

Belisama (C) Goddess of the River Mersey.

Belenos (C) God of fire and light.

Beow (S) Fertility god.

Beyla (N) Companion god of Freyr (Bee).

Bogy Beast (E) Mischief-making sprite (Bogyman, Boggart etc.).

Borvo (C) 'The Bubbling One', god of thermal springs, consort of Damona (*q.v.*).

Bragi (N) God of poetry and eloquence, consort of Iduna (*q.v.*).

Brigantia (C) Goddess of potential, handicrafts, poetry and learning, equivalent to Bride/Brigid.

Brownie (E) Domestic sprite (*see Hobgoblin*).

Bucca (C) Semi-domestic sprite (*see Puck*), of which there are two varieties, *bucca dhu*, the black bucca, and *bucca gwidder*, the white bucca.

Byggvir (N) Companion god of Freyr = John Barleycorn.

Cailleach Bheur (C) The Blue Hag of the Scottish Highlands.

Caletos (C) 'The Hard' god.

Camulos (C-I) Sky god.

Cernunnos (C-W) The horned god, lord of the forest.

Cluricaun (C) Irish fairy, intermediate between a hobgoblin and a leprechaun.

Cocidius (R-C) Equivalent to Tyr/Tîwaz/Mars.

Coventina (R-C) Goddess of the holy well at Carrowburgh, Northumberland.

Cu Sith (C) Supernatural dog, with green coat.

Dagda (I) God of the seasons, warrior, magician and artisan.

Damona (C) Goddess of cattle, consort of Borvo (*q.v.*).

Dando (C) Leader of the Celtic Wild Hunt.

Dandy Dogs (C-E) Phantom dogs, sometimes associated with Wild Hunt (*see Herla's Hounds, Gable Ratchets* and *Shuck*).

Daoine O'Sidhe (C) Irish heroic fairies.

Deva (C) Goddess of the River Dee.

Dev'la (W) Scottish Wiccan god.

Diana (R-W) Lady of the forest.

Diancecht (I) God of medicine.

Dis (R-C) God of the Underworld.

Donar (P) The oak god.

Donn (I) God of the dead, shipwrecks, guardian of crops and cattle.

Dracs (C) Spirits of the River Rhône, France.

Dunatis (C) God of fortresses.

Eir (N) Physician-goddess.

Eostre (S) Lunar goddess, patron of springtime and hares ('Easter Bunny') = Ostara (*q.v.*), worshipped at Easter. An aspect of (R) goddess of dawn, Aurora.

Epona (C) Horse goddess = Rhiannon (*q.v.*).

Esus (C) Treecutter, one of the Gallic trinity (with Taranis and Teutates, (*q.v.*).

Faunus (R-W) Lord of the forest.

Fear Dearc (C) The Red Man, luck-bringer to farms.

Fenoderee (C) The brownie (*q.v.*) of the Isle of Man.

Find (I) 'The Fair-haired One', a by-name of Lugh = Odin (*q.v.*).

Finvara (C) The King of the Dead.

Fiörgynn (S) Weather god, father of Frigg (*q.v.*).

Fjölsvið (N) 'One-Who-is-Very-Wise', by-name of Odin (*q.v.*).

Flidhair (I) Goddess of forest animals.

Forseti (F-N) The axe-god, saviour of the devout, winner of just law-suits.

Fortuna (R-C) 'Lady luck', prayed to by every gambler.

Freyja (N) 'The Lady', sister-consort of Freyr. Fertility and creativity goddess.

Freyr (N) 'The Lord', fertility and creativity god.

Friagabis (S) 'The Free Giver', goddess of plenty.

Frid (C) Sprites who live under rocks on which offerings of milk and bread are made.

Frigg (N) Queen of the Heavens, consort of Odin (*q.v.*).

Fulla (N) Goddess-servant of Frigg (*q.v.*).

Gable ratchets (E) Phantom dogs, usually malevolent.

Gathornes (C) Mine spirits.

Gaut (N) By-name of Odin (*q.v.*).

Gefjon (N) Goddess of unmarried women.

Gefn (N) 'The Giver' goddess.

Gná (N) Goddess servant of Frigg.

Gofanon (C) Patron god of metal workers and brewers (=) Gobniu.

Good people (E-C) The inhabitants of the faery kingdom.

Grim (N) 'The Masked One', by-name of Odin (*q.v.*).

Grimborg (N) Hero who reaches the princess in the labyrinth.

Gwragedd annwn (C) Harmless Water sprites who live in Welsh lakes.

Gwydion (C) God of wisdom and friend of humans.

Gwynn ap Nudd (C) God of the Underworld and the Kingdom of Faërie.

Heimdall (N) Watcher of the gods = St Michael.

Heinzelmann (S) Cooperative house-sprites.

Hela (N) Goddess of death and the Underworld (= Herla).

Helith (C-W) Phallic deity of Cerne Abbas, Dorset.

Herla's Hounds (C) Phantom dogs, white with red ears (*cf.* Dandy dogs, Shuck).

Hermod (N) One of the sons of Odin (*q.v.*), messenger of the gods.

Herne (E-W) Guardian of the forest = Cernunnos = St

Hubert, St Eustace.

Hjálmberi (N) 'The Helmeted One', by-name of Odin (*q.v.*).

Hlín (N) Goddess of infinite compassion.

Hobbedy's lantern (E) Will o' the wisp (*q.v.*).

Hobgoblin (E) A helpful and benevolent sprite, sometimes mischievous.

Howlaa (C) A sprite who wails on shore before sea storms.

Hrelsweg (N) Wind-giant.

Hyldemoder (N) The Elder Tree Mother.

Iduna (N) 'She who renews', goddess of eternal youth, consort of Bragi (*q.v.*).

Ing (S) Patronal deity of England, god of protection, identified with Freyr.

Jenny Burnt-tail (C) Will o' the wisp.

Jorth (S) Earth goddess.

Jovantucadros (R-C) 'The Lover of youth', god of young people.

Kelpie (C) A malignant Water-elemental, usually in the form of a horse.

Keridwen (C-W) Goddess of fertility, poetry and inspiration.

Knocker (C-E) A mine spirit.

Kobold (S) A house-sprite.

Landvættir (N) Land wights, Earth spirits.

Leprechaun (I) Fairy shoe-maker.

Leucetios (C) God of lightning.

Lief (W) The male deity.

Lir (I) Sea god.

Llew Llaw Gyffes (C) Solar deity = Lugh (*q.v.*).

Lofn (N) Goddess of forbidden love.

Loge (S-N) God of fire.

Loki (N) Prankster god.

Lud (C) 'King Lud', patronal deity of London.

Lugh (I) God of enlightenment = Odin. Consort of Rosmerta (*q.v.*).

Mannan mac Lir (I) Patron god of merchants and seafarers.

Maponos (C) 'The Divine Youth', hunter-god, son of

Matrona (*q.v.*) = Mabon, Apollo.

Math (C) God of the Underworld and magic.

Matrona (C) 'The Divine Mother'—the Great Mother goddess = St Mary.

Mermaid (E) Half-woman, half-fish sea fairy, usually malevolent.

Merman (E) Half-man, half-fish.

Moccos (C) The pig-god.

Mordgud (N) Keeper-goddess of the bridge of the Underworld.

Morigu (C) Goddess of war, consort of Nudd (*q.v.*).

Moss Women (N) Sprites pursued by Odin (*q.v.*).

Mullo (C) The ass-god.

Nanna (N) Consort-goddess of Balder (*q.v.*).

Nantosvelta (C) Water goddess consort of Sucellos (*q.v.*).

Neckan (N) River sprite.

Nectan (C) River deity or sprite (= Nechtan, St Nectan, St Neot).

Nehalennia (F) Fertility goddess associated with the Divine Mother.

Nerthus (S-N) 'The Earth Mother'.

Nicky Nye (E) Malevolent Water sprite.

Nixies (S) Water sprites.

Njörd (N) God of seafaring, controls wind, stills sea and fire.

Nodens (R-C) Tutelary god of the sanctuary at Lydney, Gloucestershire, god of healing.

Norns (N) The Three Fates, Urd, Verdandi and Skuld (*q.v.*), also known as the Wierd or Wyrd (S) Sisters = Shakespeare's *Three Witches* in *Macbeth*.

Nuada (I) One-handed god, chief of Irish deities = Tyr (*q.v.*).

Nudd (C) God of the sun and rivers, consort of Morigu (*q.v.*).

Nuggie (C) Scottish Water sprite.

Nykur (N) The water-horse (*cf. Kelpie*).

Oakmen (E) Wood-sprites, hostile to humans, but friendly to wildlife.

Odin (N) God of inspiration, shamanry and combat.

Ogmios (I) Solar deity of knowledge, eloquence and writing (*see Smertrios*).

Ollovidius (C) 'The all-knowing' god.
Óski (N) 'Fulfiller of Desire', by-name of Odin (*q.v.*).
Ostara (S-W) Lunar goddess = Eostre (*q.v.*).
Othr (N) Consort god of Freyja.
Ovinnik (B) Cat-deity, protector of barns.

Padfoot (E) Yorkshire Bogy Beast (*q.v.*).
Pan (G-W) 'The Great God', the universal male principle.
Peg O' Nell (E) Spirit of the River Ribble, Lancashire.
Peg Powler (E) Spirit of the River Tees.
Perkonis (P) Axe-god, Baltic equivalent of Thor (*q.v.*).
Phoebe (G-R) East Anglian deity of the sun.
Phol (S) Fertility god = Balder.
Pixies (E) The trooping fairies.
Puck (E) Intermediate between a brownie (*q.v.*) and Will o'
  the wisp (*q.v.*) = Robin Goodfellow, Hobgoblin.

Radigast (B) God of the Baltic lands.
Ran (N) Sea-goddess, consort of Ægir (*q.v.*).
Rigantona (C) 'The Great Queen', aspect of the Divine
  Mother.
Rigisamus (C) 'The Most Royal', aspect of Teutates (*q.v.*).
Rhiannon (C) Goddess aspect of Epona (*q.v.*).
Rig (N) By-name of Heimdall (*q.v.*), organizer of society.
Roane (C) Scottish Highland mermen who travel in the
  form of seals.
Rosmerta (C) Goddess of material wealth, consort of Lugh
  (*q.v.*).
Rugevit (B) God of the Baltic holy island of Rügen.

Saule (L) Sun goddess.
Sága (N) Attendant goddess of Frigg (*q.v.*).
Saxnot (S) Saxon helper-god.
Seater (S) Deity of Saturday = Saturn (R).
Seely Court (C-E) The 'Blessed Assembly', friendly spirits.
Sequana (C) Goddess of the River Seine.
Shuck (E) East Anglian phantom black dog, a portent of
  death.
Sif (N) Consort goddess of Thor (*q.v.*).
Sigtyr (N) God of victory = Odin (*q.v.*).
Silkie (E) Household spirit, part brownie (*q.v.*), part ghost,
  not entirely malevolent.
Sinaínn (I) Goddess of the River Shannon.

Sjöfn (N) Goddess of love.

Skadi (N) Goddess of winter.

Skuld (N) 'That Which is to Come': one of the three *Norns*, female Fates, the future. (*See also* Urd and *Verdandi*.)

Smertrios (C) The destroyer = Ogmios (*q.v.*)/Hercules.

Snotra (N) Goddess of good manners.

Souconna (C) Goddess of the River Saône.

Sól (N) Sun-goddess.

Sucellos (C) Hammer-god, chthonic fertility deity, consort of Nantosvelta (*q.v.*).

Surt (N) Fire-giant.

Svantovit (B) Fourfold god of the Baltic lands.

Syn (N) Goddess who shuts the door against those who are not to enter.

Tanaros (C) Fire god = St Anne.

Taranis (C) God of thunder = Thor (*q.v.*).

Teutates (C) The god of the people, one of the Gallic trinity = Tîwaz/Tyr/Mars.

Thor (N) God of lightning, defence and strength, the peasants' god = St Nicholas, Santa Claus.

Thorgerdr (N) Fertility goddess of Halogaland, north Norway.

Thunor (S) Lightning god = Thor (*q.v.*).

Tom Tit Tot (E) A malevolent black entity with a long tail.

Tîwaz (S) Sky god of battle and victory = Tig, Teiwa, Tyr (*q.v.*), Mars.

Troll (N) Malevolent Earth spirit.

Tvisto (S) Ancestor-god of northern Europeans.

Tyr (N) 'The Valiant', god of defence = Tîwaz.

Ull (N) Son of Sif (*q.v.*), god of archery and skiing, tutelary god of Ullswater in the Lake District.

Urd (N) 'That Which Was', one of the three *Norns*, the past.

Urisk (C) Half-human, half-goat spirit associated with waterfalls.

Valfather (N) Odin as god of the slain.

Váli (N) Son of Odin (*q.v.*) and Rind, bow-and-arrow-god (= Cupid/St Valentine).

Vár (N) Goddess of love-vows.

Vatviæ (R-S) Goddesses of the waters.

Veraldargod (N) An aspect of Freyr (*q.v.*).

Veratyr (N) 'God of Men', by-name of Odin (*q.v.*).

Verdandi (N) 'That Which is Becoming', the middle *Norn*, the present.

Vindonnus (R-C-S) Tutelary god of Vienna (*Vindobonna* = Woden (*q.v.*)).

Vintios (C) God of the winds.

Vitucadros (C) 'The Brilliant in Energy', the energy god.

Vör (N) Omniscient goddess.

Wachilt (B) Sea goddess.

Wayland (S) The smith-deity = St Clement.

Walburga (S) Moon goddess whose festival is May Eve, Walpurgis Night.

Wilbet (S) Moon goddess.

Will o' the wisp (E) The fairy light-bearer, ignis fatuus, *Earthlight*, etc.

Woden (S) = Odin.

Woodwives (N) Wood spirits hunted by Odin.

Yarthkin (E) Malevolent Earth spirit.

Ygg (N) 'Terrible One', by-name of Odin (*q.v.*).

Ymir (N) The primal being, from whose slain body the world is created.

Appendix 3
The Names of the Months

Northern Tradition months have had different names in different countries and at different historic periods. This appendix lists some of the variants, with explanations of the month-names:

ANGLO SAXON MONTHS

Winter Solstice = Geola = Yule

1	Æftera Geola	After Yule	(night of 1 Jan = Modranect (Mother's Night)
2	Solmonað	Sun Month	February
3	Hrethmonað	Hertha's Month	March
4	Eastermonað	Eostre's Month	April
5	Thrimilcmonað	Thrice Milk Month	May
6	Æerra Litha	Before Litha	June

Summer solstice = Litha

7	Æftera Litha	After Litha	July
8	Weodmonað	Weed (vegetation)	August
9	Haligmonað	Holy Month	September
10	Winterfilled	Winter is Filling	October
11	Blotmonað	Sacrifice Month	November
12	Æerra Geola	Before Yule	December

FRANKISH MONTHS

1	Wintermanoth	Winter Month	January
2	Horning	Horn, the Turn of the Year	February
3	Lentzinmanoth	Renewal Month	March

4 Ostarmanoth	Easter Month	April
5 Winnemanoth	Joy Month	May
6 Brachmanoth	Break Month	June
7 Hewimanoth	Hay Month	July
8 Aranmanoth	Corn-ears Month	August
9 Witumanoth	Wood Month	September
10 Windumanoth	Vintage Month	October
11 Herbistmanoth	Harvest Month	November
12 Heilagmanoth	Holy Month	December

ASATRÚ AND TAVAS KERNEWEK (CORNISH) MONTHS (MODERN PRACTICE)

	Asatrú	Cornish	English
1	Snowmoon	Genver	January
2	Horning	Whevrer	February
3	Lenting	Merth	March
4	Ostara	Ebrel	April
5	Merrymoon	Me	May
6	Fallow	Metheven	June
7	Haymoon	Gortheren	July
8	Harvest	Est	August
9	Shedding	Gwyngala	September
10	Hunting	Hedra	October
11	Fogmoon	Du	November
12	Wolfmoon	Kevardhu	December

ICELANDIC MONTHS

Midsummer's Sunday 22–28 July

1	Heyannír	(Haytoil)	July–August
2	Kornskur- damánuðr	(Corn Shearing)	
	Tvímánuðr	(Twain Month)	August–September
3	Hanstmánuðr	(Harvest Month)	September–October
4	Gormánuðr	(Slaughter Month)	October–November
5	Frermánuðr	(Frost Month)	November–December
6	Hrútmánðr	(Ram-Month)	
	Mörsugur	(Fat-Sucker)	December–January

7	Thorri	(Thor's)	January–February
8	Goi		February–March
9	Einmánuðr	(One-Month-Last-Winter)	March–April
10	Gaukmánuðr	(Cuckoo Month)	
	Sáidtið	(Seedtide)	April–May
11	Eggtið	(Eggtide)	May–June
12	Sólmánuðr	(Sun Month)	
	Selmánuðr	(Dairy Month)	June–July

Unlike the others, the traditional Icelandic calendar does not have months which coincide with the modern European calendar.

Appendix 4
The 'Parts of Man' and 'Parts of the Body'

There are eight *Parts of Man* and 12 *Parts of the Body* in the Northern Tradition, which relate the human physique to the qualities and structures of the universe. This version was recorded in the Welsh Book of *Llanwrst* by the Bard Taliesin.

THE 8 PARTS OF MAN

These are the correspondences between qualities and structures in nature and in the human being:

1	Earth	Inert and heavy	Flesh
2	Stones	Hard	Bones
3	Water	Moist/cold	Blood
4	Salt	Briny/sharp	Nerves
5	Air		Breath
6	Sun	Clear and fair	Body heat
7	Spirit		Soul/life
8	Divinity		Intellect

12 PARTS OF THE BODY

These are the corresponding temperaments, humours and qualities ruled by the human organs:

1	Forehead	Sense/intellect
2	Nape	Memory
3	Pate	Discretion/reason
4	Breast	Lust
5	Heart	Love
6	Bile	Anger/wrath

7	Lungs	Breath
8	Spleen	Joyousness
9	Blood	Body
10	Liver	Heat
11	Spirit	Mind
12	Soul	Faith

Select Bibliography

A subject such as the Northern Tradition has an enormous bibliography, approaching its various aspects from many different directions. There are original documents and translations of sacred scripture and sagas; historical and analytical treatises; comparative studies; commentaries and descriptive publications issued by groups and individual practitioners. There is also a considerable literature in the German language. This bibliography, whilst in no way claiming to be exhaustive, is a selection of publications which may be of use to the reader.

Alver, Brynulf, *Dag og Merk*, Oslo, 1970.

Anwyl, Edward, *Celtic Religion in Pre-Christian Times*, London 1906.

Arntz, Helmut, *Handbuch der Runenkunde*, Haale/Saale, 1944.

Blachetta, Walther, *Das Buch der deutscher Sinnzeichen*, Berlin, 1941.

Blinkenberg, C, *The Thunderweapon in Religion and Folklore*, Cambridge, 1911.

Branston, Brian, *Gods of the North*, London, 1955.

Branston, Brian, *The Lost Gods of England*, London, 1957.

Brøndsted, Johannes, *The Vikings*, trans. Kalle Skov, London, 1960.

Bucknell, Peter A., *Entertainment and Ritual, 600–1600*, London, 1979.

Campbell, Joseph, *The Masks of God* (4 vols.), London, 1973.

Chadwick, H.M., *The Cult of Othin*, London, 1899.

Christian, Roy, *Old English Customs*, Newton Abbot, 1962.

Cockayne, O., *Leechdoms, Wortcunning and Starcraft*, London, 1864.

Colum, Padraic, *The Children of Odin*, London, 1922.

Dickins, B., *Runic and Heroic Poems*, Cambridge, 1915.

Döring, Oscar, *Die Edda*, Jena, 1933.

Drake-Carnell, F.J., *Old English Customs and Ceremonies*, London, 1938.

Dumézil, G., *Les Dieux des Germains*, Paris, 1959.

Düwel, Klaus, *Runenkunde*, Stuttgart, 1968.

Eliade, Mircea, *The Myth of Eternal Return, or Cosmos and History*, trans. W.R. Trask, Princeton, 1971.

Elliot, Ralph, W.V., *Runes: An Introduction*, Manchester, 1959.

Ellis, Hilda R., *The Road to Hel*, Cambridge, 1943.

Ellis Davidson, H.R., *Scandinavian Mythology*, London 1969.

Ellis Davidson, H.R., *Gods and Myths of Northern Europe*, London, 1964.

Evans, George Ewart, *The Pattern Under the Plough*, London, 1966.

Evans, Hilary, *Gods, Spirits, Cosmic Guardians: Encounters with non-human beings*, Wellingborough, 1987.

Evans-Wentz, W.Y., *The Fairy Faith in Celtic Countries*, London, 1911.

Fidler, J. Havelock, *Earth Energy*, Wellingborough, 1988.

Gelling, Peter and Davidson, Hilda Ellis, *The Chariot of the Sun and Other Rites and Symbols of the Northern Bronze Age*, London, 1969.

Gomme, G.L., *Folklore Relics in Early Village Life*, London, 1883.

Gorsleben, Rudolf John, *Die Hoch-Zeit der Menschheit*, Leipzig, 1930.

Graves, Robert, *The White Goddess*, London, 1961.

Graves, Tom, *Needles of Stone Revisited*, Glastonbury, 1986.

Green, Arthur Robert, *Sundials: Incised dials or Mass-clocks*, London, 1926.

Grimm, Jacob, *Teutonic Mythology*, trans. S. Stallybrass, New York, 1966.

Grönbech, Vilhelm, *The Culture of the Teutons*, London, 1931.

Halifax, Joan, *Shamanic Voices. The Shaman as seer, poet and healer*, New York, 1979.

Harland, John, 'On Clog Almanacs, or Rune Stocks', in *The Reliquary*, London, 1865.

Herrmann, Paul, *Das altgermanische Priesterwesen*, Jena, 1929.

Hone, W., *Every Day Book*, London, 1826.

Howard, Michael, *The Wisdom of the Runes*, London, 1985.

James, E.O., *The Nature and Function of Priesthood*, London, 1955.

Jansson, Sven B., *Runes of Sweden*, Bedminster, New York, 1962.

Jones, Prudence, *Eight and Nine: Sacred numbers of Sun and Moon in the Pagan North*, Bar Hill, 1982.

Jones, Prudence, *Sundial and Compass Rose: Eight-fold Time Division in Northern Europe*, Bar Hill, 1982.

Jung, Carl, ed., *Man and His Symbols*, London, 1964.

Jung, Erich, *Germanische Götter und Helden in christlicher Zeit*, Munich, 1922.

Kosbab, Werner, *Das Runen-Orakel (Einweihung in die Praxis der Runen-Weissagung)*, Freiburg-im-Breisgau, 1982.

Kraft, John, *The Goddess in the Labyrinth*, Åbo, 1985.

Kraft, John, *Gotlands Trojeborgar*, Stockholm, 1983.

Krause, Wolfgang, *Die Runenschriften im älteren Futhark*, Haale/Saale, 1937.

Krause, Wolfgang, *Runen*, Berlin, 1970.

Krohn, Kaarle, *Skandinavisk Mytologi*, Helsinki, 1922.

Lethbridge, T.C., *Gogmagog: The Buried Gods*, London, 1957.

Lethbridge, T.C., *Witches: Investigating an ancient Religion*, London, 1962.

Lewis, I.M., *Ecstatic Religion: An anthropological study of spirit possession and Shamanism*, London, 1971.

Lockyer, J.N., *Stonehenge, Astronomically Considered*, London, 1909.

MacCulloch, J.A., *The Celtic and Scandinavian Religions*, London, 1948.

MacManus, Dermot, *The Middle Kingdom*, London, 1972.

Marby, Friedrich Berhard, *Der Weg zu den Müttern*, Stuttgart, 1955.

Mermet, Abbé, *Principles and Practice of Radiesthesia*, London, 1959.

Michell, John, *The Earth Spirit, Its Ways, Shrines and Mysteries*, London, 1975.

Odinic Rite, Instructional and Information leaflets (various), London, from 1978.

Olrik, Axel, *Viking Civilisation*, London, 1930.

Olsen, M, *Farms and Fanes of Ancient Norway*, trans. Th. Gleditsch, Oslo, 1928.

Osborn, Marijane and Longland, Stella, *Rune Games*, London, 1983.

Page, R.I., *An introduction to English Runes*, London, 1973.

Pastor, Eilert, *Deutsche Volksweisheit in Wetterregeln und Bauernsprüchen*, Berlin, 1934.

Peisheng, Wang and Weiqi, Zeng, *Wu Style Taijiquan*, Beijing, 1981.

Pennick, Nigel, *Runic*, Trumpington, 1974.

Pennick, Nigel, *Ogham and Runic: Magical Writing of Old Britain and Northern Europe*, Bar Hill, 1978.

Pennick, Nigel, *The Ancient Science of Geomancy*, London, 1979.

Pennick, Nigel, *Sacred Geometry*, Wellingborough, 1980.

Pennick, Nigel, *The Subterranean Kingdom*, Wellingborough, 1981.

Pennick, Nigel, *Labyrinths, their Geomancy and Symbolism*, Bar Hill, 1986.

Pennick, Nigel, *Earth Harmony*, London, 1987.

Pennick, Nigel, *Einst War Uns die Erde Heilig*, Waldeck-Dehringhausen, 1987.

Rees, Alwyn and Brinsley, *Celtic Heritage*, London, 1961.

Reichardt, Konstantin, *Runenkunde*, Jena, 1936.

Reuter, Otto Sigfrid, *Germanische Himmelskunde*, Munich, 1934.

Reuter, Otto Sigfrid, *Skylore of the North*, trans. Michael Behrend, Bar Hill, 1987.

Rhys, John, *Lectures on Religion as Illustrated by Celtic Heathendom*, London, 1888.

Rutherford, Ward, *The Druids, Magicians of the West*, Wellingborough, 1983.

Rutherford, Ward, *Celtic Mythology*, Wellingborough, 1987.

Schramm, P., *Herrschaftszeichen und Staatssymbolik*, Stuttgart, 1954.

Schütte, Gudmund, *Dänisches Heidentum*, Heidelberg, 1923.

Shippey, T.A., *Poems of Wisdom and Learning in Old English*, Cambridge, 1976.

Speth, G.W., *Builders' Rites and Ceremonies*, London, 1894.

Spiesberger, Karl, *Runenmagie*, Berlin, 1955.

Spiesberger, Karl, *Runenexerziten für Jedermann*, Freiburg-im-Breisgau, 1976.

Stanley, E.G., *The Search for Anglo-Saxon Paganism*, Cambridge, 1975.

Stephens, George, *The Old-Northern Runic Monuments of Scandinavia and England*, London, 1866.

Strombeck, Dag, *Sejd*, Lund, 1955.

Sturluson, Snorri, *The Prose Edda*, trans. Jean I. Young, Berkeley, 1966.

Strachan, Francoise, *Natural Magic*, London, 1974.

Syversen, Earl, *Norse Runic Inscriptions, with their long-forgotten cryptography*, Sebastopol, California, 1979.
Thom, Alexander, *Megalithic Sites in Britain*, Oxford, 1967.
Thom, Alexander, *Megalithic Lunar Observatories*, Oxford, 1971.
Thorsson, Edred, *Futhark: A Handbook of Rune Magic*, York Beach, 1984.
Tiller, Alexander, *Yule and Christmas*, London, 1899.
Tolkien, J.R.R., *Tree and Leaf*, London, 1964.
Turville-Petre, E.O.G., *The Heroic Age of Scandinavia*, London, 1951.
Turville-Petre, E.O.G., *Myth and Religion in the North*, New York, 1964.
Varagnac, André and Derolez, R., *Les Celtes et les Germains*, Paris, 1965.
von List, Guido, *Das Geheimnis der Runen*, Vienna, 1912.
von Reichenbach, C., *Letters on Od and Magnetism*, London, 1926.
von Zaborsky, Oskar, *Urväter-Erbe in deutscher Volkskunst*, Leipzig, 1936.
Wardle, Thorolf, *Runelore*, Braunschweig, 1983.
Wardle, Thorolf, *The Runenames*, Braunschweig, 1984.
Watkins, Alfred, *The Old Straight Track*, London, 1925.
Weber, Edmund, *Runenkunde*, Berlin, 1941.
Wirth, Herman, *Die Heilige Urschrift der Menschheit*, Leipzig, 1931.
Whitlock, Ralph, *In Search of Lost Gods. A Guide to British Folklore*, Oxford, 1979.
Williamson, George C, *Curious Survivals: Habits and Customs of the Past that still live in the Present*, London, 1925.
Willis, Tony, *The Runic Workbook*, Wellingborough, 1986.
Wilson, David, *The Vikings and their Origins*, London, 1970.
Wood-Martin, W.G., *Pagan Ireland*, London, 1895.
Wood-Martin, W.G., *Traces of the Elder Faiths of Ireland*, London, 1902.
Wright, Elizabeth Mary, *Rustic Speech and Folk-Lore*, Oxford, 1913.
Yeowell, John, *Hidden Gods*, London, 1979.
Zeller, Otto, *Der ursprung der Buchstabenschrift und das Runenalphabet*, Osnabrück, 1977.

Index

Aarhus, 51
Abbot's Bromley, 231
Acorn, 80
Ægir, 47,101
Ægishjalmur, 204–5
Ages of the World, 54
Air, lore of the, 103–6
Airts, 15,21–3
Æsc, 129
Agaric, fly, 163
Alag, 167
Alder, 70
Aldreth Fen, 108
Alf-blot, 106
Alfreka, 94, 183
Allfather, 99
All Fool's Day, 47–8
All Saint's Day, 19
All Soul's Day, 50
Alphabet, Etruscan, 131
Alraun, 209–11
Ammonite, 62
Amsterdam, 70
Anglicus, Bartholomæus, 87
Annwn, Descent Into, 100
Aphrodite, 87
Apollonius of Tyana, 12
Apple tree, 70
Arthur, King, 126
Asatrú, 36–42
Ash tree, 71–2
Aspen tree, 72–3
Athamé, 165
Augury, 113

Aun, 32
Awen, 207, 248

Backgammon, 141
Bacon, Francis, 60
Balder, 38–9, 80
Balderick, 164
Banner, Raven, 173–4
Barleycorn, 143–4
Barleycorn, John, 39–40, 249–52
Baton, 147–8, 170
Bay tree, 73
Beans, lore of, 139
Beech tree, 73
Bell, 178
Beltane, 34, 37–8
Benedict XIV, Pope, 129
Beow, 126
Beowulf, 121, 126
Berserkeres, 123–7
Besom, 189
Bifröst, 109, 185
Bind-runes, 199
Binding magic, 180–88
Birch tree, 73–4
Birds, lore of, 68–70
Birgit, 36
Birka, 74
Blackthorn, 74–5
Boars' Throng, 139
Bodhran, 180
Bottles, protective, 181, 183
Bramble, 75

Bran, 69
Breathing, 115–6
Bride, 36
Brigantia, 18, 36, 47
Broomstick, Witches', 189
Bryony, 88–9
Bulla, 195
Bungay, Friar, 127
Burin, 166

Caduceus, 206
Calendars, 27–8
Cambridge, 38, 51, 54, 188
Candlemas, 18, 36, 47
Canne, 147–8, 170
Capitularia Regum
    Francorum, 93, 112
Cat troughs, 106
Ceremonies, 228–258
Cernunnos, 115
Chime Hours, 22
Chivalry, 123
Circles, runic, 149
Cnut, King, 111, 173
Clothes, colour of, 161–2
Coelbren Y Beirdd, 11
Cock, 68–9, 208, 254
Cock, weather, 239
Collar, dog, 162
Colour, 129
Confessor, King Edward
    the, 94
Consecration, 214–6
Corn dolly, 217, 253–4
Corposant, 107–8, 129
Cord, Druids', 148
Cosmic Axis, 98–100, 172
Croomstick, 169
Crossroad (Blues song), 94
Crow, 69
Crystals, 64
Cubit, Northern, 142–3
Cubit, Royal, 163
Cycles, lunar, 19–20

Dance, sacred, 230

Daytime, 20
Day Star, 57
Days, lucky and unlucky, 53
Dean, Forest of, 70
Dineen, P.S., 85
Dionysus, 35
Directions, guardians
    of, 55–6
Distaff, 59
Dobbie Stone, 106
Dorflinde, 79
Dowsing, 172, 225
Dozmary Pool, 102
Dragon Project, the, 129
Dragon, Snap the, 245
Drink, sacramental, 252–3
Druids, 33, 71, 77, 80, 99,
    192
Drusus, Nero Claudius, 143
Dust, fiery, 128

Ealh, 91
Earth Mother, 60
Earth, bones of, 106
Eddas, the, 42, 79
Edward I, King, 94
Egill, 197
Egbert, Archbishop, 111
Egg, 240–1
Einherjar, 50
Eiriks Saga Rauda, 120
Elder tree, 75
Elementals, Earth, 189–90
Elm Tree, 76
Excalibur, 102
Exercises, spiritual, 114–7
Eye, evil, 79

Fawkes, Guy, 40
Fear Dearc, 163
Feng Shui, 222, 225
Ferlingate, 145
Festivals, fire, 18, 33–4, 40
Festivals, lunar, 52–3
Fibonacci series, 87
Fionn's Shield, 77

Flags, 173–4
Flails, sprite, 75
Forseti, 44, 115
Fossils, 61–2
Freigrafschaft, 146
Frey, 39, 44, 81
Freyja, 83, 106, 121
Friday, 25–6
Frigg, 39, 42
Frithsplott, 91, 219
Fylfot, 158

Gaia, 61
Gallows, 88
Ganglieri, 42
Gar, 71
Gaudi, Antoni, 15
Geneva, 208
Geomancy, 222
Gibich, King, 139
Glastonbury, 77
Goddess, lunar, 24
Goddesses, Northern, 43–4
Goethe, 78
Gonfanon, 173
Graves, Robert, 220
Great Yarmouth, 25, 37
Greenland, 121
Grevens Væng, 115
Grids, 119
Grim, 125
Grimborg, 156–8
Ground, holy, 90–91
Guising, 40
Gungnir, 25, 71
Gypsies, 175, 184

Hallowe'en, 21, 39
Hammer, sacred, 174–7
Hamrammr, 163
Hardar Saga, 127
Hávamál, 42, 127, 140, 229
Hawthorn, 76–7
Hazel, 77–8
Headband, 163
Heimdall, 50, 109

Herbs, 85–6
Hermod, 95, 117
Hitchin, 267
Hlafmasse, 39
Hlin, 43, 69
Hlutr, 122, 209
Hobby Horse, 243–5
Hof, 72, 91, 122
Hogmagog, 238
Hogmanay, 34
Holly, 78
Hood, Robin, 147–8
Hørgr, 91, 112
Hour, runic, 151
Hrafnsmal, 126
Hrolfs Saga Kraki, 124

Ice, 109
Images, 208–11, 225
Imbolc, 18–19, 34–6, 238–9
Incense, 191–3
Interlaken, 97
Ireland, 10, 61, 85, 96–7,
    126, 163, 178–9
Irmin, 84
Irminsul, 105
Ivy, 78–9

Jelling, 219
Journey, archetypal, 117
Juniper, 79
Jupiter, 112

Kal, 161
Kaufbeuren, 155
Ki, 123
Kilpeck, 125
Keltensitz, 115
Kennedy, Patrick, 163
Kitchels, God's, 235
Knives, 165

Labyrinths, 53, 141, 153–9,
    205
Lavender, 164
Leys, 91–5, 151, 183

Lightning, 106–9
Light tree, 233–4
Linden tree, 79
Lockyer, Sir Norman, 93
Lode Star, 57
Loki, 26, 39, 44
London, 51, 69
Luck, bad, 53, 80–81, 138, 235
Lugh, 249
Lughnassadh, 18–19, 38–9, 249

Magnetism, 66–7
Mandrake, 86–9
Mani, 24
Maple tree, 79
Maponos, 73
Magpie, 69
Martial Arts, Northern, 123–7
May-Pole, 37, 73–4, 241
Measure, natural, 142–8
Mercury, 112
Metals, 66–8, 86
Mete-wand, 146–7, 215
Midsummer, 248
Mint, 164
Mistletoe, 79–80
Mithras, 35
Moats, 113
Mohenjodaro, 143
Motley, 162
Mystic Plot, the, 146

Nails, 225
Nanna, 39
Need-fire, 33, 37, 113
New Grange, 119
New Year's Day, 45–6, 238
New Year's Eve, 55
Njord, 44
Nodens, 73
Norwich, 177
Nowl, 176, 245
Numbers, magic, 137–42

Oak Apple Day, 245–6
Oak tree, 80–81
Odin, 25, 39, 44, 67–8, 112, 120, 125, 131, 140, 175
Odinism, 41
Odyle, 127
O'Flaherty, Roderick, 220
Ófreskr, 163
Ogham, 77, 83
Oimelc, 35
Old Style, 28
Önd, 93, 95, 108, 114, 123, 127–9, 150, 164–5
Öndvegissulur, 221–2
O'Neill, Eugene, 258
On-lay, 167
Orientation, 54, 57
Orpheus, 12, 95
Orwandil's Toe (star), 58
Ostara, 36, 48, 53, 66

Pathworking, 117
Paths, fairy, 91
Pattern, step, 186–7
Peacock, 69
Picardt, Johan, 118
Pietarinleikki, 141
Pilebogar, 169
Pilgrims' Way, 54
Pine tree, 81
Platonicus, Apuleius, 87
Plot, Dr Robert, 31–2
Pneuma, 127
Poplar tree, 81
Pouch, 190–91
Pudding, 235
Pythagoras, 12, 86, 117

Quarter-staff, 148

Raven, 69–70
Red colouring, 184–5
Reginnaglar, 176–225
Remembrance Day, 40
Rhabdomancy, 171–2
Ristir, 166

Robes, 160–62
Robin, 70
Rosaries, 185–6
Rowan tree, 81–2, 181
Rudbeck, Olaf, 31–2
Rue, 163
Runes, 10, 31, 49, 71,
    149–52, 195–99, 225

Sacred space, 218
Saints' Days, 45–52
Samhain, 19, 29, 39–40,
    255–1
Saturday, 26
Sæter, 26, 67
Score, 140
Seax, 165
Seidr, 120–23
Service tree, 82
Shamanic lodges, 118–20
Shipton, Mother, 97
Silbury Hill, 119
Sigyn, 39
Sjöborg, 153
Skulls, 118, 224
Sleipnir, 49
Sol Invictus, 35
Soul, resident, 127
Soup, Norwegian Pea, 235
South Star, 57
Sowens, 235
Spindle tree, 82
Spiral, 203
Sprites, water, 100–102
Spruce tree, 83
Stars, 56–9
Stations of the Year, 40–41
Staves, 168–9
Stave numbers, 33
Stones, 61–5
Stonhenge Festival, 38
Subterranea, 95–100
Sunday, 23–4
Svinfylking warriors, 58, 125
Swastika, 44, 209
Sweeping, 189–90

Synods, 19

Talismans, 83, 113, 194–208,
    211–3
Tetractys, 140
Thaun, Philip de, 87
Thiazi's Eyes, 58
Thorn-apple, 180
Tinley fires, 50
Theophrastus, 87
Thor, 10, 25, 37, 43, 51, 67,
    76, 78, 80, 82, 112, 117,
    174–7, 254
Thule, 120
Thunderbroom, 189–90, 205
Thyme, 164
Tiw, 24
Torch, the (star), 57
Torch Bearer, the (star), 57
Torslunda, 124–5
Træf, 148
Trap, spirit, 182
Trees, lore of, 70–84
Triads, Bardic, 138
Triskele, 207
Tuesday, 24–5
Twelfth Night, 46

Uffington, white horse
    at, 246
UFOs, 108
Olfhednar, 123–7
Ulfius, 126
Ullr, 84, 232
Uppsala, 31, 257
Útiseta, 114

Valhalla, 148
Valknut, 44, 200
Vebond, 77, 219
Vegetation year, 18
Verstigan, R., 24
Vervain, 190
Vienna, 175, 211
Vis plasica, 62
Volsunga Saga, 126

Völva, 117, 121, 160–61
Vril, 127

Wales, 126, 176
Wand, 171–3
Warenne, Sir John de, 205
Ward Hills, 90
Warlock, 120–22
Wassailing, 46, 79, 237
Watkins, Alfred, 90–93
Wayfaring tree, 83
Wayland, 44, 51, 67, 139
Week, 23–7
Wendover, Roger de, 94
Westphalia, 146–7, 204
Wheel, 177
Whitby, 62
Whortleberry, 84
Wih, 91, 148
Wild Hunt, the, 247
Willow tree, 83–4
Will's Mother's, 108
Winds, 54–5, 103–6, 152–3
Winds, Rose of, 104
Winds, raising the, 105–6
Witch Hazel, 84

Witta Wijven, 118
Woden, 10, 25, 44, 61, 67, 94
Wolf, 123–7, 129–30, 163
Wyrd, 134

Yantras, 154
Yarrow, 163, 227
Yarthkins, 90
Ydalir, 84
Year, British financial, 28–9
Yellowhammer, 70
Yew tree, 84
Yggdrassil, 54, 71, 98, 116, 137, 196
Ymir, 1066
Ynglinga Saga, 123
York Minster, 80
Yries, 93, 113
Yuga, Kali, 148
Yule, 33–5, 40, 52, 73–4, 78, 83, 91, 189, 231–7

Zimbabwe, 13
Zürich, 155, 208